GLORIOUS INCENSE

The Fulfillment of Edgar Allan Poe

EDGAR ALLAN POE

From the portrait by Samuel S. Osgood

GLORIOUS INCENSE

The Fulfillment of Edgar Allan Poe

by
Haldeen Braddy, 1908—
Professor of English
The University of Texas at El Paso

Second Edition

KENNIKAT PRESS, INC./PORT WASHINGTON, N. Y.

GLORIOUS INCENSE

Copyright 1953 by Haldeen Braddy
Reissued in 1968 by Kennikat Press by arrangement
Library of Congress Catalog Card No: 68-16283
Manufactured in the United States of America

TABLE OF CONTENTS

INTRODUCTION TO
THE SECOND EDITION

Glorious Incense endeavored in 1953 to cover all the essentials of both Poe's biography and his works, making its sole claim as an original contribution to scholarship in its survey of his renown in foreign lands. I then tried to assemble proofs that by 1949, the centenary of his death, Irish-American Poe had won global fame.

My rather comprehensive study, first published fifteen years ago, compiled and evaluated the bibliographical records of E.A. Poe's fame up through 1949, with one exception, *Chivers' Life of Poe.* I referred to the biography edited by Richard Beale Davis, which came out in 1952 and which found its way into my text only at a late proof stage. Since the appearance of my book in 1953, the tide of writing about Edgar Allan Poe has continued without the slightest cessation. More and more, Poe grows as an international figure; worldwide interest in him continues, expanding notably in recent years. In the twenty years between 1949, the terminal date of my bibliography, and this reprint of 1968, the body of literature on Poe has reached grand proportions.

In American letters, Mark Twain and Walt Whitman notwithstanding, the volume of writings about Poe sets him in the foremost category. In world letters, books and papers about him issue from scholarly capitals around the earth. He is today a literary Titan. Along with the English poets Chaucer and Shakespeare, Poe the American now has attained dimension as one of the writers most investigated by scholars.

Not many of the numerous papers appearing annually in the learned journals partake of the nature of "discovery." One article by the prolific W.T. Bandy particularly forces on one's attention a devastating conclusion regarding Baudelaire's identification of himself as Poe's spiritual heir, now a universally accepted view. The Frenchman's essay on Poe in 1852 was not original; it derived from two articles in American magazines of the time ("New Light on Baudelaire and Poe," *Yale French Studies*, Number 10 (1953), 65-69). A firstrate example of the union of psychological analysis and aesthetic appreciation, Eric W. Carlson's "Symbol and Sense in Poe's 'Ulalume'" (*AL*, XXXV (1963), 22 ff.) depicts Poe's narrator as "symbolizing within his own mind or self the psychomachia of the modern ego" (p. 37). In a convincing demonstration, Frederick W. Conner displays that John Nichol, a contemporary astronomer from Glasgow, contributed a number "of .the most potent suggestions that went into the making of Poe's wondrous theory." *Eureka*, it will be remembered, reads little different from treatises of today, as Poe speaks of "gigantic clusters of the heavens" in terms of "'colossal atoms' that would one day merge into a final cluster of clusters and then into 'one magnificent sun'" ("Poe and John Nichol, Notes on a Source of *Eureka*," from ... *All These to Teach, Essays in Honor of C.A. Robertson* (Gainesville, Fla., 1965), pp. 194-95).

Several outstanding books on Poe deserving mention here have appeared since 1949. W.H. Auden's *Edgar Allan Poe: Selected Prose and Poetry* dates from 1950; Irving Wallace's *The Fabulous Originals*, from 1955; Edward H. Davidson's *Poe, A Critical Study*, from 1957; Vincent Buranelli's *Edgar Allan Poe*, from 1961; Sidney P. Moss's *Poe's Literary Battles*, from 1963; and *The Recognition of Edgar Allan Poe*, an anthology edited by Eric W. Carlson, from 1966. These five volumes, however, represent only a fraction of the total output: a survey by one of my graduate students, Col. Howard A. Simonides, for 1949-65 turned up a total of forty-nine books from nine different languages, printed in eighteen countries, including the United States. The foreign languages represented, besides the usual European tongues, are Swedish, Greek, Hungarian, and Japanese. In addition to the nearly fifty book-length studies, Simonides tabulated the sum of three hundred and fifty-eight articles for the same period. The separate published items in these two categories total four hundred and seven for the seventeen years between Simonides' compilation and mine in *Glorious Incense*.

Of the book titles just mentioned, Eric Carlson's bears most directly on Poe's reputation as an artist. In a compact volume, styled in its subtitle "Selected Criticism since 1829," Carlson reprints almost forty pieces by as many writers, both foreign and American, that attest to Poe's influence in diverse countries. Minus footnotes and other technical appurtenances, *The Recognition of Edgar Allan Poe* shows the anthologist's cultured knack in selecting worthwhile specimens that both edify and challenge the devotees of Poe. This anthology offers as a specimen of the editor's own labor an illuminating preface; as compiler, he wisely limits himself to terse intercalary comments throughout. Carlson's *Recognition* may be prized as the first Poe gatherum of its kind. Beyond this distinction, it contains a full range of appraisals, in multiplicity of informed opinions as well as diversity of the persons expressing them. The virtually scurrilous obituary by Poe's literary executor, Rufus Wilmot Griswold (object of the poet's "misplaced trust"), is here; the spirited defense and tribute by Charles Baudelaire, versatile French Impressionist deeply influenced by Poe, is here; "the most serious, most all-out attack" by our contemporary, Yvor Winters, is here; and the grandiloquent assay by the modern poet Allen Tate is here. Editor Carlson thereby escapes the trap of bias.

The chronology exhibited in Carlson's selections ranges from the "Comments on Poe's Poems" by John Neal published in 1829, to "The Question of Poe's Narrators," by James Gargano, published in 1963. The world-famed belletrists include also Lowell, Dostoevski, W.B. Yeats, Shaw, D.H. Lawrence, T.S. Eliot, and a half-dozen others. Another group, aside from professional critics and critical professors, presents a psychoanalytical vignette of "Morella" by a Freudian, Princess Marie Bonaparte, and a mystical elegy on *"Le Tombeau d'Edgar Poe"* by the French Symbolist Mallarmé. Carlson's variegated specimens of Poeana constitute the first gleanings from multilingual sources.

The stature of Poe as a world figure of course has long been accepted by scholars. The first pioneer in this aspect of historical criticism was C. Alphonso Smith, the initial chapter of whose biography bore the title "The World-Author" (*Edgar Allan Poe: How to Know Him*, Indianapolis, Ind., 1921). The 1953 edition of *Glorious Incense* made serious effort to trace

Poe's influence in America, Britain, France, Germany, Russia, Spain, and Spanish America. Carlson ignored both the door opened by the chapter "The World-Author" and the road pursued by *Glorious Incense*, but he is due credit for printing the texts upon which earlier scholars based their discoveries.

There remain one or two newer developments to record. Readers in the Southwest should know that the cult of Poe extended even to El Paso. In 1933 Edwin B. Hill reprinted at nearby Ysleta, Texas, Vincent Starrett's edition of a famous reminiscence. This *Memoir* on Poe was written by Captain Mayne Reid about 1843, now a collector's item for a generation. Kenneth Goldblatt, a graduate assistant in English at The University of Texas at El Paso, recently transformed his seminar paper on this memorabilium into an article. Goldblatt's "Edgar Allan Poe in the Southwest" saw print in volume five of *Western Review* (1968).

The newest development in periodical literature is the *Poe Newsletter*. The editor, Dr. G.R. Thompson, of the Department of English, Washington State University (Pullman, Wash.), announced in November, 1967, that publication would begin early in the spring of 1968. Editorial plans call for two issues each year; if contributions and response warrant expansion, the number of issues may be increased in subsequent years. The *Newsletter* will feature materials on relevant aspects of Poe both as man and as writer. It will devote itself especially to "bibliographical, source, and influence studies" and to brief essays and notes on Poe in the context of international Romanticism. Dr. Thompson's *Poe Newsletter* also will feature general news about Poe and dark Romanticism through the medium of colloquiums, symposiums, celebrations, and so forth.

If I were rewriting *Glorious Incense,* it would be obligatory to insert some changes dealing with meaning, but perhaps not as many as one might expect. On p. 34 the clause stating that "The Sphinx," a story about cholera, "narrates an imaginary incident that occurred in New York in 1832" would now read "an imaginary incident as occurring in New York in 1832." On p. 50 the date of the review by Poe of *Twice-Told Tales* should be changed to 1837 from 1847. Three basic changes concern something more crucial than phrasing or dates. On p. 92 where unexpected opposites and contradictory images are the subject, I would incorporate a vivid extract from R.H. Blyth to the effect that stones rise up; fire burns down into the water, and "The sun rises in the evening" (*Zen in English Literature* (Tokyo, 1949), p. 12). On p. 93 Meyer Shapiro ("Blue Like an Orange," *The Nation*, CLXV (Sept. 25, 1937), 323) would be credited with suggesting that "the spectrum of poetry logically includes colors that are 'blue like an orange.'" On p. 96 at the end of chapter 2, section 6, "The Scope of His Interests," I would append a passage from *Eureka* (Harrison's ed., *Works*, XVI, 311) on the fascinating idea of the Heart-Throb of the Universe, as follows:

> The process we have here contemplated will be renewed forever, and forever, and forever; a novel Universe swelling into existence and then subsiding into nothingness, at every throb of the Heart Divine.

Some other revisions also demand notice. An insertion on p. 100 would identify "Poe's extravaganzas on nosology" as deriving from "Some Passages in the Life of a Lion," à la Lawrence Sterne in *Tristram Shandy*. The author of the extended Georgian novel may have influenced Poe in this instance and elsewhere, as maintained to me in a recent letter from Professor Burton R. Pollin, one of the emerging Poe experts. Another inadvertence appears in *Glorious Incense* on p. 106 where I incorrectly give *Pinakidia* as the title instead of *Marginalia*. On p. 126, after the sentence about Slavic Symbolists, the findings of Oleg Maslenikov should be added. Maslenikov's treatise on Symbolism in Eastern Europe gages the impact of Poe on such noted Russians of that school as Vladimirov, Petrovsky, and Bugoyev (*The Frenzied Poets*, (Berkeley, Cal.), 1952, p. 68). On p. 131 the middle initial of biographer John H. Ingram is garbled as "F."

One change I would not have to make, in spite of Edward Wagenknecht's misquotation from *Glorious Incense*, namely that Poe "had the story at first hand from Mrs. Stanard," which Wagenknecht follows with his own aside, "Professor Mabbott says Poe actually had the story from Mr. Stanard" (*Edgar Allan Poe*, (New York, 1963), p. 230). The verity is that *Glorious Incense* (p. 151) prints "Mr. Stanard," not "Mrs. Stanard" as incorrectly alleged. But despite this glaring instance of setting to rights the accurate, the Boston University savant otherwise rendered a worthy service to scholarly letters. He quotes more critical literature than most other authorities on Poe, although the biographer has little that is strictly fresh in his book. In sifting the legend to erase the popular image of

Poe as "an atheist, a diabolist, an immoralist, or a Gothic monster" (p. 221), Wagenknecht was successful, although Arthur H. Quinn had pretty well put the quietus on this legend in his biography of 1941. Mayne Reid (p. 34) also suffered miscitation by Wagenknecht, who had the captain writing, "The innocent mirth in which we all indulgence when Bacchus gets the better of us." The word Reid penned was "indulge," which is what I printed (p. 164), taking it from Starrett's edition (*op. cit.*, p. 5).

Another item would stand unaltered: that is, the date 1846 for Poe's suit against Dr. Thomas Dunn English. John Ostrom in reviewing my work (*AL*, XXV (1954), 508 ff.) charged that I had misdated the event. All one needs for refutation is to cite reviewer Ostrom against himself. For example, in his notes to *The Letters of Edgar Allan Poe* (Cambridge, Mass., 1948), Ostrom used, correctly this time, the same date as I did (I, 291 n.); and then he rightly repeated 1846 in a second epistolary mention (II, 325). Ostrom's other charges against me seem equally groundless and, in any case, unfit subject matter to expand on here.

If I had it to do over, the section on p. 208 labeled *Bibliography* would now be titled *Selective Bibliography*, which better describes my method in arranging the list. Bibliographical references not contained therein abound in the section called *Notes*. A reader sufficiently enterprising to read this section can encounter here unexpected items which, hopefully, will reward him for his time. To revise *Glorious Incense* meticulously and bring its documentation up to the minute falls far beyond my present aim. The truth is that my note cards long ago overran into a second filing case; to print all these data would require a separate monograph, possibly a later undertaking for me or, say, an enterprising apprentice researcher in a Poe seminar. Meanwhile, future readers of *Glorious Incense* should be forewarned that the list beginning on p. 208 is only a *Selective Bibliography*.

Proofs of the reach of Poe's fame accumulate year by year; they pose a problem too complicated for resolving in this Introduction. It might be possible to compress in the covers of one large volume all of the evidential material now available, or it might be more effective, I think, to initiate smaller and more tightly-defined projects. Here on the Texas-Mexico Border, I see bright hopes in an extension of the findings in *Glorious*

Incense into an up-to-date book on *E.A. Poe in South America*, or perhaps an essay on *E.A. Poe in Modern Mexico*.

Certainly there is much interest in Poe in Central and South America. In 1957, four years after the publication of *Glorious Incense*, I received a gift from Hector Strazzarino, an author native to Montevideo, Uruguay. Strazzarino's package contained two items; first his manuscript in Spanish on *Diálogo en las regiones Celestes*, a short undated drama with three characters: "Poe, Chopin y Virginia Poe (que no habla) [who does not speak]." This dialogue, according to author Strazzarino, comprises the last chapter of the book *Dos Vidas paralelas (Poe y Chopin)*, first published in the magazine *Germinal*, Havana, Cuba, October, 1951. The second item sent me was a copy of a small book, *Cuatro Poetas Cuentistas insignes* (Montevideo, 1955). The last (pp. 109-40) of the four litterateurs treated is "Horacio Quiroga, 'El Poe oriental'" (the others: Amado Nervo, Alejandro Puchkin [sic], and Robert Louis Stevenson). The chapter on the Poe of the East proved to be a most welcome acquisition; Strazzarino's findings afforded substantiation of my earlier claim in *Glorious Incense* (p. 122) that Poe's imprint could be detected in the art of Horacio Quiroga.

No doubt data on Poe's influence in other countries also could be developed into individual projects. Much of the pitiless darkness in Louis-Ferdinand Céline's French novel, *Le Voyage au bout de la nuit* (New York, 1934), particularly its scenes in the psychiatric ward, reminds one of Poe's madhouse fantasy, "The System of Dr. Tarr and Professor Fether." Patrick F. Quinn's *The French Face of Poe* (Carbondale, Ill., 1957) makes no move in the direction of linking Poe and Céline or of even evaluating any Gallic literary echoes. But the resemblances between the melancholy of Poe and the disgust of Céline are too strong to ignore. As for Poe's bequest to his own countrymen, I hold that he fathered Ambrose Bierce's touted bitter humor just as certainly as he sired Bierce's pessimism about American democracy (Richard O'Connor, *Ambrose Bierce, A Biography* (Boston, 1967), pp. 3, 6, 182-201). Similarly, I detect a link between Poe and George Sterling. Fritz Leiber once delineated Sterling's *A Wine of Wizardry*, published long ago by A.M. Robertson (San Francisco, Cal., 1909), as a "fantasy tinged with supernatural horror in the manner of Coleridge's 'Kubla Khan'"; but a handier model existed in the macabre poetry of Sterling's precursor, Edgar Allan Poe (for a text, see

Dale L. Walker and Al Frick (eds.), *A Wine of Wizardry and Three Other Poems* (Fort Johnson, N.Y.), 1967).

A matter of considerably less importance is the abundance of textbooks on Poe. These deserve no consideration in terms of scholarship; they add nothing to the lustre of Poe's name. The edition of his works compiled and edited by T.O. Mabbott for issue by the Harvard University Press doubtless will become, on the other hand, a landmark in Poe scholarship. Mabbott's many-volumed enterprise is destined to be a matchless acquisition for all Poe fanciers. There are many eager, indefatigable minds busy in the field today — newer students like William Bittner, Richard Cary, Carroll D. Laverty, William B. Todd; and older ones like Jay B. Hubbell, Floyd Stovall, Arlin Turner, and Harry R. Warfel. Certainly Mabbott stands in the forefront of living Poe authorities.

Two topics mentioned in *Glorious Incense*, Poe's alcoholism and his narcoticism, loom as challenging puzzles. His dipsomania provokes little debate. As for drug addiction, I pursued my own research and consulted a friend, Mr. Robert S. O'Brien, of the Bureau of Narcotics. What I learned was that persons over-indulging in drugs suffer impairment of the senses. In disturbing the sensorium, narcotics distort in particular both the conception of space and the sensation of time. The poet's resorting occasionally to laudanum may explain "Dream-Land," where he evolves a phantasmagorial region "Out of Space — out of Time" (Haldeen Braddy, "Poe's Flight from Reality," The University of Texas *Studies in Literature and Languages*, I (1959), 400). One must further admit that Poe's alcoholism may have hastened his death.

Sensitivity to alcohol may injure the body in many ways and lead to tuberculosis of the lungs (of the bone, the intestines, or the like); it may cause heart failure or an infectious tumor of the brain. In a letter to me (April 30, 1958), T.O. Mabbott favored the diagnosis of brain damage.

> Poe's death is not mysterious if you throw out the lies about it. Widow Meagher never had a tavern — I investigated for a note in the *Poems* (Harvard University Press), as he was said to have composed verses there. And a friend of mine has been working on his illness. Dr. Valentine Mott said Poe had a brain lesion and would not live long. Mott was sent for to England to operate on Queen Vic [toria]. A brain lesion produces manic-depressive states. Insanity was considered disgraceful by Baltimore "socialites" — and it is the occasional manic attacks that are what Poe hints about, rather than

opium....Neilson Poe said a single indulgence led to Poe's final spree.

In *Glorious Incense* I specified consumption as the major cause of Poe's death (pp. 184 ff.). His disease, it is clear, may have manifested itself in some other form — as perhaps tuberculosis of the intestines; as possibly, a lesion of the brain (or tuberculous tumor); and as conceivably a weakened heart. But all the theories just reviewed are patently guesses; and unless new proof is brought to bear on the case, I cannot retract my considered conclusion, namely that tuberculosis of the lungs killed both Edgar and Virginia.

To turn to a lesser matter, the worst mistakes in my book reveal themselves as errors in spelling, omissions of the article, and misplacements of English diacritical marks, French accents, and German umlauts. Such blemishes gall and frustrate an author. Many of them are fortunately too minute to weigh heavily against the usefulness of the volume. At all events, I now cannot correct them. Attempts to emend these lapses might well result in new ones.

Glorious Incense is flawed mechanically; and my judgments, though honest, may be challenged by new voices of dissidence. Mabbott once wrote me (April 11, 1958) that *Glorious Incense* "is of real help on *many points*. Few works are so valuable in general, save Campbell's — (and Phillips, when you winnow the wheat from the chaff!)." I therefore continue to believe that the patient prober into Poe's "forgotten lore" will be rewarded if he overlooks the rough exterior and focusses his attention on intrinsic values of the research.

Poe himself was very *avant garde*, as timely as tomorrow's headlines. In *Eureka* he was a scientist speaking of atoms, if not the atomic age; in his own notes to "Tamerlane" he long before the hippies experienced the psychedelic "trip" when, as he testified, he could "hear the sound of darkness" and "see music" (Eric W. Carlson (ed.), *Introduction to Poe* (Glenview, Ill., 1967), p. 565).

Haldeen Braddy

The University of Texas at El Paso
January, 1968

Preface

Glorious Incense, the Fulfillment of Edgar Allan Poe is
the chronicle of a gifted young man who succeeded in his
ambition. By working hard, constantly writing and incessantly revising, Poe in his maturity lived a busy, gratifying
life, the kind he preferred. This is seen in the letter written
to his friend F. W. Thomas during his last year on earth:
"Depend upon it, Thomas, literature is the most noble of
professions. In fact, it is about the only one fit for a man.
For my own part there is no seducing me from the path. I
shall be a litterateur at least, all my life; nor would I
abandon the hopes which still lead me on for all the gold
of California."

As a literary genius, Poe merits serious consideration.
In his *belles lettres* he was the inventor of fresh forms and
new effects; in his critical and utilitarian works he displayed
one of the best minds of the century. Before his death, Poe
saw his fame beginning to arise in both the United States
and Europe. The likelihood is that he recognized then that
his life was a triumph. It seems safe to predict that in the
future he will come more and more to be held, not as a
pretender concealing himself behind a façade of false
erudition, but as a writing man with a modest claim to
learning and a firm one as a thinker.

The nature of my investigation is chiefly historical. In
various libraries—El Paso Public, Henry E. Huntington,

Los Angeles Public, New York Public, Tulane University, University of Southern California, and others, particularly the excellent collection of Poeana at Texas Western College —I have examined the more important writings on Poe in the century since his death in 1849. My study is thus a literary survey of critical opinions of him from roughly 1850 to about 1950, with a few incomplete references to publications since the latter date. Without meaning to take sides in examining the materials available on Poe, I have attempted to show that many of the conventional views of him, persistent though they be, are basically unsound. Nowhere do I set out to give him the accolade. His finer compositions are, I think, among the very best America has produced, and that is very good indeed. At the same time I now and again have been critical of his art and his opinions. But where I have sought most for an objective approach, namely in the biographical section, I have perhaps been least so. For this I can make no true apology, for I believe that he deserved better treatment from his contemporaries than he received. Possibly he was no hundred percent gentleman, but I can not say that he was not respectable. In poetry Byron was his idol. It appears that Poe also endeavored to live like that poet and that he was condemned by a narrow-minded America for doing so. For the rest, I should be pleased if interested students found this book useful as a digest, or a review, of the elements which have served to establish Poe at last among the immortals.

The Samuel S. Osgood portrait serving as a frontispiece here is reproduced through the courtesy of The New-York Historical Society, New York City. Dean James Southall Wilson, of the University of Virginia, distinguished authority on portraits of Poe, testified to me, in a letter dated January 5, 1950, as to the authenticity of the Osgood portrait.

My obligations to earlier students of Poe, to specialists like Professors Quinn, Mabbott, and the late Killis Campbell, are many. I received encouragement from Professor Gay Wilson Allen, of New York University. Professor Nelson Adkins, of the same institution, kindly shared with me some of the findings of his projected study, *Poe and His Biographers*. Professor Thomas Ollive Mabbott, of Hunter College, generously loaned me his own annotated copy of the Harrison edition of Poe's works. In 1949 Professor Joseph Doyle, of Washington and Jefferson College, gave me material from his forthcoming biography of George E. Woodberry, an early Poe scholar. In 1950 Mr. David Post, American Vice Consul, sent me information about Poe's reputation in Mexico.

I owe grateful thanks to a number of friends who have examined my manuscript for errors. These readers are Professor George Arms, of the University of New Mexico; Miss Ada Rutledge, of the *New Mexico Quarterly;* Professor Thomas A. Kirby and especially Professor Arlin Turner, both of Louisana State University. My friends at Texas Western College, El Paso, also have helped me, namely my former students, Mr. and Mrs. R. E. Patton, and Mr. Francis Ehmann, as well as my colleagues, Professors Caleb Bevans, Francis Fugate, Joseph Leach, Baxter Polk, E. T. Ruff, John Sharp, C. L. Sonnichsen, and William West. Professor Leach aided me both in stages of the composition and with the final revision. Throughout my labors, note taking, writing, revision, I have been helped by my wife, Virginia Bell Braddy, to whom this book is affectionately dedicated.

Haldeen Braddy

Chapter One

Aim and Attainment

1. Poe's Works

Most readers remember Edgar Allan Poe as the author of several exciting horror tales, a handful of morose love lyrics, and three or four provocative critical essays. Perhaps this is how he should be remembered, for the supreme excellence of this small number of his writings is beyond denial. The position these selections now occupy in American literature appears permanent. Poe's place has not been usurped by any of the able writers of verse or horror stories and detective fiction who have been active since his time. Few American writers, if indeed any, are more universally read than Poe, because he is liked by every class of reader—the layman, the literary critic, and the scholar.

Poe himself hardly expected to win everlasting immortality with so limited a representation of his complete works. His prolific output includes seventy short stories, sixty-two poems, and over 250 critical and miscellaneous pieces.

Besides these, the works include one verse tragedy, *Politian* (1835-36); one philosophical treatise, *Eureka* (1848); and one scientific compilation, *The Conchologists's First Book* (1839); and finally, two published leaflets: *Prospectus of the Penn Magazine* (1840) and *Prospectus of the Stylus* (1848).

Poe's chief works, verse and prose, are contained in nine separate printings that appeared during his lifetime. His poems were issued in book form four times, in the following order: *Tamerlane and Other Poems* (1827), *Al Aaraaf, Tamerlane, and Minor Poems* (1829), *Poems* (1831), and *The Raven and Other Poems* (1845). During Poe's life the stories were printed in book form five times, as follows: *Tales of the Grotesque and Arabesque* (2 vols., 1840), *The Prose Romances of Edgar A. Poe* (1843), *Tales* (1845, 1849), a pirated reprint in London called *Mesmerism "in Articulo Mortis"* (1846), and an anonymous publication entitled *The Narrative of Arthur Gordon Pym* (New York and London, 1838). Quinn has observed that Poe also projected, but never published, a volume of tales called *Phantasy Pieces* (1842).

In the enumeration of the tales here, such additional titles as the fragmentary narrative "The Lighthouse" (first discovered by Woodberry and analyzed by Mabbott) and the sketch "The Atlantis" (recently brought to light by Quinn) have been omitted as inconsequential.[1] Similarly, in counting the poems, I have excluded a number of Poe's newly-discovered "tippling" verses (first cited by Mabbott)[2] as not of sufficient merit to qualify. On the other hand, I have classed the two long prose narrations, "The Narrative of Arthur Gordon Pym" and the "Journal of Julius Rodman," as tales. A group of verses attributed to him, though adding no lustre to his name, has been reckoned in totalling the sum of Poe's poetry. These poems appear in standard editions as his works. In the present inquiry they may be best treated in a briefly descriptive roll call, as they do not measurably advance Poe's place in *belles lettres*: "Elizabeth," (an acrostic to his cousin, Miss Herring), "To Sarah" (published in the *Messenger* above the signature "Sylvio"), "The Departed" (in the *Broadway Journal* the signature "L" is attached), "Alone" (ascribed to Poe by E. L. Didier), "A West Point Lampoon" (attributed to Poe by H. B. Hirst), "Latin Hymn" and "Song of Triumph" (incorporated in "Four Beasts in One—The Homo-Cameleopard"), and "Fragment of a Campaign Song" (attributed to Poe by Gabriel Harrison)[3]. The number of his poems, sixty-two, which excludes the "tippling" verses, is not greatly exceeded by that of his tales, seventy, which includes "Pym" and "Rodman."

The sum of Poe's compositions is in excess of 385 titles—possibly a round figure of 400 if all the ephemeral sketches, leaflets, and scraps of doggerel are entered in the count. Conceivably, the poet sought to achieve fame by producing a bulk of writing overpowering in its mass. The variety, range, and scope of his production is indubitably a marvelous accomplishment. The fact that the great majority of his writings is brief renders his attainment no less remarkable, for wherein these may fall short in length, they compensate with intensity of expression. Deep sources of creative energy were exhausted in composing them, and only a man of indomitable determination could have brought to completion so many literary projects. A question as to Poe's aim is thus perhaps justified: did the poet believe that by keeping before the public a stream of new titles from his ever-flowing pen he was increasing his chances at lasting renown?

2. His Craftsmanship

Lambert A. Wilmer's paper, "Recollections of Edgar A. Poe" (first published in the Baltimore *Daily Commercial*, May 23, 1866), is a tribute to the poet's industry during his Baltimore sojourn from 1831 to 1835. Wilmer said: "He appeared to be one of the most hardworking men in the world. I called to see him at all hours, and always found him employed." What was the nature of the work? Poe was trying to learn to write. And he was learning by the hard but best method, revising. There is hardly another writer in American letters who labored so prodigiously and who revised so incessantly as this indomitable craftsman.

Poe's mania for work resembles a scientist's passion for experimentation and accuracy. He sought perfection in every literary undertaking. Many writers have revised their poetry; Poe repeatedly revised his prose, as well. He constantly changed the titles of his tales and often added much interior description. Not certain in some instances which phrasing was preferable, he experimented, sometimes inventing a new title to supplant the old and sometimes returning to the orginal after a trial with the new. As examples of the first type of revision, "A Succession of Sundays" was changed to "Three Sundays in a Week," "The Visionary" to "The Assignation," "Life in Death" to "The Oval Portrait," and "Conversation of Eiros and Charmion" to "The Destruction of the World." These changes are marked improvements, since each revised title is more concrete. Illustrating the renaming process when it was less successful, "A Tale of Jerusalem" was temporarily changed to "A Pig Tale," "Metzengerstein" to "The Horse-Shade," and "Berenice" to "The Teeth." These three new titles were introduced in the projected *Phantasy Pieces.* As Quinn observed, "in each of these instances the new title is not an improvement and was not retained."[4] There are other changes of titles kept in later printings which look neither better nor worse than the original: "Epimanes" was changed to "The Homo-Cameleopard," "Van Jung" to "Mystification," "Siope" to "Silence—a Fable," "Signora Zenobia" to "How to Write a Blackwood Article," and "The Scythe of Time" to "A Predicament."

In Poe's poetry revision of titles occurred infrequently. Obvious improvement took place when "The Song of the Newly Wedded" became "Bridal Ballad" and "The Doomed City" became first "The City of Sin" and finally "The City in the Sea," but not when "A Dream Within a Dream" became either "Imitation" or "To——." There is little to choose between 'Hymn" and its alternate, "Catholic Hymn." Poe's procedure illustrates, not always an attainment of, but certainly an unflagging quest for exactitude.

Sometimes in the stories Poe undertook extensive revisions of details. When "Life in Death" became "The Oval

Portrait," a passage on the effect of drugs was omitted. Why it was is not known. The information which he withdrew is of too vague a nature to suggest a personal knowledge of the actual drugs. The most likely explanation is that he decided, correctly, that the description added nothing to the tale's effectiveness.

There are particular indications that in revising his texts Poe strove to reduce the purple passages. He omitted in "Berenice" the distressing description of the hero's return to the death chamber to look at the heroine. In the revised "Morella" the narrator no longer "shrieked" the name Morella; he "whispered" it. The altitude of the spectral vessel in "Ms. Found in a Bottle" was "one hundred times" that of the hulk on which the narrator floated until Poe thought better of it, and substituted the more moderate figure, "fifty times." Besides these important revisions, he introduced others, together with numerous verbal alterations and constant shifts of punctuation marks, in such additional tales as "Lionizing," "The Man That Was Used Up," "The Fall of the House of Usher," "The Duc de l'Omelette," "Ligeia," "King Pest,' and so on. All the modifications resulted in improvements—at least in Poe's opinion. The changes incorporated in "A Predicament" and especially in "How to Write a Blackwood Article" make these selections sound more learned. The significant reason for Poe's doing this, suggests Thomas H. McNeal, was that Poe wished to point up the satire on Margaret Fuller as the historical prototype of the fictional Zenobia.

There were more revisions in the poems than in the tales. Regarding these, Campbell said:

> Certainly no other American poet ever recast his work so freely or republished it so often once it had found its way into print . . . Of the forty-eight poems collected by Poe . . . ,no fewer than forty-two were republished or were authorized to be republished at least once; and of these all but one, "Sonnet—To Zante," were subjected to some sort of verbal revision upon publication.[5]

Often Poe's recasting tendency led to conflicting results. The first published text of "The Bells" comprised only 18 lines; the final form contained 113. The textual history of

"Tamerlane," illustrating the opposite principle of condensation, is hardly less arresting: in 1827 it included 406 lines; in 1829, 243 lines; in 1831, 268; and finally in 1845, 243. There are other examples of his unpredictable procedure. "Fairy-Land" in 1829 had 46 lines, in 1831, 64, and in 1845 the original 46 lines; "Romance" in 1829 numbered 21 lines, in 1831, 66, and in 1845 again 21 lines. "Lenore" appeared early in simple ballad form, next in an ode-like style, and last in a long-line stanza. Then "Lenore" and "The Raven" were also printed in a short-line stanza with caesuras. In recasting both "Israfel" and "The City in the Sea," Poe evened the stanza length. Uniformity was aimed at and caught in these poems, though this was not an invariable practice with Poe.

Poe's favorite revisions concern phrasing. He possessed the true poet's flair for the exact word in the exact position, substituting "started" for "wondering" in "The Raven" (61), "quivering" for "dying" in "The Conqueror Worm" (34), "grains of the golden sand" for "some particles of sand" in "A Dream Within a Dream" (15), and "yon brilliant window-niche" for "that little window-niche" in "To Helen" (11). Two famous lines (9-10) in the last poem once read:

> To the beauty of fair Greece
> And the grandeur of old Rome

before becoming the magnificent:

> To the glory that was Greece
> And the grandeur that was Rome.

But sometimes his alterations were less felicitous. In the last line of "Annabel Lee,"

> In her tomb by the sounding sea,

Poe later replaced with the phrase, "By the side of the sea." Also, in line 12 of "Dream-Land,"

> For the dews that drip all over,

he lost alliteration by changing 'dews" to "tears." Poe's revisions, however, were usually improvements over earlier readings.

The attention Poe devoted to his manuscripts indicates that he was profoundly interested in posterity's judgment of his style. A man who worked so conscientiously as did

Poe unquestionably respected the writing profession. Many of his brilliant passages that appear to be the immediate result of spontaneous inspiration evolved, instead, as the product of labored revision. The finished, highly literary—and indeed sometimes artificial—quality of his style was due largely to hours spent in polishing and repair. Poe's relentless quest for the absolute mode of expression became a natural procedure of his artistic thinking. He had a passion for the perfect. But his recastings bring to light something else, too—his passion for the decorative; hence his habit of prefixing a motto to individual poems and tales and of adopting such assumed names as Lyttleton Barry, E. S. T. Grey, Thaddeus Perley, Peter Prospero, Henri Le Rennet, Sylvio, and Quarles.

Poe's letters give a final proof that he was a stylist, not by inspiration, but by craft. The carelessness of their workmanship leaves a lasting impression of Poe's temperamental instability. He is by turns euphorically enthusiastic and profoundly depressed, too ambitious and too defeated. He wheedles his patrons, rebuffs his critics, and slanders his enemies. The letters unmistakably attest that he achieved a literary style only when he rewrote and revised his manuscripts.

His communications to Mrs. Whitman are different from all the others in being carefully styled, the marked restraint of these suggesting that there was the ulterior consideration of security in his proposal of marriage to her. His most feveredly ardent outcries were directed to two women already married—Mrs. Osgood and Mrs. Richmond. Yet even after the death of Poe's wife Virginia, his emotions for these two sweethearts were insufficiently inflamed to move him to write a single immortal passage of impassioned love.

J. S. Wilson, author of the Introduction to John W. Ostrom's edition of the letters (1948), is judicious in averring that "Altogether, this correspondence of one of America's first men of genius suggests the life of a literary hack." Submerged as he was by his responsibilities to his family, his duties to his editors, and his obligaton to his women friends, Poe was in the letters unable to view life and letters in philosophical or objective terms. The failure to rise in a dreary world above demands of the moment to a serious contemplation of his high place as a genius prevented Poe from delivering, spontaneously, enduring pronouncements on art, although these are normally expected from a writer as richly endowed with natural gifts as Edgar Allan Poe. Most great authors are skillful in their personal correspondence, and Poe is here certainly unlike Baudelaire, his greatest champion and disciple. Poe's genius forsook him when he turned to writing letters. Baudelaire's artistic convictions became an indissoluble part of his personality and always burned within him, demanding forceful expression. No such unquenchable flame fired the mind of Poe. He lacked the philosophical breadth of the Frenchman, and a comparison betrays the immaturity of the American's outlook. Poe is a lesser and more decadent figure than the Baudelaire who framed an original definition of beauty in a reply addressed to an unknown correspondent (August, 1851):

> As man advances through life and begins to see things from a higher angle, then everything which the world has agreed to call beauty loses much of its importance for him, and also carnal pleasure, and other trifles of that sort. In the eyes of the clear-sighted and disillusioned man each season has its beauty, and it is not spring which is the most enchanting nor winter the most evil. Henceforth beauty will not mean for him the promise of physical pleasure and happiness. It is Stendhal who says that beauty will be henceforth the form which seems to promise most kindliness, most loyalty in fulfilling one's share of the bargain, most honesty in keeping trust, most *finesse* in intellectual perception. Ugliness will mean cruelty, avarice, falseness, and stupidity.[6]

Poe could reach this height in his deliberate writing, as in "The Poetic Principle," where he describes Taste "waging war upon Vice solely on the ground of her deformity—her disproportion—her animosity to the fitting, to the appropriate, to the harmonious—in a word, to Beauty".[7] But in the letters he never approached it. For this reason the materials in Ostrom's two volumes supply the final truth that Poe the letter-writer was lamentably mediocre.

3. Best-known Selections

Poe's three most popular poems are probably "The Raven," "The Bells," and "Annabel Lee." "The Raven," which only yesterday was a favorite for public recitations, has remained popular because it is viewed as an autobiographical report on the lonely, tragic poet himself. "The Bells" is a phenomenal execution in onomatopoeia, and it retains its appeal wholly on the basis of melody and stylistic novelty. "Annabel Lee" is likewise melodic, and this singing quality partly accounts for its popularity. A further explanation of its renown is that the heroine of "Annabel Lee" is usually thought to be Virginia Clemm, though Sarah Elmira Royster (Shelton) is as strong a candidate.

Most literary critics prefer "To Helen," "Israfel," "The City in the Sea," "The Haunted Palace," "The Raven," and "Ulalume." "To Helen," a poem of only fifteen lines, recommends itself on the basis of its melody and imagery ("How statue-like I see thee stand"). "Israfel," in second place, requires an intelligent reader, for the poem contains a partial expression of Poe's poetic creed. "The City in the Sea," ranking third, has won high praise as Poe's most notable poem dealing with the world of spirits, its most famous verses depicting a shrine

> Whose wreathed friezes intertwine
> The viol, the violet, and the vine (22-23).

The gothic atmosphere of "The Haunted Palace," in fourth position, helped to inaugurate in American poetry the "dark tradition." Originating in the foreign clime of Europe, the gothic element hovers near the foreground in the fifth and sixth poems, "Annabel Lee" and "The Raven," but the evocation of darkness gained its best American expression in the poem placed seventh, Poe's "Ulalume," where darkness falls "down by the dank tarn of Auber, / In the ghoul-haunted woodland of Weir."

Scholars usually like three poems, "Eldorado," "The Conqueror Worm," and "For Annie." "Eldorado" is usually linked with the "gold-excitement of '49," but instead of referring to California and gold-hunters, the poem speaks of a land "Over the Mountains of the Moon" and of a knight who "met a pilgrim shadow." Accordingly "Eldorado" is clouded by the darkness that characterizes all of his poetry. "The Conqueror Worm" is Poe's most graphic picture of the inevitable end of man's mortality. The "Angel throng," helpless to prevent such a tragedy, shows human beings destroyed by the worm, symbolizing the serpent of evil. This gloomy outlook is historically important, Quinn says, since it marks "one step in the poetic treatment in America of the relations of God and man." However this may be, nobody will cavil with Quinn in his opinion that "For Annie" is one of Poe's finest poems, and his further statement that here Poe "reproduced an emotional state by a short throbbing measure, in which the very incoherencies mirror the mood":[8]

> And the lingering illness
> Is over at last—
> And the fever called "Living"
> Is conquered at last   (3-6).

In youth, according to contemporaries, Poe displayed more than trifling talent in his occasional drawings. One of the individual features of his poetry is its picture-like quality. This is apparent in "Eldorado" and "For Annie," and is conspicuous in "The Conqueror Worm":

> But see, amid the mimic rout,
> A crawling shape intrude!
> A blood-red thing that writhes from out
> The scenic solitude!   (25-28).

The graphic quality is a signal merit of Poe's verse, and doubtless his penchant for imagery is related to an early interest in drawing.

Five remaining poems are frequently mentioned: "Lenore," a ballad with a medieval element not uncharacteristic of Poe; "Spirits of the Dead," a poem which finely evokes the dark tradition; 'To One in Paradise," a sentimental lyric replete with autobiographical suggestions; "Bridal Ballad," a poem composed from the point of view of a woman; and "Al Aaraaf," a composition whose abstruse contents forbid the wide appreciation it deserves as an extensive predication of Poe's esthetic beliefs. These last five poems bring the total to fifteen selections, upon which the claims for Poe as a major American poet are based.

At first glance Poe's fifteen poems may appear a contribution slight in volume. But when one pauses to consider the impossibility of naming fifteen outstanding poems by most other American poets, even such writers as Longfellow, Whittier, Bryant, and Lowell, Poe's attainment becomes emphatically more imposing. Only Whitman is an apt figure for comparison, because he is clearly a singular exception to the above list. For fifteen of Poe's sixty-two poems to survive is decidedly not a poor percentage. The unique feature of Poe's claim as a major American poet is that, with the exception of "The Raven," "Al Aaraaf," and "The Bells," his poems are all remarkable for brevity. The fifteen poems discussed here comprise a combined total of only 1206 lines. This is worth pondering. Is there another poet in the literature of the world who, with less than 1500 lines, has reached the summits of fame attained by this American poet? Poe's feat is little short of astonishing. It is of course also a perfect illustration of his critical dictum, announced in "The Philosophy of Composition" (1846), that brevity is an indispensable characteristic of the effective poem.

Poe's tales are more popular than his poems—not so much because they are easier to read, for the poetry is quite intelligible, but because the tales contain more variety. The poems, preoccupied with death and the dead beloved, are remarkably limited in scope.

One type of Poe's fiction is what might be called police prose. Poe occupies a permanent place among authors of this genre because of the excellent results he achieved in the field. He holds the preeminent historical position because he, more than any other writer at home or abroad, was responsible for the invention of the so-called "mystery thriller." Taking possibly an idea—but little else—from Voltaire's *Zadig*, Poe founded the detective story. His superior ability is demonstrated in three famous tales: 'The Murders in the Rue Morgue," "The Mystery of Marie

Rogêt," and "The Purloined Letter." The series introduces the incomparable detective, C. Auguste Dupin, whose name Poe drew from a paper in *Burton's* on the life of Vidocq, the French Minister of Police.[9] Dupin, an erudite amateur detective of crime, is the original of a celebrated line of scholarly detectives which includes A. Conan Doyle's Sherlock Holmes and S. S. Van Dine's Philo Vance.

Poe contributed all the requisite ingredients to first-rate criminal literature. He not only featured as the central character a brilliant detective but further added a befuddled Prefect of Police as the literary prototype of the stupid Police Chief,[10] who is today another indispensable fixture of the mystery story. Poe worked without established literary models, relying upon his power of imagination and his own knowledge of contemporary crime. His police plots thus have no precedents in literature. "The Mystery of Marie Rogêt" is based on the actual murder case in August, 1841, of Mary Cecilia Rogers, Poe changing the scene from New York to Paris.[11] Both "The Murders in the Rue Morgue" and "The Purloined Letter" are even more original.

Poe's mastery in writing these three detective stories has made them perennial favorites. None of the numerous anthologies of mystery stories which are issued almost yearly neglect to pay homage to Poe as the founder of this form of popular literature or to include one of his tales as a specimen of the best that has been done in the field. His thorough mastery of the art of mystery fiction is also shown by his lesser known tale, 'Thou Art the Man," a burlesque of the detective story.[12] It was characteristic of the romantic genius of the gifted Edgar Allan Poe that he should write three masterpieces and then cap his unprecedented performance with a burlesque of the very plots which he had executed with such admirable success.

Hardly less popular are Poe's horror tales. Not even H. P. Lovecraft, his ablest imitator and a writer of truly exceptional talent, has superseded the master Poe, auhor of such well-remembered "tension tales" as "The Pit and the Pendulum," "The Cask of Amontillado," "The Black Cat," and "The Tell-Tale Heart." With its unoriginal situation of a captive tortured by the increasing arc of a swinging pendulum in compressing walls, "The Pit and the Pendulum" fails to reach the final titillation of terror when the prisoner is at last providentially rescued. Poe's careful description of the implements of torture omits nothing in its terrifying detail.

A full shock of horror is extracted from the situation in "The Cask of Amontillado" when in the wine crypt Montresor forever entombs the drunken Fortunato with a wall of stone and mortar. The setting is in an Italian city during a gay carnival—a scene sharply incongruous for the horrendous perpetration of murder. The complete emotional orbit from gaiety to terror is circumscribed with cold, scientific exactness. Possessing a fine psychological sense of calculated irony, Poe ends his "shocker" with a faint jingling of carnival bells on Fortunato's motley from behind the victim's sepulchre.

The device of the wall used in "The Cask of Amontillado" (a story first printed in November, 1846) Poe may have heard someone describe, or he may have picked it up in his readings. It is in both J. T. Headley's *Letters from Italy* (1845) and Bulwer's *Last Days of Pompeii* (1834). Poe's treatment of this oft-repeated theme is as effective as Balzac's in "La Grande Bretêche," one of the prize short-stories of modern French literature. The arresting circumstance in this story is the idea of burial alive, a topic which evidently fascinated Poe, since he had already used it in both "The Black Cat" (1843) and "The Tell-Tale Heart" (1844). A version of this plot with which Poe was familiar appeared in Charles Dickens' "The Clock-Case."[13] Corpses real or apparent, bodies that remain dead or that again come to life, are stock figures in the prose of Edgar Allan Poe. Other patent examples are "Berenice," "Ligeia," "Never Bet the Devil Your Head," "The Oblong Box," and especially "The Premature Burial," which cites a full number of allegedly historical incidents that earlier occurred. He even reverts to the subject in his essay on "The American Drama." He probably composed these tales because they were easy to write and were welcomed by magazine editors. But he

was intelligent enough to know that the triteness of his
subject would become apparent after its too frequent repetition in succeeding stories. For this reason, Walter F.
Taylor claims that in "Loss of Breath" Poe is satirizing his
own style in a fantastic burlesque of the hackneyed theme of
living burial.[14]

"The Cask of Amontillado," "The Black Cat," and "The
Tell-Tale Heart" grip us with terror because Poe has created
scenes of horror that are psychologically correct in every
detail. Sound is perfectly handled before the last faint tin-
kling of Fortunato's motley in "The Cask of Amontillado."
The auditory display of hysteria proceeds alternately from
laughter to screams, from cries to whispers, and so downward
to a last scarcely audible jingling of Fortunato's bells. The
ticking of a watch at the conclusion of "The Tell-Tale
Heart" drives the criminal to an unexpected confession of
murder. Visual effect is exploited in "The Black Cat," so
that at its end darkness dominates everything. Whereas
Poe's detective stories command respect, intellectually, for
their originality of plot, his "tension tales" stir the emotions
largely because in them are mustered together all the
qualities of gothicism and, in his three best examples, the
tremendously effective psychological factors of sight and
sound.

Two excellent pieces of psychological fiction are among
Poe's stories which maintain their esteem today. These are
"The Fall of the House of Usher" and "William Wilson."
The first story, presenting an old house falling into decay,
is hardly noteworthy, this feature being common in the
gothic romance. The sickly hero and heroine would be
equally unremarkable if their illness were consumption since
this disease is a commonplace in the romantic school of
literature which the French designate as *"l'école de poitrine,"*
The notable thing about "The Fall of the House of Usher"
is Poe's entry into abnormal psychology in his treatment of
madness. The story, like those in the other groups, is chiefly
the product of Poe's creative imagination.

Extraordinary as is "The Fall of the House of Usher" in
its depiction of of utter ruin and decay, "William Wilson"

in its methodical demolition of factors physical, spiritual, and mental was ahead of its time in the treatment of a mental disorder. The story, a precursor of the phychological fiction of today, was written well over fifty years before Freud began publishing his theories. As for literary origins, Poe may have consulted an article on Byron by Washington Irving in the *Knickerbocker Magazine* (August, 1835). Blanche Colton Williams regarded Calderon's "El Encapotado" as a forerunner of "William Wilson."[15] In both Poe's tale and Nathaniel Hawthorne's "Howe's Masquerade" critics have noted that a figure is described in the act of unmasking himself. Certainly "Howe's Masquerade" (1838) did not borrow from 'William Wilson," as Poe suggested, since Hawthorne's story antedated Poe's by over a year. Perhaps it was simply a coincidence. Oscar Wilde may have been influenced by "William Wilson" in composing *The Picture of Dorian Gray* (1891), a famous novel about a young man with a split-personality.

The vogue of psychological fiction, a field in which Poe made a significant contribution, is possibly the outstanding literary phenomenon of the first half of the present century. Poe's experimental stories about mesmerism, a topic much discussed in his time, are of slight artistic value. The mesmeric trance is as close to psychoanalytical hypnotism as Poe's age came, and Poe touched on the subject in several tales, such as "Some Words With a Mummy," "Mesmeric Revelation," and "The Facts in the Case of M. Valdemar." It is, finally, a kind of clairvoyance, or prevision, which is the basic theme of "A Tale of the Ragged Mountains."

After mastering the technique of psychological fiction, Poe turned on his creation and satirized it, burlesquing the whole subject in "The System of Dr. Tarr and Prof. Fether," which describes a lunatic asylum. The trend which Poe started has currency today, a recent example of a satire on the psychiatrist being H. G. Wells' novel, *The Croquet Player* (1937).

Poe's success extended to his experiments with the pseudo-scientific tale. Inevitably, since scientific knowledge is so constantly increasing, some of Poe's ideas now appear old-fashioned. A specific example is "The Balloon-Hoax," whose subject, a balloon trip, has become outmoded in an air-minded age. The story has now only historical value. Yet "Hans Phaal," another tale of a balloon, continues to excite our curiosity. It may do so partly because its realistic style creates what Coleridge described as a willing suspension of disbelief. More probably, it is because the major factor in this story is the hero's successful landing on the moon, a goal not beneath the notice of twentieth-century scientists.

Three other popular stories, classified here as pseudo-scientific because of the nature of either their subject matter or their style, are "MS. Found in a Bottle," "A Descent into the Maelstrom," and "The Gold-Bug." The first two are tales of the sea and are undistinguished for originality of plot. "MS. Found in a Bottle" (1833) appears based on *Symzonia* (1820), by Captain Adam Seaborn (? Poe's friend Symmes), and "A Descent into the Maelstrom" (1841) on an anonymous tale "Le Maelstrom" in *Le Magazin Universel* (1836).[16] The South Pole is mentioned in "MS. Found in a Bottle"; both a rugged hurricane and a fearful whirlpool figure realistically in "A Descent into the Maelstrom." The element of adventure combines with an observation of natural phenomena to make these sea stories two of Poe's most famous contributions to pseudo-scientific fiction. "The Gold Bug" is the tale of a fortune found and of a hero's re-establishing himself in society, its happy ending being a remarkable departure from the dark tradition.

These are the best-known short stories of Edgar Allan Poe. Now, over a hundred years later, they rank among the masterpieces of American prose fiction. This is not to deny that Poe wrote many other excellent tales; one is obliged to concede that his romances, "The Spectacles" and "Why the Little Frenchman Wears His Hand in a Sling"; his fantasy, "A Thousand-and-Second Tale of Scheherazade"; his allegory, "King Pest"; his impressionistic episode, "The Man in the Crowd"; and his dramatic sketches, "The Conversation of Eiros and Charmion," "The Colloquy of Monos and Una," and "The Power of Words"—do together display Poe as an author both versatile and prolific. It is only that

Poe's thirteen best-known narratives have firmer recommendations to lasting renown.

Poe's best-known poems (15) loom as neither more nor less significant than his best-known stories (13). The relative number in each class may be, to some extent, arbitrary. Perhaps another reader would name thirteen poems and fifteen tales. The added stories might be "Berenice," "Ligeia," or "The Masque of the Red Death." In Poe's own opinion, he was primarily a poet. Unquestionably, he was, at least, an equally accomplished teller of tales.

4. Autobiographical Echoes

Self-revelation in the works of Edgar Allan Poe has value for its bearing on his life as well as the understanding of his art. There is more autobiography in his poetry than in his prose. The reason for this is twofold: his verse is, first, largely lyrical in type and, secondly, most often of an occasional character, being addressed to real persons in actual life.

The use of autobiography became a major fault in Poe's earliest poetry, when he too frequently employed the personal pronoun. This rhetorical device characterizes the tyro in poetry, and Poe in later revisions sought to eliminate passages which were too personal in either form or content. A clear illustration of the latter occurs in "Romance" (1829, 1831, 1843), where Poe in a last revision cancelled the reading of 1831 about "being an idle boy lang syne, / Who read Anacreon, and drank wine." Much of Poe's early occasional verse nonetheless suffers from autobiographical coloring. His numerous dedicatory poems to this and that lady may have momentarily lifted him from the doldrums in the flush of creative excitement or even have swelled with emotion the palpitating bosoms of his female admirers; but they communicate hardly anything to the present-day reader. Such poems as "An Acrostic," "Elizabeth," "To F—," "To F—s S. O—d," "To M. L. S.," "Song (To——)," and the three selections awkwardly captioned "To—" ("The bowers whereat"), "To—" ("I heed not"), and "To — — — " ("Not long ago") contain among them all scarcely one line worth remembering. Their contribution to the Poe biography, because of the uncertainty or unimportance of their dedication, is likewise negligible.

The numerous lyrics addressed to women attest to the personal character of Poe's poetry. Sarah Elmira Royster (later Mrs. Shelton) was his first and perhaps his last sweetheart. According to tradition, she inspired the following eight works: "Tamerlane" (1827), "Song (To—)" (1827), "Spirits of the Dead" (1827), "To—" (1829), "To One in Paradise" (1834), "To Sarah" (1835), "Ballad" (1835), and "Bridal Ballad" (1837). Mrs. Osgood inspired five works: "To F—" (1835), "To F-s S. O- d" (1835), "Stanzas" (1845), "A Valentine" (1846), and "Ulalume" (1847). The first two poems, "To F—" and "To F-s S. O-d," were in earlier drafts intended for another person, most probably Mary White, daughter of the owner of the *Messenger*. Two other works, "The Sleeper" (1831) and "Lenore" (1831), owe their inspiration to Mrs. Jane Stith Craig Stanard, whose untimely death left a deep impression on the poet. The famous stanzaic "To Helen" (1831), since it reflects a general attitude, may apply to Mrs. Stanford and two or three other women.[17] Two works each commemorate respectively his affection for his cousin Elizabeth Herring, his friend Mrs. Mary Louise Shew, and his wife Virginia. Miss Herring was remembered in "An Acrostic" (?1830) and "Elizabeth" (?1830); Mrs. Shew, in "To M. L. S." (1847) and the blank verse "To — — (—)" (1848); and Virginia, in "Eulalie—A Song" (1843) and possibly "Annabel Lee" (1849). One work was devoted to each of a group of six women. The second Mrs. Allan, whose given name was Louisa, is celebrated in "Lines to Louisa" (?1831); Miss Hunter, a school girl at Rutgers Female Institute, in "To Miss Louise Olivia Hunter" (?1847);[18] Mrs. Estelle Anna Lewis, whose pen name was Sarah Anna Lewis, in "An Enigma" (1848); Mrs. Whitman, in the blank verse "To Helen" (1848); Mrs. Annie Richmond, in "For Annie" (1849); and Mrs. Clemm, in " (Sonnet)—To My Mother" 1849). As proof that the amorous lyric intrigued Poe, it should be noted that twenty-eight of his sixty-two poems were inspired by women.

Men, on the other hand, influenced Poe hardly at all. Some critics believe that his estrangement from Mr. Allan is reflected in both "A Dream" (1827) and "The Happiest Day—the Happiest Hour" (1827). "A West Point Lampoon" (?1831), a work attributed to Poe, is a satire of a man named Locke, who was an Assistant Instructor of Tactics at West Point. But these are the only two allusions of this kind to men in his poetry.

In fact, one looks in vain among the works of Poe for definitely autobiographical material other than that contained in the poems to women.

Descriptive passages in "Tamerlane" (1827), it has been suggested, may be based on the author's observation of natural scenery at Charlottesville. Some students examine "Dreams" (1827) and "Alone" (?1829), an attributed work, as autobiographical expressions of narcissism. Poe's religious beliefs may be mirrored in "Stanzas" (1827) and "Hymn" (1835). On unfirm grounds "Sonnet—To Zante" (1837) is sometimes regarded as his farewell to Richmond.

One or two general conclusions about autobiography in Poe's works now may be drawn. First, Poe endeavored to improve his art during revision by relying less and less on narration in first person and by omitting a personal reference to wine as possibly injurious to his reputation. Secondly, autobiography in the poems has to do so much with his regard for women that Poe ranks in American letters with Emily Dickinson as a perspicacious poet of love. One may credit in full Poe's frank statement in 1845 that "With me poetry has not been a purpose, but a passion."[19]

The short stories are in tone markedly impersonal, though some autobiography, particularly in the naming of people and places, may be gleaned from them. His few scattered references to liquor and opium are as casual as those to coffee, tea, and tobacco. In "How to Write a Blackwood Article" Poe evidently had read about opium, because he cites an imaginary article, "Confessions of an Opium-eater" (apparently in no way related to De Quincey's work by the same name). Perhaps it was this work which prompted him first to mention narcotics in "Ligeia" and in the cancelled version of "The Oval Portrait" for the pupose of increasing their credibility.

One must proceed cautiously in interpreting the stories as autobiography. Just as no reader would seriously insist that Poe's detective and horror tales are evidences of his personal participation in crime, one should not argue that the madness of his characters, as those in "The Fall of the House of Usher" and "William Wilson," indicates any possible insanity in his own family history.

Evidences of autobiographical echoes in his European fiction are a different matter. Pauline Dubourg, who is a laundress in "The Murders in the Rue Morgue," has the same family name as the Misses Dubourg who taught Poe when he was a schoolboy in London. The dazzlingly analytical brain of the detective Dupin, whose name possibly derived from that of Marie Dupin in the life of Vidocq, has been identified with the brilliant mind of Poe, the cryptographer, but the relationship is uncertain. In sharp contrast, the descriptions of school life in "William Wilson" are based closely upon the author's own adventures at the University of Virginia as well as at the Manor House in London. The headmaster of this school, the Reverend Bransby, seems to be the prototype of the Dr. Bransby in the story. An unexpected feature of the narrative is its false autobiography, Poe in the final version giving 1813 as the year of his birth.

There are additional stories whose characters may be related to people well known to Poe. First of all, his foster father John Allan may have been, as Agnes Bondurant proposes, the original of the person described in "The Business Man."[20] Some critics believe that he is referring to his wife Virginia in "Eleonora." Mrs. Annie Richmond is probably the lady described in "Landor's Cottage" inasmuch as a character of her temperament is here called Annie. Among other possible allusions to real persons, N. P. Willis may be the man satirized in both "Lionizing" and "The Duc de l'Omelette." Mabbott cites reasons for his belief that the fictional Mr. Snap in the Introduction to "The Tales of the Folio Club" represents Poe's friend John Neal.[21] A literal reference occurs in the "Literary Life of Thingum Bob, Esq.," where the editor of the *Knickerbocker Magazine* is expressly named Lewis G[aylord] Clarke.

There remain a number of stories which have to do with places and happenings with which he was familiar. Besides the allusions to Charlottesville and the University of Virginia in "William Wilson," an autobiographical reference opens "A Tale of the Ragged Mountains": "During the fall of the year 1827, while residing near Charlottesville, Virginia . . .," although there is nothing further in the story worthy of notice in this respect. London is mentioned in "The Assignation" (or "The Visionary"). The setting of "Why the Little Frenchman Wears His Hand in a Sling" is next door to 39 Southampton Row, London, where the Allan family had apartments in 1818. As for descriptions of American scenes, the Villa pictured in "Morning on the Wissahiccon" can still be seen in Philadelphia. Amity Street, Baltimore, is said to be the original of the Valley of the Many Colored Grass in "Eleonora." Poe's knowledge of the sea was probably utilized in "The Oblong Box," "The Narrative of Arthur Gordon Pym," and elsewhere. His own habit of canoeing as well as his appreciation of luxuriant natural beauty are doubtless reflected in "Morning on the Wissahiccon" (or "The Elk") and in "The Domain of Arnheim" (or "The Landscape Garden") His home in Fordham may be idealized as the building in "Landor's Cottage"; the figures of dimension in the story fit the actual proportions of Poe's Cottage in the Bronx. His seeing in Baltimore a rain of meteors in 1833 and of Halley's comet in 1835 was probably recorded in "The Conversation of Eiros and Charmion" (1839). South Carolina—Fort Moultrie on Sullivan's Island as well as Charleston—seems to have made a particularly strong impression on Poe. Charleston is the port of departure in "The Oblong Box." The beach at Sullivan's Island likely suggested the landing place of the travellers in "The Balloon-Hoax." The stately oaks in Christ Church Parish, Charleston, appear to be described in the climax of "Metzengerstein." Poe's most famous portrayal of Sullivan's Island

occurs at the opening of 'The Gold Bug." The reference
to cryptography in "The Gold Bug" is also autobiographical,
for in 1841 Poe wrote two series of articles on the subject
for *Graham's*. His futher interests in science are shown in
"The Imp of the Perverse" and "The Power of Words."

In retrospect, the narrative called "William Wilson" is the
only extensive piece of autobiographical prose. Merely
scraps of additional information could be assembled from
the other stories, so that further speculation about these
works is unprofitable. The personal notes in the prose, it is
clear, do not significantly enlarge our knowledge of Poe's
life. They do demonstrate that his art to a minor extent
only derived from his own experience, a situation in sharp
contrast to that evident in large numbers of the poems,
for which women inspired him.

5. Indebtedness to His Times

What part did the contemporary scene take in Poe's
literary art? The resolution of this question must appear
in any attempted final appraisal of the man.

Edgar Allan Poe was so avowedly a romanticist that it
would have been a contradiction of his esthetic principles to
deal more than superficially with the present and the near.
He recognized their value in the creation of atmosphere
when he pronounced verisimilitude a prime requisite of the
art of story telling. But he refused to believe, with the
realists, that the picturing of actual life is the main aim of
art.' One would be surprised to find in his works many illustrations of the real world in which he lived. If these were
present, it would be in open violation of his dictum. Poe,
so much a misfit in the world in which he lived, may have
intended his writings as an escape not only for his readers
but for himself. This view would account for the distaste
for reality shown in much of his work.

Poe's esthetic theories are so carefully applied to the
poems that local references in them to his period are nebu-
lous.[22] The most probable historical connection occurs in a

minor poem, "Fragment of a Campaign Song." Gabriel
Harrison attested to its authenticity on March 4, 1899, over
fifty years after its purported composition; he claimed that
Poe improvised this piece as propaganda favoring General
William H. Harrison's election as President. The student
must be alert to locate any further allusion to contemporary
happenings in all Poe's verse. "Eldorado" was influenced
by the gold excitement of '49; but the "gallant knight,"
"Gaily bedight," is obviously a typical figure from an earlier
age, most probably a conquistador—certainly not a mid-
century prospector who panned for gold in California. In
fact, there are direct allusions in three minor poems to only
three personages then living. Henry T. Tuckerman, a
fellow writer, is referred to in "An Enigma" in the phrase
"*tuckermanities.*" Miss Letitia E. Landon, a local poetaster,
is the person in "An Acrostic" designated by the initials
L.E.L. Napoleon is characterized as "The king Napoleon"
in the cancelled 1829 version of "A Dream Within a Dream."
Whatever evidential material there is of Poe's indebtedness
to his times resides elsewhere than in the poetry.

A bonafide specimen in poetic drama is *Politian.* The
plot was founded on a tragedy of ante-bellum Kentucky and
became the source of a number of contemporary plays. Poe
may have turned to the plot because of its sensational appeal
rather than through a desire to employ material from actual
life. A husband, Jeroboam O. Beauchamp, on November 7,
1825, killed Solomon P. Sharp for having seduced his wife
prior to their marriage. Both man and wife were taken to
prison and convicted of murder. Beauchamp's spouse took
her own life while still a prisoner; Beauchamp himself was
sortly afterward executed on July 7, 1826.[23] *Politian,* which
mentions America and her discoverer ("one of Genoa"), is a
clear-cut example of what one usually means by an author's
indebtedness to his own land and his own time.

Concerning Poe's references to his milieu in the tales,
Killis Campbell said:

> Poe's indebtedness to his times is even more palpably
> revealed in his stories. No one can read the American
> newspapers of the thirties and forties of last century with-

out observing how often the subjects of ballooning, of
voyages into remote parts of the world, of premature burial,
of mesmerism, of the pestilence, and of mystification of
some sort recur there.[24]

There are only two plausible references to his Southern up-
bringing in all the tales, these being in "William Wilson"
and "The Tale of the Ragged Mountains." Aeronautical
exploits figure in six stories: "Hans Pfaall," "The Balloon
Hoax," "The Man That Was Used Up," "The Angel of the
Odd," "The Thousand-and-Second Tale of Scheherazade,"
and "Mellonta Tauta." The first two alone utilize aerial
feats prominently; in the other four tales the aerial elements
are incidental in the plot. Voyages into distant parts occur in
"MS Found in a Bottle," "The Journal of Julius Rodman,"
and "The Narrative of Arthur Gordon Pym," where all the
predominant features come, not from personal observation,
but from printed books. Six tales—"Berenice," "Loss of
Breath," "Ligeia," "The Fall of the House of Usher," "The
Premature Burial," and "Some Words with a Mummy"—
concern burial dead or alive. Again, the explanation of
these is literary tradition and not reliance upon testimonials
of the era. As for "Berenice," an editorial in the Baltimore
Visitor (February 23, 1833) cites the crime of "robbing
graves for the sake of obtaining human teeth," assuredly a
practice sufficiently well known to belong within the realm
of Poe's general knowledge. A literary precedent for "Loss
of Breath" exists in Voltaire's *Candide* (1759). A story in
Fraser's Magazine (April, 1834) entitled "The Dead Alive";
Sir Walter Scott's *The Bride of Lammermoor* (1819); an
anonymous tale in *Blackwood's* (October, 1821) called "The
Buried Alive"; and the *Encyclopedia Americana* (1829-33)
afforded literary models, respectively, for "Ligeia," "The Fall
of the House of Usher," "The Premature Burial," and "Some
Words with a Mummy." Mesmerism, a development of
nineteenth-century experiments, was treated mainly in
"Mesmeric Revelation" and "The Facts in the Case of M.
Valdemar." But as Sidney E. Lind and Mabbott have
observed, Poe in the two tales turned again to printed
sources: for the first to C. H. Townsend's *Facts in Mesmerism*

(London, 1840) and for the second to the anonymous "Seeress of Prevorst" (New York, 1845).[25] To accept any number of these narratives as transcripts of an age is to stretch a theory unnecessarily.

Poe did, however, reflect clearly his awareness of his times in many subordinate, miscellaneous references to current fashions, local happenings, contemporary personages, and political, religious, and scientific developments of the day. The feminine vogue for bustles received passing mention in "The Thousand-and-Second Tale of Scheherazade," "The Spectacles," and "Mellonta Tauta." The cholera pestilence of the thirties is the background for "The Sphinx" and "Shadow" (the Black Death of the Middle Ages underlies 'The Masque of the Red Death" and "King Pest"). Americans and Englishmen mentioned in the tales include Thomas Jefferson, John Randolph of Roanoke, Commodore Matthew Fontaine Maury, John Jacob Aster, and the Prince of Wales as well as Lady Morgan. Democracy is attacked in "The Colloquy of Monos and Una"; Transcendentalism is satirized in "Never Bet the Devil Your Head"; and mechanical engineering is celebrated in "The Thousand-and-Second Tale of Scheherazade."

Comprehensive treatments of contemporary lore, though scarce, suggest one narrative procedure in Poe's methodology. The best instance is his confessed elaboration in "The Mystery of Marie Rogêt" of a sensational murder that occurred in the early forties, although S. C. Worthen observed in *American Literature* (1948) that "Some of the minor statements in Poe's fairly correct summary of known facts are erroneous." "Von Kempelen and His Discovery," so Poe told Evert A. Duyckinck in a letter of March 8, 1849, was composed as a "check to the gold-fever." "Mystification" may be construed less certainly as a satire on the nineteenth-century custom of duelling. "X-ing a Paragrab" reads as though it may have been intended as a travesty on the idiosyncrasies of one of the poet's editors, but this is purely conjectural.

These evidences warrant the conclusion that Poe sometimes utilized contemporary lore as either dominant or incidental details of his plotting. Poe at other times adopted a fictional procedure. Most often he exercised the privilege of a creative genius and produced imaginary settings in keeping with the needs of his art. "The Sphinx" narrates an imaginary incident that occurred in New York in 1832. "The Narrative of Arthur Gordon Pym" fictionally represents the hero as departing from New Bedford for the South Seas in June, 1827. "The Balloon Hoax" imaginatively records an aerial feat as being performed in the Atlantic area on April 6, 7, and 8, 1844.

In a final connection, it may be noted that a number of Poe's works are grounded on folklore, whose ultimate origin greatly antedates the nineteenth century. Thus the devil figures in five stories and the Negro in six. The unbonneted rider of "Metzengerstein" is traceable to the tale of Roushan Beg or the legend of Ichabod Crane. Three tales, "King Pest," "Hop Frog," and "The Devil in the Belfry," are properly classified as sagas of the folk. The hoax of "Hans Pfaall" is like the tall yarns of the West. The occult pervades "The Black Cat." "A Tale of the Ragged Mountains" belongs to the genre of the "Arabian Nights."[26] Of all these examples, one might reasonably expect Poe's treatment of the Negro to be most accurate, for he knew the colored man well. As a child, he had a Negress for nurse; as a youth, he engaged in the sale of a colored servant; and as a University student, he had his own personal slave. But in his works, when he came to describe the Negro, Poe based his treatment upon the conventional conception.

Poe's technique, as a matter for the record, was seldom realistic. Although some of his tales are said to be typically American or even peculiarly Southern, his settings actually range from anywhere to nowhere, from Hungary to the South Pole. In "The Mystery of Marie Rogêt," the most convincing illustration in prose of his use of a contemporary incident, he went to pains to create a Parisian atmosphere and to change the setting from New York to Paris. It is a serious mistake to emphasize his Virginia upbringing as composing a special trait of his work. The art of Poe contains an unexpandable minimum of Southern qualities.

What little local color his work possesses is due to the impress
of folklore, not to that of his environment. But even the folk
element is slight. His narratives lack throughout the quali-
fying traits of homely figuration and colloquial language.
His characters are not in the same classification with either
Uncle Remus of Harris's famous tales or, say, Joe Christmas
of Faulkner's *Light in August*. In point of fact, Charles S.
Sydnor, a contributor to *A History of the South* (1948),
claims that "Poe, the greatest of the poets, was the least
Southern of them."

In the last analysis, realistic happenings of the day
whether coming from contemporary newspapers or the folk,
influenced Poe less than almost any other writer of his
century, certainly less than either Irving or Hawthorne, each
of whom utilized folklore widely. Of course his critical
works, to be discussed later, are a different matter. Edgar
Allan Poe's stature today is that of a major romantic writer,
and to interpret him as anything else obscures his funda-
mental greatness.

6. Literary Models

Any explanation of Poe's success as a writer must include
the question of his literary sources. Although by no means
overshadowing other features in the portrait of Poe as an
artist, the models stand as probably the single greatest influence among the external factors contributing to his genius.
It is only when one further considers such personal attributes
as the author's own imagination, taste, experience, and
writing habits that the literary sources are seen in correct
proportions as ultimately of secondary importance. Much of
Poe's work conveys the impression of originality. And even
in handling materials drawn from various quarters he
managed to be more than an obviously derivative writer.

Many of the poems are without literary antecedents.
Approximately half of them, as noted beforehand, were inspired, not by literature, but by women of his acquaintance;
yet even among these, there is at least one instance in which

Poe utilized a literary source. The stanzaic "To Helen," written in honor of Mrs. Stanard, appears indebted in phraseology to two poems by Coleridge.[27]

The poetry of Lord Byron was perhaps Poe's chief literary inspiration. Byron's influence extends beyond mood and atmosphere and is detectable in theme and style. First, there is "Tamerlane," the character of whose hero he may have known from drama, as the plays by Marlowe, Nicholas Rowe, and "Monk" Lewis were available.[28] The closest parallels in style are, however, in Byron's *The Giaour, Manfred* (Act III), *Don Juan,* and *Childe Harold. The Giaour* is said to have influenced two separate passages in "The Sleeper." Again, phrases in "To One in Paradise" may owe something to Byron's "The Dream," "The Island," and *Don Juan.* The hero in Poe's "The Lake: To—" (1.19) hints once at suicide, and Byron's hero in *Manfred* (I, II, I) meditates killing himself. The influence of *Manfred* is more readily detectable in "Spirits of the Dead." Indications of Poe's having borrowed from Lord Byron recur in "Romance," "Dreams," and "A Dream Within a Dream," which are similar in title but not conclusively so in theme to Byron's "To Romance" and "The Dream." A more convincing resemblance exists between "The Coliseum" and Byron's description of the coliseum in *Childe Harold* (IV, II, cxlv.). For the motto of "Stanzas" Poe used a quotation of four lines from Lord Byron's *The Island.* In a statement in "The Happiest Day—the Happiest Hour" ("An essence-powerful to destroy") Poe paraphrases a line in *Manfred* ("An essence which hath strength to kill"). Finally, several passages in "The City in the Sea" may be derived from Byron's account of the end of the world in his poem *Darkness.* However critics may evaluate the extent of the Byronic influence, its presence is not to be denied.

Lord Byron influenced Poe in both his poetry and his attitudes. The Englishman's example accounts in large measure for the American's youthful dandyism. The concept of the blasted man, *l'homme fatal,* reduced to disillusionment and thoughts of death, is implicit in the definition of dark romanticism. And if Poe drew the idea from any one source, it was from Lord Byron.[29]

Poe's instinctive response to melodic line brought him inevitably to the study of Thomas Moore's Irish songs. Next in importance to Byron, Moore prompted many of Poe's lyrical musings. The opening stanza of the Irish poet's "While Gazing on the Moon's Light" supplied the model for lines 5-23 in "Evening Star," where Poe on a midsummer midnight finds the moon repellantly cold and shifts his gaze to the proud Evening Star. Both *Lalla Rookh* and *The Loves of the Angels* afford more likely verbal parallels than Milton's *Paradise Lost* for Poe's emotionalism in the youthful "Al Aaraaf." "The Light of the Haram," from *Lalla Rookh,* furnished Poe the central idea of "Israfel," a poet's song being likened to the lute of Israfel. Moreover, "Israfel" opens with a slightly inaccurate quotation ostensibly from the Koran (the Angel Israfel "has the sweetest voice of all God's creatures") which may originate in a footnote to "The Fire-Worshippers," from *Lalla Rookh* ("The Angel Israfel, who has the most melodious voice of all God's creatures"). A passage in Moore's *Epicurean* (ch. XII) may underlie the symbolism of "Eldorado." Poe's borrowings from this Irish poet are often quite direct and, as Hoover H. Jordan recently has shown, both important and widespread.[30] In fact, after writing "Fairy-Land," Poe confessed his indebtedness in the revealing statement that he had utilized "the works of Thomas Moore."

Poe's poetry proves his familiarity with other romantic poets of England. His announced belief in the existence of a supernal beauty, towards which the poet should aspire, led him to the contemplation of Shelley's sublimely intellectual credo. Unmistakable appearances of Shelleyean elements in Poe's style are less marked than the agreement in their poetic principles would suggest. The proposed resemblance between "For Annie" ("the fever called 'Living' ") and both *Prometheus Unbound* ("Death is the veil . . . , and it is lifted") and *Adonais* (". . . he doth not sleep - / He hath awakened from the dream of life") is too indefinite to be significant. The flower symbolism in "For

Annie" doubtless came, not from Shelley's "Remembrance"
nor even from Ophelia's memorable words about rosemary,
but from the folklore of flowers, which often is known by
children before they turn to books.   The connections with
Shelley are disturbingly oblique, though possibly one reader
may have a better ear than another for detecting literary
echoes.   I see no ulterior intention in Poe's "Israfel"; yet
Mabbott says: "The direct reminiscence of Shelley's "Sky-
lark" suggests he was answering Shelley, and it is just possible
that Poe thought of Shelley as Israfel."[31]

This type of heavily veiled reference is too abstruse for
ready penetration.   Campbell's notion that in "Fairy-Land"
Poe was influenced by *Prometheus Unbound* (II, i-ii) has
little to recommend it, especially since it tends to contradict
the poet's own expressed indebtedness to the works of
Thomas Moore.[32] Similarly, in "The City in the Sea" possible models in the Scriptures, in Dante, and in Byron obvi-
ate the likelihood of Poe's particular reliance on Shelley's
"Lines Written Among the Euganean Hills."   Furthermore,
the employment of silence to signify death in "Sonnet—To
Silence" and the traditional views on dreaming expressed in
"Dream-Land" were certainly topics which Poe could independently entertain without recourse to *Prometheus Unbound.* The full import of Poe's relations to Shelley can be
better measured in terms of an occasional identity of mood,
for Poe was inspired in his ambitions less as a slavish imitator
of Shelley's works than as an admirer of Ariel's rebel spirit.

The other major romantic poets, Wordsworth, Coleridge,
and Keats, figure inconspicuously in this review.   The opening three lines of "To Sarah" have been compared with the
first stanza of Wordsworth's "Expostulation and Reply," but
the relation is too vague to cite positively.   The works of
Coleridge were fertile ground for Poe, who in his title "A
Dream Within a Dream" may have drawn upon Coleridge's
"Recollections of Love," where the twelfth line mentions
"A dream remembered in a dream."   James Routh construes
"Fairy-Land" as a burlesque of Coleridge.[33]   Scholars have
regarded Keat's *The Eve of St. Agnes* (276-278) as a model
for two lines in "The Sleeper" (37-38), but Poe's poem will

strike most readers as entirely free of this indebtedness. Keats's *Lamia* has been cited as a source of "Sonnet—To Silence"; nevertheless ideas which these poems have in common belong well within the realm of popular knowledge.

There is evidence that Poe borrowed from such transitional literary figures as Cowper and Hood. It is Cowper's "The Stream, Addressed to a Young Lady," not Byron's "Stanzas to the Po," which most adequately parallels the situations in Poe's "To the River," where the waters tremble from the beams of the lady's soul-searching eyes gazing into them. Likewise, Thomas Hood's sonnet on "Silence" accords too closely in title and theme to Poe's "Sonnet—To Silence" for the agreements to be mere happenstance. But evidence of any further special indebtedness to either Cowper or Hood is unknown.

Poe's reliance upon the later neo-classical poets is problematical. There is reason to believe that he knew the works of Pope, whose "The Dying Christian to his Soul" may have occasioned some of the moral reflections uttered in the otherwise original "Lines to Louisa."

Poe knew such older English authors as George Peele and Milton and such German and French writers as Goethe and Bürger, Béranger and Chateaubriand. The blank verse "To — (-)," in lines on "dew / that hangs...on Hermon hill," misquotes a passage from Peele's "David and Bethsabe (1599). The angelology in "Al Aaraaf" is most easily accounted for in descriptions from *Paradise Lost*. Three lines from Goethe's "Meine Göttin" supply the motto for "Al Aaraaf." The title of the narrative "Lenore" may derive from Bürger's *Lenore,* a popular ballad mentioned in two of Poe's reviews for the *Messenger. Le Refus,* by Béranger, supplied the motto for the story "The Fall of the House of Usher":

> Son coeur est un luth suspendu;
> Sitot qu'on le touche, il resonne.

These French verses are the probable source of line twelve in "Israfel": "Whose heart-strings are a lute." *Itinéraire de Paris à Jérusalem* and *Génie du Christianisme,* two prose works by Chateaubriand, are linked with "Sonnet—to Zante" and "The Bells." From thence came Poe's use of the tradition that the island of Zante, together with the Italian "Isolo d'oro" and "Fior di Levante," took its name from the hyacinth. "The Bells" has for a possible model an excerpt in Chateaubriand's *Génie*.[34]

Some doubt surrounds the question of a literary model for "Annabel Lee." The poem is autobiographical, being a lament on the loss of his beloved, either Elmira Royster or his wife Virginia. Yet R. A. Law located in the Charleston *Courier* (December 4, 1807) a poem "The Mourner," signed D. M. C. This poem is in four stanzas, the third suggesting "Annabel Lee" in several obvious particulars:

> "But the smile of contentment has never return'd
> Since death tore my Anna from me;
> And for many long years I've unceasingly mourn'd
> In the cot by the side of the sea."[85]

Poe's lament, it is clear, owes something to either "The Mourner" or one of its now unknown later imitations.

Though a group of contemporary American writers—Pike, Hirst, Cone, and Chivers—may have influenced a few of Poe's poetical compositions, none of these deserves more than passing mention. The source of line eight of "Eulalie—A Song" ("Than the eyes of the radiant girl!") some critics trace to the thirty-eighth verse of Albert Pike's "Isadore" ("Thy sweet eyes radiant through their tears"). A further parallel between these two poems is said to be Poe's "While ever to her dear Eulalie upturns her matron eye" (20) and Pike's "Which thou didst lovingly upturn with pure and trustful gaze" (42). These random agreements in a word or two are surely without any particular significance. The two closing lines of the blank verse "To Helen":

> I see them still—two sweetly scintillant
> Venuses, extinguished by the sun!

have been linked, questionably, with the tenth and eleventh lines of H. B. Hirst's sonnet "Astarte":

> . . . thy argent eyes
> (Twin planets swimming through love's lustrous skies).

"The Conqueror Worm" probably derived its title from a poem by Spencer Wallis Cone, which was reviewed in *Burton's* while Poe was an editor. Cone's verses referring to the corpse of a warrior contain the line: "And let him meet the conqueror worm." The name "D'Elormie," employed in "Bridal Ballad" and in the story "The Man That Was Used Up," may have come from the title of G. P. R. James's novel *De L'Orme* (1836). Lastly, the alleged indebtedness of Poe's poetry to the lyrics of Thomas Holley Chivers is unlikely, though Chivers regarded his own "To Allegra Florence in Heaven" as the model followed by "The Departed," a work attributed to Poe. Campbell suggested that the author of "The Departed" was Chivers himself[36] and at least cast reasonable doubt on Poe's heavy dependence on Chivers.

A few famous poems seem to employ multiple sources. In writing "The Raven" Poe was acquainted with "Lady Geraldine's Courtship" by Mrs. Browning (to whom he dedicated a volume of poems) and also with *Barnaby Rudge* by Charles Dickens. There is a pet raven in *Barnaby Rudge* named "Grip," whose symbolistic possibilities Poe recognized in reviewing this novel in *Graham's* (February, 1842). Coleridge's "Ancient Mariner" may have inspired the use of the repetend in Poe's poem and in other ways may have affected its eerie atmosphere. But the suggestions are unconvincing which connect "The Raven" with Chivers' lyrics, Pike's "Isadore," the *Noctes Ambrosianae* (*Blackwood's*, 1829), and two of Tennyson's juvenilia. The genre of "Ulalume" is the best-known literary type involving a debate between the body and the soul, a type of poetry much favored in the Middle Ages. Poe develops the ballad's theme with so much originality that its medieval origin is unobtrusive. The imagery of leaves "withering and sere," which reappears throughout "Ulalume," he could have taken, as Nelson Adkins points out, from a poem "To the Autumn Leaf" (1837) by W. G. C. (probably Willis Gaylord Clark), which opens:

> Lone trembling One!
> Last of a summer race, withered and sere.[37]

Poe was well acquainted with W. G. Clark, editor of the *Philadelphia Gazette*, but the reference to autumnal leaves as "withered and sere" is surely an observation which he could make independently ten years later.

The suggested sources of "Eldorado" are Sir Walter Raleigh's *Voyages to Guiana*, an anonymous "Tom-a-Bedlam" song, the song "Man from Galway" in Charles Lever's *Charles O'Malley*, the poem "The Unseen River" in H. B. Hirst's *Coming of the Mammoth*, and a passage from Moore's *Epicurean*. Poe's unusual coinage in "The Bells" has been compared with descriptions in *Fraser's Magazine* (three times between 1830-1835), *The New Monthly* (1826), Paulson's *Daily Advertiser*, De Quincey's *Confessions*, Dickens' *The Chimes*, W. G. Clark's "Ollapodiana" papers in the *Knickerbocker Magazine*, and "Misocrotalus's" "A Letter to the Bells of a Parish Church in Italy."[38]

Perhaps one general statement is justified regarding the matter of Poe's literary borrowings. Not infrequently the multiplicity of suggested models vitiates the likelihood of his having had any source at all. Numerous illustrations indicate that the theme in question was possibly a matter of common knowledge and therefore not traceable to a specific literary original. Whatever Poe may have owed to other writers, he utilized these borrowings with so much artistry that even compositions of proved indebtedness retain the flavor of Poe's own poetic genius.

Poe's short stories are testimonials to his industry, orginality, and rare talent for fusing materials of varied origin into unified compositions. "The Oval Portrait," "The Island of the Fay," and "Landor's Cottage" were probably inspired by contemporary paintings, so that there are really only twenty-nine derivative tales. The fact that thirty or more of his seventy stories have no known basis in earlier literature—a number including some of his best fiction, "The Purloined Letter," "Eleanora," "The Man of the Crowd," and "The Black Cat"—may well demonstrate Poe's singular originality.

Yet Edgar Allan Poe had his literary masters. What Byron and Moore were to his poetry, Brown and Disraeli were to his prose. As often as not, the imprint left on the works by the whole romantic, gothic tradition is evident in such intangible qualities as mood and atmosphere. Poe's predilection for dark settings recalls the gothic scenery of Charles

Brockden Brown's novels. Scholars tie the situation of "The Pit and the Pendulum" to one in the twelfth chapter of Brown's *Edgar Huntly* (1799). The plot, however, was more readily available to Poe elsewhere, if not in J. A. Llorente's *Critical History of the Inquisition* (1817) (which L. Gallois translated in 1826), then perhaps in two contemporary stories from *Blackwood's*, "The Man in the Bell" and "The Involuntary Experimentalist." The latter two Poe mentions himself in "How to Write a Blackwood Article." Poe clearly perceived, as he showed in "A Predicament," that the melodrama of "The Pit and the Pendulum" was too strained; so he burlesqued it. His treatment of Disraeli, by whom he was deeply influenced, followed the pattern set in his use of Brown.[39] First, he seems to have selected, from *Vivian Grey*, in particular, materials like the horse in "Metzengerstein," the appointments of rooms and their furnishings in "Bon-Bon," and the main situation in "King Pest." Moreover, in "Four Beasts in One," Poe seems possibly to have been familiar with the camelopard in Disraeli's two novels *Alroy* and *Pompanilla*. Then he proceeded to burlesque *The Young Duke*, by Disraeli, in the "Duc de L'Omelette."

Horace Walpole, Mrs. Radcliffe, and Bulwer Lytton are three other English authors with whose prose narratives Poe may have been familiar. For gothic coloring in "Metzengerstein," he may have consulted Horace Walpole's *The Castle of Otranto*. For features of the old husband Mentoni in "The Assignation," he may have followed the description of Montoni in Mrs. Radcliffe's *The Mysteries of Udolpho*. In both "Shadow—A Parable" and "Some Passages in the Life of a Lion," he may have relied on Bulwer's "Too Handsome For Anything." And then, in a fashion now not unexpected, Poe in "Silence—A Fable" proceeds to burlesque Bulwer's "Monos and Daimonos."[40]

The continental writers best known to Poe were the French satirist Voltaire and the German romancers Tieck, Novalis, and especially Hoffmann. In "Bon-Bon" he mentions Voltaire's real name, "François Marie Arouet." In "Silence—A Fable" he evidently gleaned the name Zaire

from the Frenchman's drama *Zaire*. The variant names
Froissart, Croissart, Voissart, and Moissart in "The
Spectacles" may be contrasted with those in Voltaire's
Zadig, where the play on names is differently worded:
Nabussan, Nussanab, Nabassum, and Sanbusna. The char-
acter Zadig, as noted earlier, was the probable model for
Poe's detective, Dupin. A comparison of "Loss of Breath"
with Voltaire's *Candide* may be valid but to do so is to
stretch the parallel as far as it can conceivably go. Tieck's
work, *Journey into the Blue Distance,* is cited by title in
"The Fall of the House of Usher." A quotation from
Novalis's *Moralische Ansichten* is correctly translated in the
motto prefixed to "The Mystery of Marie Rogêt." Though
his theory has won approval in few quarters, Palmer Cobb
believed Poe was considerably in debt to Hoffmann. Cobb
linked both "Metzengerstein" and "William Wilson" with
Die Elixiere des Teufels, "A Tale of the Ragged Mountains"
with *Magnetiseur,* "The Assignation" with *Doge und
Dogaresa,* and "The Oval Portrait" with *Die Jesuiterkirche
in G——.*[41]

For the most part, Poe in his stories was not a slavish
imitator of any one special literary school or any particular
author. The range of his reading was wide. Before the
composition of "The Masque of the Red Death," he may
have perused J. K. B. Eichendorff's *Ahnung und Gegenwart*
(1815) or W. H. Ainsworth's *Old Saint Paul's* (1841) together
with Willis' letter in the *Mirror* (June 21, 1832) about a
"cholera waltz," "cholera gallopade," and a figure imperso-
nating the pestilence. According to one proposal, he was
in "Morning on the Wissahiccon" attracted to this river
by Fanny Kemble's *Journal* and some verses which had
appeared in *Burton's.* The skit "X-ing a Paragrab" has for
analogue an anonymous piece "Xtraordinary Play upon Xes"
in the *Mirror* (September 12, 1840). In both "Three
Sundays in a Week," based on the anonymous "Three Thurs-
days in One Week" (*Public Ledger,* October 29, 1841), and
"The Thousand-and-Second Tale of Scheherazade," he
employed statistics from Dr. Dionysius Lardner's *Course of
Lectures* (1842), to whom he may refer in the first story as

"Doctor Dubble L. Dee." "Hop Frog," which owes something to "P's" "Frogere and the Emperor Paul" (*New
Monthly Magazine,* 1830), is based principally on an incident
in Froissart's *Chronicles.*[42]

Since models for "Tell-Tale Heart," "The Cask of Amontillado," and "The Premature Burial," as well as both "Pym"
and "Julius Rodman"[43] have been earlier discussed, there
remains for consideration only the rather second-rate work
"A Tale of Jerusalem," said to be a burlesque of an episode
in Horace Smith's *Zillah, A Tale of the Holy City.* Poe's
narrative of three Jews who, after paying the Philistines for
food, receive in exchange a hog derives from the Jewish
Talmud.[44]

Poe students can look forward to a final statement about
Poe's literary sources from T. O. Mabbott, who has many
new and sometimes revolutionary findings to include in his
projected critical edition of the complete works of Edgar
Allan Poe.

7. Development as a Writer

It is traditional to assume that a writer over the years
shows progressive developments and that his works may be
divided into separate, distinct periods. At best the procedure
is often arbitrary. Such an approach to the art of Poe is
particularly fallacious. As a writing man, he could work
hard at revisions, but he did not at the same time succes-
sively generate new styles of composition. Besides this, he
died too early to undergo radical changes in his literary
theories.

An interesting trait of Poe's writing is that frequently his
early poetry is as good as or better than the later work.
"The Raven" (1845) belongs among his later compositions,
but is it as good a poem as the early stanzaic work "To
Helen" (1831)? It is possible that Poe was a better poet
in 1831 than he was in 1845. If so, what brought about the
degeneration? One scholar, Gay Wilson Allen, believes that
Poe's critical theories had an adverse effect on his poetical

productions. In a recent letter to me Allen says: "I personally think that the critic ruined the poet." It is notable that "The Raven" was composed at about the same time as the biographical "Memorandum" which Poe sent to Griswold. Perhaps the poem suffered from Poe's avowed determination to damn himself in the eyes of his readers—his desire to obtain public notice, regardless of its damaging character. Obviously he was self-conscious when he wrote "The Raven," as evidenced by his analysis of its technique in "The Philosophy of Composition," written in the following year. In the "Preface" to *The Raven and Other Poems* (1845), Poe confessed: "I think nothing in this volume of much value to the public, or very creditable to myself."[45]

About the only instance where Poe ran true to traditional form in the development of an idea is in his treatment of the subject of death. A great deal of his poetry is suffused with the graveyard atmosphere encountered in earlier British poetry. Much of what he said about love, his favorite topic, was well within the channel of contemporary tides of taste. There is assuredly something feminine in his preoccupation with the tepidly erotic; most male poets are more concerned with the world of ideas and affairs about them; and only women with narrowly circumscribed lives experience a range of emotions so strictly limited to love. Poe's individual contribution is that he inflected the melancholy tradition in an original manner when he mourned the loss of his loved one. The theme of the *princesse perdue,* the princess of long ago, came in Poe's hands to have less and less to do with a human woman. In "To Helen" (1831) her features are not modern: she has the "classic face"; her coloring is not of human shade; her hair is "hyacinth hair"; and even her body is depicted as rigid, not alive: "How statue-like I see thee stand." In the later "Bridal Ballad" (1837) she is not animated but has the "pallid brow." In the yet later "Ulalume" (1847) the princess has dissolved into his "sweet sister" and "Psyche." In "Annabel Lee" (1849) he can only return to his beloved in an imaginative flight:

> And neither the angels in Heaven above
> Nor the demons down under the sea,

Can ever dissever my soul from the soul
Of the beautiful Annabel Lee. (30-33)

The romantic idea of the far-away princess, *la princesse lointaine,* Poe brought to its absolute terminus. His princess is farther than far-away; she is irrevocably dead, irretrievably lost. In "The Philosophy of Composition" he wrote that "The death of a beautiful woman is, unquestionably, the most poetical topic in the world." However one may regard the pronouncement, the quotations afford a conspicuous instance of Poe's progressive development of an idea. I have detected no parallel example of the procedure elsewhere in his poetry.

The statements about the poems rather aptly fit the tales. "The Mystery of Marie Rogêt" (1842) is a prose masterpiece, whereas other stories similarly based on local history, like "Von Kempelen and His Discovery" (1849) and "Never Bet the Devil Your Head" (1841), are among his lesser works. It is not the historical occasion, then, which explains the value of the invidual composition. Neither is the chronology of a work a reliable determinant; for his later tales, in which he might be expected to profit from his writing experiences, are not invariably superior to his earlier ones. "A MS. Found in a Bottle," though printed as early as 1833, is on all scores more effective than a much later treatment of a like theme, "Mellonta Tauta" (1849), which is in its nature and purpose coldly philosophical. In brief, one is unable anywhere in the prose to isolate stages of progressive improvements that might be said consistently to characterize his stylistic development. About all that one may claim is that he had a distinctly unusual penchant for short rather than long compositions. "Pym" (1838), written in response to information from Harper and Brothers that American readers wanted long prose narratives, did not launch him on a career as a novelist. Although both "Pym" and "Rodman" have merit, Poe's forte was the short story.

There are perhaps multiple reasons why Poe almost exclusively cultivated the short prose narrative. Brevity of form coincided with his theory of effectiveness. The failure of the fragmentary "Pym," historically important as an early American sea novel, was doubtless another consideration. It must be recalled that only five years beforehand he had won an award from the *Baltimore Saturday Visiter,* which on October 19, 1833, printed his "MS. Found in a Bottle" as the premium-winning story and that in general he had experienced relatively little difficulty in selling his tales to current periodicals. Although there was the matter of ready money to be quickly accrued from the sale of short compositions, I believe that Poe's thirst for immediate fame prevented him from devoting the time that was necessary for developing a technique to handle the large scope of a novel. As a magazine editor himself, Poe naturally had a more intimate knowledge of markets for tales than for novels. There is the further circumstance that he worked by fits and starts and that he probably never possessed enough energy to sustain him through the completion of a writing chore as dimensional as a novel. Besides, Poe's few intimate friends did not include book publishers, who might have influenced his writing habits.

Despite the spatial limits of his works, Poe in his lifetime wrote enough to emerge, undeniably, as a major writer. The appeal of his poetry, usually too personal to possess universality, is not remarkable for its breadth, nor did he inspire a school of imitators. It was Walt Whitman who set the tempo for the modern school of free-verse poets, Carl Sandburg being his most obvious heir, whereas the style of Poe, though claimed as an influence on Hart Crane, has not established, in America at least, a similar cult of followers.

Yet there are, today, a large number of Poe devotees among the *literati,* many of his twentieth-century readers expressing intense admiration for the peculiar qualities of his dark poetry. The occasional radio recitation of such poems as "The Raven" may be gaining acclaim for Poe among auditors who would not otherwise know of him or his works. Rachmaninoff's impressive symphonic arrangement of "The Bells" has exerted a fine effect on Poe's reputation as a lyrical poet.

It is as a writer of short stories that Poe remains best known. The popularity of his plots is shown by their being utilized by later authors. Guy de Maupassant's "Beside Schopenhauer's Corpse" recalls "Berenice;" Joel Chandler Harris's "Tellmenow Isitsoornot," "A Thousand-and-Second Tale of Scheherazade;" and, most recently, Eric Knight's "Never Come Monday," "Three Sundays in a Week." His prose style early attracted eminent literary imitators abroad and at home. His followers in England include A. Conan Doyle and Robert Louis Stevenson; in America, Fitz-James O'Brien, Thomas Bailey Aldrich, Ambrose Bierce, and Howard Philipps Lovecraft. In our time Hollywood has popularized Poe with cinematic versions of titles like "The Murders in the Rue Morgue" and "The Black Cat." The Decca recording company has recently issued a valuable album of "The Cask of Amontillado," with Sidney Greenstreet as narrator.

The reputation of Poe as a story teller is now quite perceptibly on the increase. His skillful craftsmanship conforms with the best practices of successful twentieth-century authors, whose methods he anticipated, particularly in narratives of imaginary voyages, police prose, and psychological fiction. The short stories of Poe are peculiarly adaptable to the needs of today—to the screen, the radio, the phonograph, and even television. The Menzies-Finney Company has selected "The Tell-Tale Heart" to be first in a series of telecastings which later will feature "The Pit and the Pendulum." The spirit of Edgar Allan Poe was never more intensely alive, nor his technique ever more worthy of study, than now.

Chapter Two

Theorist and Technician

1. Esthetic Principles in Practice

After Poe learned to write, he formulated for others the principles which had been of service to him in mastering that art. His criticism, though at times elementary, is practical. It is sound because it had been tested in his own workshop before it was recommended to beginning writers. Poe claimed, with only partial truth, that it originated in age-old literary traditions. His principal tenets, stated with exactness and clarity, merit thoughtful investigation, for a correct appraisal of his ideas is an important step towards a just estimate of the man.

Today Edgar Allan Poe's reputation as a superior theorist rests upon his doctrine of brevity for effect. Throughout his later career Poe maintained that all effective writing reveals in its form a requisite compactness. In 1847, in a review of Hawthorne's *Twice-Told Tales*, he announced that a poem or a story does not increase in value commensurate with the length it atttains but must observe a due proportion. Poe said: "Common sense, in the time to come, may possibly insist upon measuring a work of art rather by the objects which it fulfils, by the impression it makes, than by the time it took to fulfil the object . . . ."[46]

In an earlier review of *Twice-Told Tales* in 1842, Poe had predicated his convictions more exactly, stating that a rhymed poem should not "exceed in length what might be perused in an hour" and that "Within this limit alone can the highest order of true poetry exist." This dictum, obviously invalid as a universal principle because it would exclude from the realm of poetry practically all verse forms except the lyric, Poe refuted four years afterward in "The Philosophy of Composition" (1846), where he recognized the necessity of admitting works of larger scope. Meanwhile, in the paper of 1842, he applied his theory to prose, acknowledging that "We may continue the reading of a prose composition .. . . much longer than we can . . . a poem." His recognition of the effect produced by short prose narratives, while it ignores the impressions of completeness conveyed by a novel, discloses a basic aspect of Poe's modernity. A magazinist himself, Poe foreshadows present-day editors who advertise the reading time of their wares.

Further in his analysis of Hawthorne, Poe explained that brevity conforms with the normal duration of man's experiences when he is highly excited. He now banished the epic as an outworn vehicle, an art form fallen into disuse because its narrative was too prolonged to sustain excited interest: "Epics were the offspring of an imperfect sense of art, and their reign is no more." With an identical argument he disposed of the novel. He declared that since " it cannot be read at one sitting, it deprives itself, of course, of the immense force derivable from totality."[47]

In his dismissal of epic and novel, the critic Poe handed to posterity an ultimatum which had been brought home to the writer Poe. With short stories he had tasted the flavor of real success; with the long "Pym" and "Julius Rodman," the bitterness of disappointment and failure. His theory is vulnerable on the grounds that the experiences of authors differ and that readers are normally indifferent to the matter of length provided the selection creates human interest.

Poe in the course of time was wise enough to consider further the danger of arbitrarily evaluating everything by its brevity, though the issue was never squarely faced. In "The Philosophy of Composition" (1846), he shifted his position slightly, as from one critical foot to the other, recommending for a poem "a length of about one hundred lines." His arithmetic meant a round number, for he gave as an example "The Raven" with " a hundred and eight." He neglected to mention "The Bells," 113; "Tamerlane," 243; and "Al Aaraaf," 264 lines. In 1842, when speaking of the epics, he had stated that " a long poem is a paradox." How, then, could he in 1846 still uphold this principle in the face of having himself composed two long poems like "Tamerlane" and "Al Aaraaf"?

In this manner Poe, by necessity, pondered the structure of the epic. Perhaps he talked the matter over with his old friend Charles Anthon and from him learned that in *Prolegomena in Homerum* (1795) Friedrich Wolf, the celebrated German scholar, interpreted the *Iliad* and the *Odyssey* as blendings of separate hymns or poems. At any rate, Poe in 1846 wrote differently about the long poem, which he now explained as "merely a succession of brief ones." He then declared that in the *Iliad* "we have, if not positive proof, at least very good reason, for believing it intended as a series of lyrics." Poe here revealed himself as a pundit in drawing his illustrations from the Greek classics. He also revealed himself as an authoritarian, for he believed that he had discovered in art an indispensable element, a *sine qua non* of literary criticism.

But Poe erred in his formulations by proposing his analysis of the *Iliad* as an elucidation of all epics. Momentarily tantalizing as his theory is, it is not an absolutism, and the short-sightedness of the ambitious young critic is hardly anywhere more evident than in his reduction of *Paradise Lost* to "a series of minor poems." Robert K. Root recently observed that Alexander Pope sometimes varied the style of his larger works by the employment of sonnet-like "heroic paragraphs,"[48] and Root here avoided the pitfall which ruined Poe when he let his acute observation rest there. With Root's evidence, Poe would have described Pope's mock-epics as "a series of irregular sonnets." There is a residuum of truth in Poe's dictum on brevity; but he over-stated its advantages, stretched the illustrations to suit his theory, and became hypnotized by a mechanistic attitude more applicable to science than to art.

The rules laid down in "The Philosophy of Composition" belong to a common sense, or Scotch, school of criticism. Of course all good writing should be original, brief, lifelike, intense, and compelling in the totality of its effect. Stated thus, the principles are worthwhile for a beginning writer, to whom Poe's remarks have greater practical value than to an accomplished student of esthetics. His artistic views are too mechanistic—writing can be evaluated by its length— and too sensationalistic—art is measurable by the excitement it produces.

Other authors might inculcate morality or describe the beautiful; Poe aimed his shots at the reader's nervous system. Compositions with brevity, verisimilitude, and totality were required, because they contributed most to an intensification of the quality of "effect." To him a poem became a machine for creating an "effect," for charging the emotions to nervous pitch. His intentions, carried out with completest results in "The Bells" and "The Raven," brought to his later poetry a brassier quality than it had owned before.

The limitations of Poe's art may have grown out of the narrowness of his theory rather than the poorness of his workmanship. For this reason, it is sometimes claimed that the critic ruined the poet. Certainly his later poems tend to lack delicacy and refinement. In artistic intensity the early stanzaic "To Helen" (1831) is superior to "The Raven" (1845). It is in "Ulalume" (1847) alone that the old manner is recaptured and presented with a gain in effectiveness, particularly in atmosphere, by the addition of mechanical echoes and studied repetitions.

"The Bells" (1849) is an experiment in onomatopoeia
as well as crescendo. We are supposed to hear the bells and
we do. In "The Raven" we are supposed to see and to
hear the bird and we do both. These poems and such tales
as "Ligeia," "The Fall of the House of Usher," and "The
Tell-Tale Heart" are all mechanistically arranged to startle
the reader, dilate his pupils, and disturb his nerves. Poe,
who practiced in his works what he preached in his criticism,
was unquestionably *l'avant garde,* his doctrine of "effect"
linking him with the present, not the past.

Poe applied some of his critical principles, namely originality and realism, to the contemporary theatre. In his
essay on "The American Drama" (1845) he struck out
vigorously against Sheridan Knowles for perpetrating "the
most preposterous series of imitations of the Elizabethan
drama, by which mankind were ever insulted or beguiled."
He next recommended that playwrights develop new methods
and create fresh innovations.[49] In some eight papers— which
touch on Sophocles's *Antigone,* Mrs. Anna Cora Mowatt's
Fashion as well as *Faint Heart Never Won Fair Lady,* N. P.
Willis' *Tortesa the Usurer,* Longfellow's *Spanish Student,*
and the Shakespearean imitation, *Katherine and Petrucchio—*
Poe attacked "closet drama," ill-constructed plots, and lifeless
characters. According to N. Bryllion Fagin, a close student
of the theatre, Poe then espoused standards which are now
observed by the best modern dramatists:

> He believed in realistic drama, containing plausible plots
> and presenting characters that are recognizable human
> beings. He insisted on acting based on direct observation
> of nature rather than on hackneyed theatrical traditions.
> Had he been able he would have cleared the stage of
> tricksters and pretenders . . . . Mr. Poe spoke for these
> things a long time ago.[50]

As for Poe's own incomplete play *Politian* (1835-36),
perhaps the less said the better. In basing the plot on a
contemporary tragic happening which had been treated the
year before by his friend Chivers in *Conrad and Eudora*
(1834), Poe violated, with sad results, one of his own principles, namely originality. The drama is a failure, just as are

"Pym" and "Julius Rodman," the two long prose works which exceeded his specifications for length.

Poe's principal ideas about criticism are expressed in "The Philosophy of Composition" (1846) and in a lecture of 1848 called "The Poetic Principle" (printed in 1850). This second essay has won acclaim for its statement of the theory of art for art's sake. The idea, basically Platonic, assumes the existence of a supernal "loveliness" towards which man aspires. The abstraction was not, like his practical criticism, Poe's own original discovery. Indeed, he despised the cloudiness of this type of idea, as his hatred of American Transcendentalism testifies. He had, however, respect for Coleridge, a powerful exponent of the theory; and it was Coleridge who involved him in a dilemma which for a time threatened to invalidate his proposal that the aim of art was, not to apprehend the beautiful, but to excite the reader.

As early as 1836, in a review of Drake and Halleck, Poe waxed Platonic in declaring that a heavenly design comprehends human existence:

> To look upward from any existence, material or immaterial, to its *design,* is perhaps, the most direct and the most unerring method of attaining a just notion of the nature of the universe itself.

It was in his later strictures on Longfellow in 1842 that Poe introduced a perception of the "Beautiful" as the poet's prime objective:

> An important condition of man's immortal nature is thus, plainly, the sense of the Beautiful . . . . It is a wild effort to reach the beauty above. It is a forethought of the loveliness to come.

In his yet later address on "The Poetic Principle," already referred to, he arrived at a modification of his earlier words:

> An immortal instinct deep within the spirit of man is thus plainly a sense of the Beautiful. There is still a something in the distance which he has been unable to attain . . . . It is no mere appreciation of the Beauty before us, but a wild effort to reach the Beauty above.[51]

If this were everything, one might argue that Poe, like his mentor Coleridge, was a Platonist and a spokesman of art for art's sake. But this is not everything. At no place in Poe's creative work is there a firm exposition of Platonic beauty. "Al Aaraaf," in which the heroine Nesace sings in praise of God and prescribes that only ideal thought can become "A partner of thy throne," might be supposed a logical poem for its discussion. Yet Poe himself, in a letter to Isaac Lea of May 27, 1829, depicted the star Al Aaraaf as a "medium between Hell and Heaven . . . ," where it may be left, somewhat this side of ideal "loveliness."

There is, however, no inconsistency in Poe's esthetic credo, if one examines the whole of the evidence. The opportunity to reconcile his doctrine of excitement with the Platonic theory came near the end of the essay, "The Poetic Principle," where Poe was obliged to discuss the conditions existing when the poet is inspired. Poe avidly seized it. In order that the reader might not lose his meaning, he placed the most significant words in italics, as follows:

> It has been my purpose to suggest that, while this principle itself is strictly and simply the Human Aspiration for Supernal Beauty, the manifestation of the principle is always found in *an elevating excitement of the soul* . . . .[52]

This theory of excitation, one may well believe, is a rather exact statement of what actually happens to the poet. According to A. E. Housman, the creative experience electrifies the human body in a series of nervous flashes. Housman said that sometimes when he was shaving a strong "inspiration" made the bristles on his face rise unexpectedly. It is this brief sensation which the poet seeks, in the form of art, to convey to his readers. To put the matter simply, it is the sensation aimed at in Poe's doctrine of brevity for effect.

2. Metrics

The third prominent specimen of Poe's criticism, "The Rationale of Verse" (1848), is a technical treatment of versification. With 'The Philosophy of Composition" and "The Poetic Principle," it forms, as Paul Elmer More observed, "one of the few aesthetic treatises in English of real value."[53] Poe's remarks, first printed in 1843 in *The Pioneer* under the title "Notes on English Verse," are today remembered for two reasons: first, his essay was among the first serious discussions of prosody in American literary criticism; secondly, his theory of the relations between verse and prose is a prediction of Amy Lowell and the modern school of Imagist poets.

The ideas incorporated in "The Rationale of Verse" are largely the outgrowth of what Poe learned from writing and from laboriously revising his own works. His versatility as a poet was displayed in workmanship that employed heroic couplets ("Al Aaraaf"), four-stress couplets ("Spirits of the Dead" and "Dream Land"), "free-stress" stanzas ("To Helen" and "Israfel"), seven-stress lines ("Lenore"), blank verse ("The Coliseum"), eight-stress trochees ("The Raven"), three-stress anapests ("Ulalume"), parallelism and alliteration ("Annabel Lee"), and other experimental forms ("Evening Star" and "Bridal Ballad"). Poe may be slightly indebted to British criticism, particularly to Coleridge, but little, as is sometimes claimed, to a group of minor American poets, like Drake and Halleck, Samuel Woodworth, E. C. Pinkney, and N.P. Willis. These personages and others Poe mentions in his essays, papers, and book reviews—sometimes with a word of comment on their skill at composing verses. Yet Poe's use of blank verse in "The Coliseum" is scarcely, if at all, reminiscent of that employed by N. P. Willis in "The Widow of Nain"; and while the "melody mad" Israfel, with its lines of uneven length, may owe something of its rhythmical effect to the influence of Coleridge, it does not imitate *The Rime of the Ancient Mariner*.

Poe's critical principles are, indeed, original to an unusual degree. The instances of his indebtedness are few and sometimes doubtful. In "Letter to B—" (1831) he may echo Wordsworth's misquotation of Aristotle—poetry is the "most philosophical of all writings"—because Aristotle said only that it was more philosophical than history. "Exordium" (1842), a series of critical dicta, reflects no special reliance on outside authority. His contention in "Preface" to *The Raven and Other Poems* (1845), that poetry originates in the passions, doubtless derived from his personal experience; but not so his references in "The Philosophy of Composition" (1846) to the Classical Unities of time, place, and action, which stem ultimately from Aristotle and Horace. Possibly "What Is Poetry?"—a paper by his friend John Neal—inspired Poe's specific comparisons of poetry and music in "The Poetic Principle" (1850);[54] but these are the only important places of his borrowing. The major part of Poe's critical work was thus generally original. "The Rationale of Verse" (1848), though discussing an old subject, is remarkable for its fresh approach and its daring utterances.

Rationalism became a fetish with Poe. "The subject is exceedingly simple," he declared, "one-tenth of it, possibly, may be called ethical; nine-tenths, however, appertain to the mathematics; and the whole is included within the limits cf the commonest common-sense." His predication neglects to differentiate between the two main schools of prosodists, those who emphasize tempo and those who emphasize accent. He erred in propounding a mechanistic formula. As Gay Wilson Allen expresses it, Poe in his attempt "to solve the problems with mathematical percision would force us to read poetry with a metronome."

By *long* and *short* syllables, Poe meant *accented* and *unaccented* syllables. In scanning verses an old-fashioned custom places a macron, long mark, over the syllable receiving the beat and a short, upturned one over the unstressed elements. A dilemma arises in Poe's oversimplified description of *long* and *short* syllables. "The *natural* long syllables are those encumbered" by consonants, he says. This statement, to which modern critics object, is accurate in a limited, historical sense. In Old English a vowel is *long by position* when followed by two or more consonants. One of Poe's mentors at the University of Virginia, Professor Blaetterman, was among the first scholars to introduce the study of Old English into the United States. Blaetterman may well have explained to the student Poe the useful rule that in early English a syllable may be *long by position,* or naturally so. In this same essay, "The Rationale of Verse," Poe mentions Chaucer's versification, so that his remark on prosody may have been intended as an historical observation. The rule about consonants has no practical utility in modern scansion.

Though the meaning of "The Rationale of Verse" is not immediately obvious, Edward H. O'Neill, a recent Poe commentator, was unjustified in regarding the poet on this account as an ignoramus.[55]

Poe's essay on versification casts further light on his personality in its reflections of the author as a scientist. In "The Philosophy of Composition" and "The Poetic Principle," having reckoned the value of a work in direct ratio to its transitory effect of high excitement, Poe now wanted in this essay to measure versification with similar exactness. To do so, he proposed it as his discovery that in a series of verses the accents on syllables would be of such differing duration that their value might be readily denoted in fractions. The principle was based on the fact that it requires longer to pronounce certain sounds than others. Poe largely ignored the circumstance that versification in English is accentual, not quantitative. Again according to Gay Wilson Allen, Poe's system is an arithmetical formula:

> (1) each foot of an iambic line has the value of 1 1/2
> (1=the time of the long syllable and 1/2 the time of the
> short syllable); (2) each foot of the trochaic line has the
> value of 1 1/2; (3) each foot of the anapest = 2 (1 = the
> time of the "long" syllable and 1/2+ 1/2 the time of the
> two "short" syllables); (4) each foot of the dactyl = 2; (5)
> the value of the "caesura" depends upon the rhythm of
> the line—thus its value is either 1 1/2 (in an iambic or
> trochaic line) or 2 (anapest or dactyl). Poe uses these num-
> bers to mark scansion "accents," leaving the "long"
> syllables (*i. e.*, whole units) unmarked, but indicating a
> "1/2" by a small "2" *underneath* the syllable, a "1/4"
> (unaccented syllables of a bastard iambus or trochee) by
> a small '4,' etc. The "caesura" is marked by placing the
> number *over* the syllable, either 3/2 (*i. e.*, 1 1/2) or 2.
> For example:

$$\text{Many are the} \mid \text{thoughts that} \mid \text{come to} \mid \overset{3}{\text{me}}\ ^{2}$$
$$\underset{6}{\text{Ma}}\text{ny}\ \underset{6}{\text{are}}\ \underset{6}{\text{the}} \mid \text{thoughts}\ \underset{2}{\text{that}} \mid \text{come}\ \underset{2}{\text{to}} \mid$$

$$\underset{2}{\text{In}\ \text{my}} \mid \text{lone}\underset{2}{\text{ly}} \mid \text{mus}\underset{2}{\text{ing}}$$

And they | drift so | strange and | swift ^{2} ^{3}

_2   2   2

There's no | time for | choosing

_2   2   2 ^{3}

Which to | follow | for to | leave ^{2}

_2   2   2

Any, | seems a | losing.

_2   2   2

What invests Poe's treatise with particular meaning for our time is that he broke with the traditions. From a modern point of view, "The Rationale of Verse" is a manifesto elucidating the aims of twentieth-century "Imagists," who agree with Poe that "it is no paradox that the more prosaic the construction of verse, the better."[56] Poe's own poems inspired few disciples; he set a better example in his theory than in his practice, which two are thus sharply at variance.

> In practice his rimes are few and inaccurate, his stanzas loose, and his rhythms often do not obey the rigid restrictions of his doctrines. His chief contributions as a practioner of versification are his truly original achievements in 'tone color,' his use of the repetend and refrain, and possibly his adaptation of parallelism and reiteration for lyrical purposes.[57]

Amy Lowell, the leader of the Imagists, relied fully on Poe in endorsing his expulsion of archaisms, contractions, inversions, and accents wrongly placed. More recently, "The Rationale of Verse" has influenced the poetical ideas of Ezra Pound, whose poetic manifesto was partially copied from Poe, and T. S. Eliot, who expressed his indebtedness in his book, _From Poe to Valery_ (1948).

3. The Journalist

Poe's journalistic writings reveal aspects of his personality seldom suggested in his _belles lettres_. They show that in his generation he knew and was known by practically every author, consequential or otherwise. His remarks on books and related topics introduce a Poe who is wide-awake and who is keenly aware of the passing literary scene. The theory that he was remote from his times, though applicable to many of his exotic tales and supernormal poems, hardly tallies with the record of his journalistic experiences. As critic he was an American championing American causes. Though never a rabid rebel, he was to some extent even a Southerner. It is in "his literary criticisms that much evidence can be found of his relationship to the South."[58] "The conception of him as a lonely exotic, while it sets him off against an increasingly commercial and unintellectual world, does not take into account the services he rendered his generation as critic and editor."[59] In the role of political commentator—and here the incipient rebel is detectable— he constantly urged that the United States break with the traditions of the Old World. He was a shrewd critic of politics and saw inevitable weaknesses in the democratic theory.

The dominant impression borne out by his association with a number of leading magazines, like the *Messenger* (1835), *Burton's* (1839), *Graham's* (1841), and the *Broadway Journal* (1845), is that Poe was an enterprising editor, a man occasionally erratic in his personal habits but from day to day both prompt and observant in the able performance of routine duties. Poe the journalist was one of the earliest critics in the United States to encourage an appreciation of the native ingredients in contemporary American letters.

During Poe's employment with the *Messenger* circulation expanded from about five hundred to thirty-five hundred copies. At the end of his second year with *Graham's* (1842), largely as a result of his efforts, the subscription list had grown from five to forty thousand. Alertness to the pace of the times was a major characteristic of Poe's journalistic talent.

Doubtless this early success inspired him to entertain the idea of founding a magazine of his own. Far from being a literary nomad, Poe moved from one magazine to another because he was dissatisfied with low standards and because he hoped to improve his chances of becoming an independent publisher. He wanted a respectable periodical that would install him as the arbiter of American letters. His plans, first, for the *Penn Magazine* (1840), and, secondly, for *The Stylus* (1843), though never realized, may very well constitute Poe's fondest dream. Anyone who interprets Poe's disappointments with successive journals as proof that he was either a temperamental transient or an unreliable worker grossly misreads the facts. Of course he quit some jobs, was fired from others, developed enemies like Griswold, and never became the arbiter of American letters. But it must be granted that as long as he lived he caustically attacked the shoddy and the commonplace, stringently opposed the importation of British vogues, and upheld firmly his dream of a superior literary magazine. Poe's talent for satirical mimicry, his flair for badinage and buffoonery, and his contempt for bourgeois tastes resemble those of H. L. Mencken during the heyday of *The American Mercury*.

Poe's years of editorial labor left on the man a mark that was partly revealed in his prose style. Irritated by occasional misunderstandings with his employers and by his failure to establish an independent magazine, he expressed his irascibility in either a severity of tone or its opposite, a mock-seriousness. Even in a supposedly objective treatment like "The Rationale of Verse" he launched what Gay Allen calls "a guerilla attack on the English hexameter (especially Longfellow's)." It became so basic an element of his style to interpolate personal attacks, with nose-thumbing at pedants, that his criticism seldom appears highly serious. His finest essay, "The Philosophy of Composition," has been called his greatest hoax,[60] because it purports that one may write a poem like "The Raven" merely by following a formula, whereas it is highly unlikely that Poe composed the poem in quite so objective a manner as he describes.

Even Poe's works in *belles lettres* were now and again tinctured with journalism, and a number of his tales and poems were executed in haste for temporary appeal to the current public taste. With Napier Wilt, I hold to the view that Poe cultivated the dark tradition because there was then a market in America for that type of literature. Hence it is ridiculous to interpret his preoccupation with the gothic as evidence of his own abnormality. Wilt says:

> . . . the greatest care should be used in reading into Poe's use of horrible and morbid situations and details a reflection of the horrible and morbid situations in his own mind. If the use of horror in fiction can be taken as an indication of horror in the mind of the author, then most of the tale-writers of the first half of the nineteenth century were verging on insanity.[61]

It was doubtless Poe's journalistic sense which impelled him to feed the taste of the moment by submitting to his readers the poem "Eldorado" and such stories as "Julius Rodman," "The Duc de l'Omelette," and "Hans Pfaal." These works, cited to display Poe's indebtedness to his native country and to "tall tales of the West,"[62] were valuable in their day as fictional journalism rather than as romantic Western travel lore. Poe's faint connections with the comic spirit arising in the West surely do not make him a native writer in the same sense as Mark Twain. Today "Julius Rodman" and other "Western" tales interest only the literary historians. The "timely" quality of his work after a hundred years has lost much of its original appeal. This is particularly true of Poe's humor, which is never comedy but farce or burlesque. Sometimes the satire is greatly strained, as in "How to Write a Blackwood Article," which belongs, not to the genre of the short story, but to pretentious journalism.

It would be a mistake to overemphasize the journalistic components in the greater works of Poe. Despite his thorough knowledge of the magazine trade, whose tricks he might have adopted for sensational purposes, he observed standards of taste greatly elevated above the low status of current flashy journalism. As witness to this truth, there is his rejection of lurid plots concerned with rape and other erotic abnormalities. "The sexlessness of his works," Krutch states, "has, of course, often been noted . . . ."[63] It appears that Poe may have been personally acquainted with Mary

Rogers, who in her purple past had been "promiscuous" and had undergone at least one abortion.[64] Nothing at all is said about this episode in "The Mystery of Marie Rogêt," which is therefore an excellent illustration of Poe's refusal to descend to yellow journalism. His account of Mary Rogers (*i. e.*, Marie Rogêt) is not a report of her transgressions, not a circumstantial chronicle of historical data, but an imaginative work of mingled fact and fiction which is artistically original. Neither can one, like Cooke, interpret Poe's omission of the sex motive as unique since there is a corresponding silence about the matter in the works of such literary men as Herman Melville and Mark Twain. In a recent discussion of Poe, Hawthorne, and Melville, H. B. Parkes makes a suggestive observation: "A normal and healthy sexuality is, in fact, conspicuously absent not only from these writers but from almost the whole of nineteenth-century American literature."[65] In excluding from his works lurid references to the sensational, Poe was motivated by artistic principles, not by the demands of offensive journalism; and he was also patently conforming to the best moral tastes of his time.

More concrete representations of Poe's journalistic work appear in such gatherums of biographical characterizations and literary chit-chat as *The Literati, Autography, Marginalia,* and *Pinakidia.* Relatively few of his remarks are worth repeating for preservation during our time, and many of the contemporary persons that he mentions are now lacking in literary interest. Posterity has inherited less from these works than any other, yet Poe's barbed wit occasionally shines through from dull pages about the small events of a bygone day. Here and there Poe drew a vivid characterization or voiced a witty, provocative saying, and fresh discoveries sometimes occur in these materials. They have been less combed by investigation than Poe's other works, and in quality they deserve little.

The Literati of New York City was published in six installments of *Godey's Lady's Book* (May-October, 1846). Largely devoted to short biographies of the literary people forming the Knickerbocker Group, the collection announced at the outset that an author may be popular with the public but not with the critics. Poe then stated, by way of illustration, that Hawthorne is a great writer little recognized by the press, whereas Longfellow is a lesser figure with a large public following. He next undertook brief descriptions of a number of individual authors, being most severe with his enemy Thomas Dunn *Brown* (*i.e.,* English), whom he called "an ass." Criticism like this was, in some quarters, distasteful. John Esten Cooke, who had a passing acquaintance with Poe, capitalized on this type of scurrility and cited it as a distinguishing trait of *The Literati.* "It is impossible to read the series of criticisms," Cooke declared, "and fail to see that invective is the author's favorite style."[66] Poe's general tone is hardly at a uniformly scurrilous level. In fact, he praised such friends as George H. Colton, [67] N. P. Willis, Charles F. Briggs (*alias* Harry Franco or "Ferdinand Mendoza Pinto"), Piero Maroncelli (*alias* Silvio Pellico),[68] Catherine M. Sedgwick ("the Miss Edgeworth of America"), Emma C. Embury (*alias* "Ianthe"), and Professor Charles Anthon. These abbreviated vignettes are perhaps not equal in grade to the best portraits that today sometimes appear in *The New Yorker,* but occasionally a Knickerbocker name becomes lustrous because of its close association with Poe.

The signatures and letters which compose *Autography* made their initial appearance in four separate texts—in the *Southern Literary Messenger* (February, 1836), and in *Graham's Magazine* (November, December, 1841; January, 1842). There are in all 134 separate authors, though some of the names occur more than once. This book of "signatures," which was edited in 1926,[69] is fine reading for an antiquarian or anybody else interested in discovering how widely and how well Poe knew his fellow countrymen. Many other than literary persons are included. For the historian, *Autography* is an index to Poe's sound comprehension of his world and the men of affairs surrounding him. To the student of literature, *Autography* is instructive because of the narrative device there adopted to introduce a tiresome succession of thumb-nail sketches. On the opening page a fictitious Joseph A. Miller pays the editor Poe a visit. Miller has a collection of autographs which he says have appeared previously in the London "Athenaeum." As Poe talks with this affected fellow, the middle initial of Joseph A. Miller's name is given, humorously, as Joseph B. Miller, Joseph C. Miller, and so on throughout the alphabet. Miller finally persuades Poe that the autographs are really American, not English as earlier implied, whereupon the American editor decides to print them. Each autograph is attached to a letter as a simulated reply to an imaginary correspondent.

Marginalia, first published in periodicals like the *Democratic Review* (1844) and the *Messenger* (1849), is a series of critical notations. Poe's notes are organized under such diverse titles as *Defoe, The Drama, Antigone, Plagiarism, Rhetoric,* and *Men of Genius. Marginalia* opens with Poe confessing that he liked to write reminders on slips of paper to paste in books; but he quoted, in French, the statement of Bernardin de St. Pierre that "if you wish to forget anything upon the spot, make a note that this thing is to be remembered." In other words, he believed that nonsense is "the essential sense of the marginal note." Following these light prefatory remarks, there are the articles themselves, arranged in no particular order or sequence. In his first he observed that in general a person retains little of what he reads but by application can learn to read by pages rather than by words. He then ranged from Thomas Moore (who has "facility in prosaically telling a poetical story") and Tennyson (who is "The greatest of poets") to an argument in favor of international copyright. He sought to dismantle John Wilson, the British editor of *Blackwood's,* for miswriting Lowell's name (*John* Russell Lowell). He said of Carlyle that "In ten years—possibly in five—he will be remembered only as a butt for sarcasm." Finally, he believed that an author could be quite successful if he wrote a book describing "My Heart Laid Bare" but thought nobody dared because "The paper would shrivel and blaze at every touch of the fiery pen."

Pinakidia, which appeared in the *Messenger* (August, 1836), illustrates Poe's early penchant for assembling random notes. Its contents, showing the "sheer fudge" that Lowell disliked in the poet, purport to analyze plagiarism, the notations being given under the titles of *Odds and Ends, Stray Leaves, Scraps,* and *Brevities.* Poe stated that the title *Pinakidia,* meaning "Tablets," was used for a similar purpose by Dionysius of Halicarnassus. Among the extracts included, there is an inexact reference to *La Mort de Cesar* by Voltaire. Poe drew for materials upon *Disraeli's Curiosities of Literature,* Baron Bielfeld's *Elements of Universal Erudition,* Jacob Bryant's *Mythology,* James Montgomery's *Lectures on Literature,* and James Fenimore Cooper's *Excursions in Switzerland.* [70] In its failure to be either amusing or informative, *Pinakidia* is a journalistic attack on plagiarism undistinguished in idea, form, or style.

There are two other minor works, *Fifty Suggestions* and *A Chapter of Suggestions,* which probably belong in the category of journalism. *Fifty Suggestions,* which ran in *Graham's Magazine* (May - June 1845), is a compendium of rather poor epigrams. A typical example is the observation that "loving our enemies" implies "hating our friends." Poe was considerably more his vitriolic self in noting that G. P. R. James's novels express the same thought "again and again in every possible variety of phrase." Truth appears in his notion that there cannot be "more things in Heaven and Earth than are dreamt of" in the philosophy of Andrew Jackson Davis.[71] Although himself childless, Poe subscribed to an old saw in remarking that children are like beef-steaks, beating them makes them tender. One of his scholarly theories is that Miss Barrett's "Lady Geraldine's Courtship" imitates Tennyson's "Locksley Hall." For a last citation, Poe agreed with Edmund Spenser that love is madness.

A Chapter of Suggestions, originating in *The Opal* in 1845, is slighter in bulk than its companion piece but more provocative. About the middle of his chapter Poe defined a good plot as *"that from which no component atom can be removed, and in which none of the component atoms can be displaced, without ruin to the whole."* This same idea Poe treated more fully in his review of Bulwer's *Night and Morning.* Another one of his suggestions—the desire to live fast is in men of genius "a psychal want, or necessity"—may have been prompted by the fevered "drive" of Poe's disease;

it pretty aptly describes the principle that he lived by.
Though seldom vocal about a subject like religion, he began
the chapter with the declaration that every man experiences
at least once a crisis in which the soul separates itself from
the body and regards itself "as a portion of the universal
Ens," explaining that "it is our *sense of self* which debases
and keeps us debased." This concept joins with his longing
for something afar to suggest that he at times entertained a
religio-esthetic belief. The entries conclude with a passage
from Newton: "If Natural Philosophy should continue to
be improved in its various branches, the bounds of moral
philosophy would be enlarged also." *A Chapter of Suggestions* represents the most seriously thoughtful selection in the
curious hodge-podge that makes up Poe's journalistic works.

At least three remaining articles, "The Philosophy of
Furniture," "Street Paving," and "Some Secrets of the
Magazine Prison-House," belong in the present classification.
"The Philosophy of Furniture," reprinted in 1845 in the
Broadway Journal from an earlier version, is a pseudo-expert
analysis of the subject in a typically critical vein. Poe said
that the English are supreme in internal decorations of
residences, whereas "The Yankees alone are preposterous."
The Americans, he complained, have no aristocracy of blood
and hence lack taste. In "Appallachia" (*i. e.,* America) the
cost of an article is "Nearly the sole test of its merit in a
decorative point of view." He railed against the well-
furnished apartment in the United States which overplays
"glare" and "glitter." He concluded with an ideal room
where "Repose speaks in all." This chamber is oblong
(thirty feet long, twenty-five broad), has one door and two
windows, contains a few draperies, and reveals many paintings on the wall to relieve the expanse of paper. A fairly
conventional room, it would appear; but Edward Shanks
believes it is the same as the one described in "The Raven."[72]

"Street Paving," also from the *Broadway Journal* (1845),
states that no real progress has been made in the last two
thousand years in roadmaking and that the method of paving
is not materially different from that used by the Romans.
Poe then went into minute detail about the construction of

Roman roads. The exposition terminates with Poe wondering why Kyanized wood pavement has not been laid in some of the public streets of America. Poe avowed that he had written this article without any "book before him" and so was "by no means positive about the accuracy of our details."

"Some Secrets of the Magazine Prison-House," likewise from the *Broadway Journal* (1845), is too obvious to be effective as satire. "The want of an International Copy-Right Law, Poe began, "has had the effect of forcing many of our best writers into the service of the Magazines and Reviews . . . ." This and following statements were undeniably true, though it is doubtful that his objections were sufficiently influential on his contemporaries to improve conditions. He remarked that pay in the United States was notoriously low: some "publishers pay *something*—other publishers nothing at all." Since editors waited months before replying and often postponed payment until long after publication, he said that it was quite possible for a young author to die before being paid for a manuscript. He ended in ironical fashion, hoping his readers would not infer that he wrote from personal experience or that he referred "to any magazine publisher now living, it being well known that they are all as remarkable for their generosity and urbanity, as for their intelligence, and appreciation of Genius." Poe's disavowal of reference to a person "now living" reads like that of a modern novelist—"any resemblance between this and a person now living or dead is purely coincidental."

It is in the byways of this unclassified material that a student may look with most hope for a fresh discovery.[73] Possibly the boundaries[74] of these so-called journalistic works should be enlarged to include such compositions as "The Conversation of Eiros and Charmion," "The Colloquy of Monos and Una," "The Power of Words," "Diddling," and "Maelzel's Chess-Player"—imperfect illustrations of the short story with which they are often classified. The least one can say is that in these articles Poe was obliged by his subject matter to evince powers as a writer not called upon when he wrote the imaginative tales and poems. Poe's alert reasoning, his practicality, his prudence, and his priceless wit and satirical flair occur rarely outside these journalistic works. Had he polished and revised them as carefully as he did his best writings, the results might have established him as the Swift—or at least the Defoe—of his age. Taken as they are, these sundry compositions introduce a man whose mind teemed with practical ideas particularly during the 1840's, indeed up to the year of his death. The work of the journalist Poe, today generally neglectèd by the average American reader, is in literary history the significant product of a versatile mind.

4. Book Reviews

Poe's numerous book reviews form a large division of his journalism. They introduce the text of his appraisals of contemporary American and British authors, the principal materials of the "Little Longfellow War,"[75] several important side-lights on his own irrepressible spirit of individuality. They are also worthy of examination for their quality, style, and scope.

These works roughly illustrate two forms of expository writings: first, the conventional review, dealing almost solely with the book in question; and secondly, the longer critical reviews, which merit greater attention because they became vehicles for Poe to present doctrines of his own, in near or remote connection with the specific books involved. Occasionally an item of first-rate significance in relation to Poe's attitudes may be gleaned from the more obscure short reviews; but it is the long review, similar in content to his critical essays, which ordinarily supplies the reader with additional data about Poe as a writer and thinker.

Poe the reviewer was an unpredictable person. Perhaps he wrote too many reviews on too many different subjects. His unpredictability was nonetheless a sort of virtue, for when he came to estimate current literature, it prevented him from falling back on hackneyed formulas. Sometimes it may have been difficult for readers to rely completely on the exactness of his critical judgments since in the next number of the journal he might surprise them with a reversal of his earlier opinion.　His analysis of Hawthorne, in a review in two parts, is illustrative: first, he praised Hawthorne as "original at all points;" next, Poe grew finicky and charged him with burdening his later stories with undesirable allegory.　What is the reason for his notorious deviation from accepted critical standards, which is to make a point and stick to it?

One possible explanation is that Poe was over-worked. He expended a great deal of sheer physical strength in his office as commentator on news in the book world. His restless spirit was bound and disciplined by the necessity of producing reviews on schedule.　Poe's industry was recently commended by Edmund Wilson, who said: "He deals vigorously and boldly with books as they come into his hands day by day, as Shaw did with the plays of the season, and manages to be brilliant and arresting even about works of no interest; he constantly insists, as Eliot does, on attempting, in the practice of this journalism, to formulate general principles."[76]　In reviewing well over two hundred books, Poe commented on such diverse topics as disease, drama, esthetics, etiquette, games, literature, manners, poetry, politics, prejudice, printing, religion, science, and slavery.　In view of the large number of books he handled and the speed with which he treated them, it was doubtless difficult for Poe in every case to remember what he had said in earlier reviews.

Unevenness of style in the critical reviews is another of Poe's weaknesses.　In the remarks on Bryant's poems in 1837, his exposition is lucid, direct, and unimpeded by the superfluity of literary quotations which came to burden his later work.　Throughout his discussion, Poe captured the spirit of Bryant's verses, without wandering away, as he did in his treatment of Halleck in 1836, into irrelevancies on ideal beauty or egregious revisions of his author's metrics.　Poe's observations are made with sincerity of expression and firmness of phrase.　Yet directness was not his usual method; nor is it that of T. S. Eliot, one of his admirers.[77]　Poe's reviews sometimes included much extraneous lore; but his tendency was to scrutinize each book carefully, and to evaluate both main design and minute detail. Plainly, the tenor of his criticism was to lift the literary standards of his time. In being exercised over minutiae, he admonished contemporaries to prepare their manuscripts carefully and to respect the principles of scholarly accuracy. He did not always illustrate these virtues himself.

Although many of the reviews show the individuality of Poe's authorship, one cannot say that he developed, by craft or through inspiration, a style which unerringly identifies the unsigned reviews as certainly his own compositions. Several selections accepted for inclusion in Harrison's edition are now known, principally as a result of Mabbott's discoveries, to be the writing of other reviewers.[78] There is in particular the oft-discussed question of the authorship of a review of "The Poets and Poetry of America," which appeared in two parts, the first in 1842 and the second in 1843.[79] Fresh information has come to light recently which may bear on the ascription of the work to Poe. A letter, dated October 2, 1848, by Amos Bardwell Heywood, the brother of the poet's "Annie," reports that Poe "lectured in Lowell, I think in July, upon 'Poets and Poetry' of America."[80] This testimony of a contemporary informant indicates the possibility that Poe may have drawn his title from the book.

One peculiarity of Poe's critical notices is their reliance on outside materials. In his review of Drake and Halleck (1836), Poe's distinctions between Imagination and Fancy are possibly indebted to A.W. Schlegel and certainly to the fourteenth chapter of Coleridge's *Biographia Literaria*. In his review of Stephens's *Arabia Petraea* (1837), he depended on his friend Professor Anthon for data about Hebrew lore. In his review of Bulwer's *Night and Morning* (1841), he cited by name Augustus Wilhelm Schlegel, disagreeing with the German critics's definition of a plot "as a simple complexity." In his review of Longfellow's *Ballads and Other Poems* (1842), he again mentioned Schlegel and referred to "the desire of the moth for the star," a quotation from Shelley. His review of Washington Irving's *Astoria* calls for special notice, for Poe not only paraphrased long passages from

Irving but even reproduced some parts of Irving's original verbatim.[18]   None of these borrowings in any way hampers the expression of Poe's meaning, although it is unusual for a reviewer to turn as often as he did to outside authority.

Poe's comments on his important American contemporaries are notable for their severity, the chief exception being his laudations of Hawthorne.   In 1847 *Godey's* carried a later revision of Poe's opinions, in which he regarded *Mosses from an Old Manse* as overladen with symbolism, but the tenor of his utterances as a whole was commendatory. Hawthorne's tales, which he examined before writing "The Philosophy of Composition" (1846), may have indirectly influenced Poe to propound his doctrine of effect.   It is worthwhile to remember that Hawthorne's first novel, *Fanshawe,* though a failure, duly observed the principle of brevity.   The reading public of the middle nineteenth century, as explained by the letter to Poe from Harpers, was unreceptive to the short novel.   How seriously Hawthorne viewed Poe's recommendations, I do not know; but his greatest novel, *The Scarlet Letter,* has been commended today on the basis of both its intense expression and its medium length, two qualities of paramount significance in Poe's esthetic philosophy.

Poe's remarks on James Fenimore Cooper, though nearly dismantling the novelists's reputation, correctly predicted that his fame would survive in reduced form and that he was not a major writer.   Poe approved *Sketches of Switzerland* but was unimpressed with Cooper's gifts as a novelist.   The novel *Mercedes of Castile* he pronounced "well nigh worthless."   In 1839, when reviewing *The History of the United States Navy,* Poe lambasted Cooper's "miserably executed literary productions, each more silly than its predecessor." In 1843, at the opening of his review of *Wyandotte, or the Hutted Knoll,* he contradicted his generalization by saying that "Mr. Cooper has never been known to fail, either in the forest or upon the sea."   He was observant when praising Cooper's Indians and when perceiving that "The negroes are, without exception, admirably drawn."

Poe's review of *Wyandotte* is memorable, further, for its distinction between popular and lasting books. By making his forceful comparison in 1843, he possibly anticipated by five years a part of the differentiation that De Quincey's "Literature of Knowledge and Literature of Power" (1848) has made famous throughout the literary world. De Quincey of course knew Poe, but I am unable to say with certainty that he read this little-known review of Cooper's minor novel. Possibly De Quincey developed the idea independently, for the distinction between the two is foreshadowed in his *Letters to a Young Man* (1823), a work unmentioned by Poe. Poe's shrewd definitions of popular and lasting art, though extraneous to the precise subject of the review, are much more valuable than his statements about Cooper. The introduction of this material illustrates Poe's tendency in criticisms to move from the particular to the universal—in this instance a constructive movement accomplished with clarity and precision.

Although delivered in his customarily denunciatory manner, Poe's review of L. A. Wilmer's *The Quacks of Helicon* (1841) is better balanced than his analysis of Cooper. Poe had a natural penchant for satire, and his discourse opens with a hearty welcome to this satiric work by an American writer. He next encouraged other writers to cultivate this particular field in the United States. As for Wilmer, Poe stipulated that he was too imitative of Dryden. He especially inveighed against Wilmer's use of "gross obscenity" as "a part of the slavish and indiscriminate imitation of the Swift and Rochester school" but lauded him for denouncing the "coteries in New York." It is likely that Poe's animosity towards the "Knickerbocker Clique" resulted from his ill treatment at their hands after his demolition of *Norman Leslie,* by Theodore S. Fay,[82] one of their members. Adopting irony as his mode of assault, Poe judged Wilmer's promiscuous censure to be his greatest sin, declaring that "Mr. Morris *has* written good songs. Mr. Bryant is not *all* a fool. Mr. Willis is not *quite* an ass. Mr. Longfellow *will* steal, but, perhaps, he cannot help it. . . ." Poe's chastisements of individual personalities were sometimes phrased distastefully.

He certainly was closer to larger truths when he complained against editors who falsely extolled books which they had not read. He correctly defamed the press for its extravagant indulgence in *puffery*, whereby native poets and poetesses flatulently became our "Miltons" and our "American Hemanses." More often than otherwise, Poe's reviews become lively reading when they drop the topic he is discussing and take up, as here, a graphic fact or two on the literary fashions of the book trade as a whole.

What is to be said about Poe's opinions of the books then being issued by his first biographer, R. W. Griswold? When examining *The Female Poets of America* in 1842, he regarded Griswold as "a man of taste, talent, and *tact.*" He further commended the good taste of the editor's selections, although he did think that Miss Alice Carey and Miss Talley, a close friend of his, deserved more representation than they received. His later two-part review of *The Poets and Poetry of America* contains in part two his famous condemnation of the editor. Poe said that if Griswold "is spoken of hereafter, he will be cited as *the unfaithful servant who abused his trust.*"

Why did he change his favorable early opinion? In July, 1843, Griswold received from Graham an appointment to the position formerly held by Poe. Poe, evidently too sensitive to view the circumstance objectively, permitted his envy and personal sense of injury to influence the direction of his critical thinking. He may also have been jealous of the attentions Griswold devoted first to Mrs. Osgood and then to Mrs. Whitman.[83]

The worst features of Poe's journalism are his personal attacks on writers of established renown, in particular his false allegations about Longfellow's writing practices. On January 13 and 14, 1845, Poe reviewed *The Waif in the Mirror,* introducing among his comments of appreciation the charge that Longfellow was a plagiarist. A friend of the New England poet, who signed himself "H," replied; and the editor Willis on January 25 printed the text of his reply together with Poe's "Post Notes by the Critic." On the following February 8, Willis published his own views on the matter, which amounted to an apology to Longfellow. In the *Mirror* for February 15—as a reply to Charles F. Briggs in the *Broadway Journal* of the same date—Poe again reverted to the controversy—apparently as a publicity stunt to gain readers since Briggs' article and Poe's answer appeared simultaneously. On February 22, Poe's editorial in the *Weekly Mirror* carried only a veiled allusion to Longfellow. Meanwhile, a correspondent named "Outis" sent to the *Mirror* a long article comparing "The Raven" with some sentimental verses entitled "The Bird of the Dream." The article cleverly imitated Poe's manner and convincingly refuted his charges against Longfellow, but Poe opportunistically accepted the epistle of Outis as a cause for prolonging the debate and for attracting attention to the *Broadway Journal,* of which he had just become an editor. Poe also wrote denunciatory notices of Longfellow's two books, *Hyperion: A Romance* and *Voices of the Night.*

Poe's rebuttal of Outis ran in five weekly numbers of the *Broadway Journal* (March 8, 15, 22, 29, and April 5) under the glaring headline: "IMITATION—PLAGIARISM —MR. POE'S REPLY TO THE LETTER OF OUTIS.— A LARGE ACCOUNT OF A SMALL MATTER—A VOLUMINOUS HISTORY OF THE LITTLE LONG-FELLOW WAR." Everything in the articles was to Poe's discredit. He pointlessly contrasted Longfellow's *Spanish Student* and his own imperfect drama *Politian.* He unjustifiably reiterated that Longfellow's translation of William Motherwell's "The Bonnie George Campbell" was a misrepresented reproduction of the German original of O. L. B. Wolff. Poe's tone thereafter bordered increasingly on bad taste. He intended an insult in declaring that "Outis is a Yankee." He was disrespectful in alluding to "Mrs. Outis and her seven children" and to "Mrs. Longfellow and hers." But to dwell further with the controversy itself is to exaggerate its importance. Actually, in his "Editorial Miscellany" in the *Broadway Journal* for August 16, 1846, Poe vainly tried to repair the injury he had inflicted, claiming that he had been one of Longfellow's "warmest and most steadfast" defenders. His review of *Ballads and Other Poems* (March-

April, 1842) had inoffensively registered his dissatisfaction with Longfellow's *didacticism*, but he now felt obliged to make reparations. He found the occasion in 1849, when reviewing *A Fable for Critics*, to link Longfellow with Lowell "as, upon the whole, perhaps our best poets." Meanwhile, Longfellow did not deem it fitting to reply, though he was aware of the attacks, as is shown by his *Journal* for December 10, 1845: "If he [Lowell] goes on in this vein, Poe will soon begin to pound him." The lamentable result for Poe was that he lost the friendship of both Longfellow and Lowell and that he created an ugly impression among many fair-minded critics. On the other hand, Longfellow appeared at his best in a letter of September 28, 1850, addressed to R. W. Griswold, who mistakenly asserted that Poe thought Longfellow's "The Beleagured City" was based on "The Haunted Palace." Longfellow, evincing no ill feeling towards the recently deceased poet, corrected Griswold's aspersion of Poe's memory by promptly disclaiming "that Mr. Poe ever accused me of taking my poem from his."[84]

In the last year of his life Poe vented his sharpest ire on Lowell's *A Fable for Critics*, which book he quarrelsomely reviewed in the *Messenger* for March, 1849. In an earlier review of Lowell's *Poems* he had placed the New Englander *"at the very head* of the poets of America." But now Poe, the only Southern author included in *A Fable,* castigated Lowell unmercifully for his omission of writers from the South. "Mr. Lowell is one of the most rabid of the abolition fanatics," the reviewer averred; and if he owned slaves, his wrong-headedness "would manifest itself in atrocious ill-treatment of them, with murder of any abolitionist who should endeavor to set them free." As for Lowell's style, Poe stated: "In Mr. Lowell's prose efforts we have before observed a certain disjointedness, but never, until now, in his verse—and we confess some surprise at his putting forth so unpolished a performance." He recorded as a major objection that Lowell's "malevolence appears." It is, however, Poe who rankled at the reference to him as "Poe with his Raven, like Barnaby Rudge. . . ." Smarting from Lowell's estimate of him as "two-fifths sheer fudge," the reviewer

levelled a last counterblast at the book, in which, he concluded, "Mr. Lowell has committed an irrevocable *faux pas* and
lowered himself fifty per cent in the literary public opinion."

Throughout the reviews Poe was overly influenced by his
personal likes and dislikes.　It is here that one discovers his
cardinal fault: he censured superiority and commended
mediocrity.　Thus his appraisal of Lowell missed the mark;
his review of *The Lost Pleiad,* by his friend Chivers, exceeded it, in claiming these poems to have lofty merit.　In
reviewing the verses of Mrs. Osgood, he again exceeded it in
declaring that no poetess in America is "so universally
popular as Mrs. Osgood."　His notice of *Tortesa, the Usurer*
overpraises N. P. Willis's drama as "by far the best play from
the pen of an American author."　His reviews of books by
other friends degenerate into a series of flatulent puffs:
Simms's tales, *The Wigwam and the Cabin,* "do credit to the
author's abilities"; Mrs. Mowatt's verses, *The Songs of Our
Land, and Other Poems,* are said to show "external taste";
Mrs. Lewis's poem, *The Child of the Sea,* "will confer immortality upon the author"; Mrs. Osgood's "grace" in *A
Wreath of Wild Flowers from New England* "is absolutely
without a rival"; and Mr. Latrobe, author of *The Rambler
in North America,* "is a scholar, a man of intellect, and a
gentleman."　Poe was most partial in the commendation he
lavished upon the bevy of his female admirers, not only Mrs.
Osgood and Mrs. Lewis but also L. E. L. (Miss Landon),
Amelia Welby, Elizabeth F. Ellet, and Mrs. R. S. Nichols.
How could Poe applaud these poetasters but carp at the
style and bicker with the opinions of such stalwart American
figures as Irving, Cooper, Lowell, and Longfellow?

The explanation is that Poe was prejudiced; he loved his
friends and despised his enemies.　It is less often true that
he sought to spur potential genius by castigation and to
wake promising talent by encouragement.　Whenever his
critical eye was undimmed by sentiment, Poe adopted a
frontal attack, displaying a hot impatience with mediocrity,
which he summarily dismissed with a caustic phrase.　He
castigated Seba Smith's *Powhatan: A Metrical Romance* as
"not worth a single half sheet of the pasteboard upon which

it is printed." In his notice of *Our Amateur Poets—Flaccus* Mr. Ward was judged "perhaps a ninety-ninth-rate poetaster." His review of *Poems,* by William W. Lord, labels the verses "Drivel." In other reviews he pronounced Henry B. Hirst's long poem, *The Coming of the Mammoth,* "The least worthy of notice" and Cornelius Mathew's poem, *Wakondah,* "gibberish." Except for small groups of friends in New York and in the South, Poe in his book notices evinced precious little respect for any living person.

In reviewing British books, Poe more usually exercised keen literary acumen. He called *Orion: An Epic Poem,* by R. H. Horne, "One of the noblest, if not the very noblest poetical work of the age." In his notice of *The Critical and Miscellaneous Writings of Sir Edward Lytton Bulwer,* he reported that he had read the two "volumes with the highest pleasure." Poe held *Rienzi, the Last of the Tribunes* to be "the best novel of Bulwer." Likewise, Poe greatly admired Tennyson, upholding in his review that "The injustice done in America to the magnificent genius of Tennyson is one of the worst sins for which this country has to answer." He neatly estimated *The Characters of Shakespeare* with the statement that Hazlitt "has done wonders, and those wonders well." He was unresponsive to Professor Wilson's *Genius and Character of Burns,* which will appeal to "lovers of mere rhapsody." He made known a scholarly interest in Milton when he objected that R. W. Griswold, in his two volumes on *The Prose Works of John Milton,* had omitted, unfittingly, the devout poet's "Christian Doctrine." In his notice of *Alciphron: A Poem* he called Thomas Moore the poet of fancy. He judged the work of Miss Barrett in *The Drama of Exile, and Other Poems* superior to Tennyson's. In yet other reviews he remarked on the good and poor qualities of such further British authors as Gibbon, Byron, Leigh Hunt, Thomas Hood, and Lord Macaulay.

It is in his review of Charles Dickens's *The Old Curiosity Shop and Other Tales* (1841) that Poe again stooped to the low trick of libel. Disliking the title, for which he proposed *Master Humphrey's Clock,* Poe playfully but maliciously impugned Dickens by alleging him to be insane: "We do not think it altogether impossible that the rumors in respect to the sanity of Mr. Dickens . . . had some slight—some very slight foundation in truth." Yet this notice is remarkable for its defense of Dickens's art of portraiture and his methods of narration, both of which are entirely different from Poe's own. Special significance is attached to the review in two installments of Dickens's *Barnaby Rudge* (1841, 1842). In the first Poe solved the plot of the mystery before seeing the last chapters of the novel. In the second he drew attention to the fact that his "pre-conceived ideas" foretold strikingly "the actual facts of the story." About the only other feature of *Barnaby Rudge* that impressed him was Dickens's introduction of a raven into the narrative. It is clear that Poe as early as 1842 recognized potentials in the bird symbolism which Dickens neglected to develop. Poe sensed that a real gain in the theatrical values would have resulted if "Its croakings might have been *prophetically* heard in the course of the drama." Poe's contradictions in attitude were perhaps best expressed in his notice of *The Posthumous Papers of the Pickwick Club,* where he averred that Dickens has nearly every desirable virtue and one thousand negative qualities.

Among the many remaining reviews Poe discussed books which are too remote from the interests of our day to deserve more than a hasty mention. These include Dr. Francis Lieber's awkwardly titled memoir, *Reminiscences of an Intercourse with Mr. Niebuhr, the historian,* and David B. Edward's book, *The History of Texas.* But Poe must have had a rare knowledge of history, for he reviewed over thirty-five books on the subject. His notices of several tomes on science may have a closer relation than has been suspected to the scientific lore that appears in his stories. It is suggestive, at least, that Poe interpreted Mrs. L. Miles's *Phrenology and the Moral Influence of Phrenology* as evidence that the subject should be taken seriously.

The wide range of his book reviews yields new information about Poe—as artist, journalist, and thinker. Often the notices point to sources that he utilized in his creative writings. One is/ constantly obliged to refer to them for their bearing on all kinds of problems, on his relations to

his contemporaries and on the habits and social customs of
that day, as well as on his knowledge of history, science,
theology, and music.[85] Poe the book reviewer was a man of
greatly varied interests, of wider reading and more intellectual depth than his contributions in *belles lettres* suggest.

5. Poe's Readings

Poe's learning relates closely to the validity of his critical
pronouncements. What did he know that enabled him to
speak as an authoritarian on classical literature? How extensive was his knowlege of contemporary foreign authors?

Poe's book reviews demonstrate that he read both widely
and carefully. In them, Poe differed from other living
reviewers in the fact that his discussions used source
materials. Thus it was that he made a thorough examination
of literature far beyond the restricted field represented by
a single book. On only one occasion, so far as I know, did
he leave an assignment unfinished, this being Coxe's *Saul*,
which poem he found "an unconscionably long one." By
custom Poe had a scholar's preoccupation with accuracy
and minutiae: he resorted to direct quotations from the
books for the purpose of dissecting the author's grammar
and diction, or even his spelling of a word, as in his notice
of Dr. Aiken's edition of Goldsmith's *The Vicar of Wake-
field.* He was sufficiently learned to evaluate a writer on
the basis of pointed comparisons between his methods and
those of the best world artists, of either ancient Greece or
nineteenth-century Italy. The record shows that Poe had
an unusually assimilative mind and that he adopted standards of criticsm advanced for his time. Poe the theorist
increases in importance, and his ideas become more worthy
of respect, when one sees in him, not a temperamental
journeyman handing down arbitrary pronouncements, but
an artist whose literary judgment was then not easy to match
among critics in America. The claims made here are fully
supported by a study of his not inextensive readings in world
literature.

Poe was familiar with the Greek masterpieces. His references bespeak an acquaintance with the works of Aeschylus, Aristotle, Euripides, Homer, Plato, Sophocles, and a number of minor Greek authors. He was in command of the major facts concerning Greek mythology, a part of his information deriving from the classical dictionaries of Lempriére and of Anthon. He remarked on P. Potter's translation of Euripides in noticing *The Classical Family Library* and on Sophocles's play as "an intentional burlesque" in two drama reviews, *The Antigone* at Palmo's and *Achilles' Wrath*. In appraising *Plato contra Atheos*, he said that Dr. T. Lewis should have included a translation to place "Plato more immediately within the *reach of the public.*" Poe's possible understanding of the tongue may explain why he was able to quote Greek in reviewing *Literary Small Talk*. He evidently appreciated classical lore, for he termed *A Dictionay of Greek and Roman Antiquities,* by Charles Anthon, "a useful book." In his notice of *Some Account of Stonehenge* he concluded with an extract from the Greek historian Diodorus Siculus. The title of his philosophical prose poem, *Eureka,* he drew from the renowned exclamation of Archimedes. In view of Poe's familiarity with Greek literature, his statement in "The Philosophy of Composition" about the internal organization of the Homeric epics is to be weighed as the comment of an informed critic.

Poe knew Latin literature even better than Greek.[86] He was well acquainted with the writings of Ovid and fairly so with Cicero's *Epistles,* the works of Horace, *The Annals* by Tacitus, Virgil's *Georgics* and the *Aeneid,* as well as compositions by such Roman satirists as Juvenal, Plautus, and Terence. His references extend to poets like Lucretius, and Seneca, and to numerous minor authors like Aurelius and Sallust. His book reviews attest that he read Latin, for he lauded Anthon's *Select Orations of Cicero;* commended J. N. Reynolds's *A Life of George Washington in Latin Prose;* and said of B. R. Hall's *A New and Compendious Latin Grammar* that "were we a teacher, we would prefer its use to that of any other Latin Grammar whatever." In his capacity as a satirist of the age, Poe brought to

American criticism a transplanted but definable atmosphere of Greek austerity and caustic Roman wit.

In the field of European letters, Poe had fullest cognizance of French. He was a competent student of the language, perusing many French authors in the original. In French literature, he appreciated the works of Balzac, Boileau, Chateaubriand, Corneille, Crebillion, Victor Hugo, Pascal, Rabelais, Racine, George Sand, Mme. de Staël, and Voltaire. He knew such other wits, philosophers, and chroniclers of France as Béranger, Bruyere, Comte, Condorcet, Froissart, Guillet, La Place, Mercier, Montesquieu, Rollin, and numerous others. Of all these, Voltaire was perhaps his favorite, and it is Voltaire's works which are praised in Poe's notice of *Literary Small Talk*.[87]

Besides French writers, Poe mentioned the Cardinal de Richelieu, whom he encountered in reviewing a novel by the Englishman G. P. R. James. The book notices establish his acquaintance with yet other Frenchmen like Lucien Bonaparte and Lafitte the Pirate; and with the fine arts in France, as exhibited in his comments on the Countess of Merlin's references to music in her two volumes, *Memoirs and Letters of Madame Malibran*. There is evidence, in two sympathetic reviews of R.M. Walsh's *Sketches of Conspicuous Living Characters of France* and of Mrs. Frances Trollope's *Paris and the Parisians* in 1835, that he esteemed the French people, their customs, and their culture.

Europe, especially France, meant a good deal to Poe. In his American tales he domesticated the exotic by transplanting intact the settings of Venice and Paris. He chose in the horror tales French titles "to create a French atmosphere, or as is more frequently the case, an atmosphere of nowhere . . . . In the *Tales of Ratiocination* French phrases are used to give what Poe himself would call a recherchée air to the mystery."[88]

Poe's knowledge of the literatures of Germany, Spain, and Italy was extensive. His principal references are to the German Goethe, Kant, Schiller, Schlegel, and Tieck—the Spanish Calderon, Cervantes, Bernal Diaz, as well as others—and the Italian Ariosto, Dante, Petrarch, and Tasso.[89] He

certainly had more than an inkling of the civilization of
each country.   Books that Poe read on Germany include
Captain Hall's *Skimmings; or A Winter at Schloss Hainfeld
in Lower Styria* [in Austria],Frederick Von Raumer's
America and the American People, and Baron de la Motte
Fouqué's *Undine.*   On Spain, or Spanish speaking countries,
Poe reviewed Lieutenant Slidell's *A Year in Spain* and its
sequel *Spain Revisited,* an anonymous writer's *Madrid in
1835,* J. L. Stephens's *Incidents of Travel in Central America,*
and R. M. Bird's *Infidel, or the Fall of Mexico.*   The reviews
discussing Italy comprise Thomas Campbell's *Life of
Petrarch* and *Ettore Fieramosca, or the Challenge of Barletta.*
Among other works from Germany and about Spain, Poe
may have consulted the German tales of Hoffmann and read
in *Godey's* (1834) an article about Juliana Morella, a child
prodigy of Barcelona.[90]

Though Poe recognized the values of Spanish and sometimes used quotations from the German literature, he indicated a preference for Italian.   The statement is supported
by the fact that at the University of Virginia Poe delivered
a translation of Tasso that drew a compliment from Professor
Blaetterman and that his review of *Ettore Fieramosca*
exhibits an intimate knowledge of Italian drama.   In this
review he pointed out that "Some of the greatest names in
Italian Literature were writers of Comedy."   He continued
by saying that in his *Encyclopédie* Marmontel betrayed
ignorance of this circumstance but that Apostolo Zeno's
collection of four thousand Italian dramas revealed the
greater portion to be comedies.   Poe's debt to Italy has been
too generally overlooked.   Italian names and settings occur
in much of his work, though more in the tales than in the
poems.   It is to Poe's experiments with the comic and the
grotesque that the Italian influence may be most specifically
traced.

Mayne Reid wrote authoritatively about another aspect of
the poet's learning.   The only literature mentioned by Reid
is Scandinavian:

> I encountered a scholar of rare accomplishments—
> especially skilled in the lore of Northern Europe, and more

> imbued with it than the southern and strictly classic. How he had drifted into this specialty I never knew. But he had it in a high degree, as is apparent throughout all his writings, some of which read like an echo of the Scandinavian 'Sagas.'[91]

Reid's claims were not fully substantiated until 1941, when Adolph B. Benson, apparently unaware of Captain Reid since he does not mention him,[92] published a paper on "Scandinavian References in the Works of Poe." Poe may have understood a little Danish and Swedish; he even knew Swedish versification, the Old Norse Sagas, and "An ancient Danish ballad"; and he referred by name to such literary and historical figures as Jacob Baden, [Jens] Baggesen, [C. M.] Bellman, Bergman, Tycho Brahe, [M. C.] Brun[n], Charles XII of Sweden, Ludwig Holberg, Linnaeus, [Julia] Nyberg, Oehlenschläger (whom he thought a German), Count Oxenstjerna of Sweden, Jonas Ramus, and [Esias] Tegnér. Among these names, Bergman's is connected with *The Conchologist's First Book;* Holberg's with "The Fall of the House of Usher"; Linnaeus' with *Pinakidia;* Baggesen's, Bellman's, Brun[n]'s, Nyberg's and Tegnér's with the review of Longfellow's *Ballads and Poems;* and practically all the others with *Marginalia.* Poe's acquaintance with Scandinavian literature provided him with models for his descriptions of life at sea and for the personal names of his seafaring characters.

Poe reviewed Leigh Ritchie's book on *Russia and the Russians* and was stirred by the vigor of that country's romantic anecdotes. There is no evidence that his readings penetrated the culture of Russia or passed in Northern Europe beyond the immediate boundaries of Denmark, Norway, and Sweden.

For information about the East Poe turned chiefly to the Bible. W. M. Forrest, in *Biblical Allusions in Poe,* demonstrated Poe's use of the scriptures in over 600 passages and his inclusion of over 200 scriptural proper names.[93] Other religious lore familiar to the poet include Sale's translation of the Koran and the philosophies of sacred church fathers like Saints Augustine, Basil, Cyprian, Epiphanius, and

Jerome. His devotion to the Bible enabled him to make
intelligent comments in reviewing J. T. Headley's *The
Sacred Mountains* and the *Inaugural Address of the Rev.
D. L. Carroll, D. D.* But when he came to write his historical essay on *Palestine,* Poe borrowed materials, not from the
Bible, but directly from A. Rees's *Cyclopaedia.*[94] Sacred writ,
however, exercised an abiding influence on the poet's
thinking, his readings therein tending to strengthen his
religious faith. In 1837 Poe nominated J. L. Stephens' two
volumes, *Arabia Petraea,* as a powerful instrument "in the
downfall of unbelief."

English writers were Poe's favorites. From an aricle by
Sir Walter Scott, he took the wording for his title, *Tales of
the Grotesque and Arabesque.*[95] To Elizabeth Barrett
(Browning), he dedicated his volume, *The Raven and Other
Poems.* In his works he made little or no mention of Jane
Austen, Robert Browning, the Bröntes, Fielding, Malory,
Richardson, Swift, or Thackeray. Of the remainder of
English literature, he had a firm working knowledge and a
profound acquaintance with parts of it. He had a fairly
thorough grasp of the contributions of Elizabeth Barrett
(Browning), Byron, Chaucer, Coleridge, Dickens, Hazlitt,
Keats, Milton, Moore, Pope,[96] Shakespeare, Shelley, and
Wordsworth.

Poe's references to English literature encompass the field
from its beginnings to his own day. At the distant extreme,
he cited the eighth-century chronicler Nennius; at the other,
the contemporary British novelist W. H. Ainsworth. His
allusion to the recital by the early Briton Nennius occurs in
Some Account of Stonehenge. The medieval English poet
known to him was Chaucer, whose poetry came to his
attention when he wrote a review of S. C. Hall's edition of
The Book of Gems, which contained selections from Chaucer
to Prior. He cited Chaucer again in "The Rationale of
Verse," where he discoursed on R. H. Horne's essay that
served "to preface his 'Chaucer Modernized.' " Poe displayed
familiarity with the masters of each important period represented in the history of English literature, for he knew such
further British authors as Francis Bacon, Lord Brougham,

Thomas Carlyle, Defoe, Disraeli, Gibbon, William Godwin, Mrs. Hemans, Hood, the eighteenth-century "Junius," Fanny Kemble, "Nat" Lee, Lord Macaulay, Captain Marryat, Scott, Southey, and Edmund Spenser. That he kept abreast of the latest literary movements is exhibited by his familiarity with such contemporary British periodicals as *Blackwood's Magazine, Edinburgh Review, Irish Chronicle, London New Monthly,* and *Popular Record of Modern Science.*

Fittingly, Poe was most intimate with American literature, of which he had an astonishing knowledge. He appreciated the contribution of each of the following major American writers: Byrant, Cooper, Emerson, Irving, Hawthorne, Longfellow, Lowell, and Whittier. He referred to a spate of minor American authors: Joel Barlow, R. M. Bird, D. L. Boucicault, C. B. Brown, C. C. Colton, J. R. Drake, Margaret Fuller, Mrs. Gove, Halleck, Mary B. Hewitt, Samuel Kettell, Dr. Lardner, Joseph Miller, John Neal, Thomas Odiorne, Anne Royal [1], Simms, Tuckerman, and countless more. He manifested a keen interest in current news pertaining to American books and authors by reading publications like the *American Magazine, American Quarterly Review, Columbian Magazine, Encyclopedia Americana, New York Evening Mirror,* and *Morning Post.*

Poe judged his countrymen by the highest standards. He allowed no jingoistic or patriotic motives to influence his sense of fine taste. Though severe with Americans, he was hardly unfair in preferring foreign to native writers. He was perhaps most stringent when he called Emerson "little more than a respectful imitation of Carlyle." He was nearer the truth when he termed Dr. R. M. Bird "a bad imitation of Sir Walter Scott." Poe's poorer opinions include his overpraise of Chivers and his extravagant compliments to his friends among the poetesses. At times he favored Lowell; on other occasions, stung by the New Englander's sense of humor, Poe momentarily lost his critical equilibrium and made hasty remarks which he later regretted. His criticism approached the right tone when he dealt with Bryant, Cooper, Hawthorne, and Wilmer. He saw fit to censure

Cooper and to praise Hawthorne; posterity has tended to accept his verdict as justified.

Is it too much to claim that Poe was in the fundamentals of his craft a learned man? His apprehension of world literature was unmatched outside scholarly circles. He attained a par with such other erudite American poets as Emerson and Lowell. His readings extended everywhere, encompassing an esoteric item like the *Chirugical Journal of Leipsic* and a commonplace folktale like *Jack the Giant Killer.* He knew Greek and Latin letters almost as thoroughly as he knew the writers of France, Germany, Italy, Scandinavia, and Spain. Poe, it is true, sometimes misquoted even French, his favorite foreign tongue. Certainly he was neither a Homer nor a Milton when it comes to intellectual proportions. But he was not a mountebank either. On the question of Poe's learning, I have scratched the surface, but there is much to be done on his knowledge of Italian and Spanish, which was greater than I have cared to take time to demonstrate. In the modern world to which he belongs, he has a fairer claim to learning than some of the other intellectuals.

The practice today, and it has been so for a long time now, is to explain a writer in naturalistic terms of his heredity and environment, to the utter neglect of intellectual influences. Poe's deep and varied readings cannot be ignored in plotting his background. Books fed his dreams, accented his conduct, and shaped his art.

6. The Scope of His Interests

Poe's chief preoccupation was literature, but in his works one sees him concerned with numerous other problems. His earlier interests merely reflect his opinions on the world about him, whereas in his later years he pondered the deepest mysteries of life.

Poe's favorable review of Mrs. Sarah J. Hale's volume on *Traits of American Life* shows that he was an acute observer of contemporary tastes. That Poe, who never forgot his youthful dandyism, gave the subject of manners more than cursory attention is a logical inference from his comment on *The Canons of Good Breeding,* which he claimed might "be read, generally speaking, with profit." He was attracted particularly to what people abroad thought of his country and its citizens. He read Lieutenant Slidell's *The American in England* and apparently enjoyed the volume, which he declared "excellent *in spite of its style.*" In a similar spirit, he perused both the Rev. Orville Dewey's experiences as a distinguished British traveler in *The Old World and the New* and Frederick Von Raumer's imperfect understanding, as a German, of our culture in *America and the American People.* Poe was never carried away by his enthusiasm for foreign culture to a disrespect for America. He seemed at least partly motivated by patriotism in his "Letter to B—" (1831), where he spoke against competition from abroad:

> . . . one might suppose that books, like their authors, improve by travel—their having crossed the sea, is, with us, so great a distinction. Our antiquaries abandon time for distance; our very fops glance from the binding to the bottom of the title-page, where the mystic characters which spell London, Paris, or Genoa, are precisely so many letters of recommendation. . . . [97]

The record shows that Poe well understood the principles of democracy. One must not be misled by his support of Southern traditions into the belief that he was un-American. References in *Eureka* to John Stuart Mill and Jeremy Bentham establish that he was familiar with the more advanced political writings of contemporary Europe. At the University of Virginia he came naturally within the immediate orbit of the political thought of its founder, Thomas Jefferson.[98] But Edgar Allan Poe did not permit geographical boundaries to limit his thinking. Seeing worthy reasons for doing so, he upheld before Lowell the culture of the South and championed Southern letters. Yet among the reviews, there is a commendatory notice of a book by an anonymous Georgian [A. B. Longstreet], *Georgia Scenes, Characters, Incidents,* which few Southerners of class would approve—evidence, perhaps, that Poe could stand free of local prejudices, as he obviously could. In his comment on *Boston and the Bostonians* Poe was especially severe with the Yankees, who should "open their eyes to certain facts which have long been obvious to all the world except themselves—the facts that there exist other cities than Boston—other men of letters than Professor Longfellow—other vehicles of literary information than the 'Down-East Review.' "[99] He here was laboring for a national literature. His diatribe was prefaced with the statement that "our friends in the Southern and Western country" have grown tired of "being ridden to death by New-England." Poe's politics, grounded on the traditions of the South, permitted division within unity, but not the subjugation of the whole country to the dictatorship of any one section. His criticism of New England at that stage of history was healthful. He energetically pointed out the bases for friction which then existed. His attitude is that of the traditional Southerner, the proponent extraordinary of state rights within a union. Poe's political principle is here at one with that of T. S. Eliot, who in his *Definition of Culture* (1949) endorses "the vital importance for a society of *friction* between its parts."

Poe's other miscellaneous writings treat matters like cryptography,[100] education, medicine, navigation, printing, and science. He discussed cryptography in some detail in a paper entitled "A Few Words on Secret Writing." He reported a number of addresses bearing on education, such as those delivered by Lucian Minor at Hampden Sydney College, by Joseph O. Chandler at Marshall College, by Thomas R. Dew at William and Mary, and by Z. Collins Lee at the Baltimore Lyceum. Poe commended S. A. Roszel's address at Dickinson College for its defense of the learned tongues and its recognition of the duties of the teacher, and the Rev. D. L. Carroll's at Hampden Sydney for its emphasis on the social qualities to be gained from college training. Poe's knowledge of medicine appears in his review of Dr. Robert W. Haxall's *A Dissertation on the Importance of Physical Signs in the Various Diseases of the Abdomen and Thorax.* In reviewing W. Newham's *Human Magnetism,* he admitted "the prodigious importance of the mesmeric influence in surgical cases" but doubted "the *curative* effects of mesmerism." He commented on navigation in reviews of Southey's *The Early Naval History of England,* Maury's *Navigation,* and *Report of the Committee on Naval Affairs.* He argued, in a paper entitled "Anastatic Printing," that new discoveries rendered international copyright laws "more imperative and more apparent." He wrote ably about science in reviews of books like P. M. Rogêt's *Animal and Vegetable Physiology,* the Rev. Henry Duncan's *Sacred Philosophy of the Seasons,* and Lemmonnier's *A Synopsis of Natural History,* as translated by Thomas Wyatt, author of *Conchology.* He spoke with glowing approval of J. N. Reynolds' *Address on the Subject of a Surveying and Exploring Expedition to the Pacific Ocean and South Seas.*[101]

These latter subjects, related to Poe's own literary interests, figured in one degree or another as background material in his creative writing: cryptography in "The Gold Bug," education in "William Wilson," medicine in "The Mystery of Marie Rogêt," navigation in "Pym," printing in "Thingum Bob," and science in many tales, including "The Premature Burial."

On the lighter side Poe was interested in anecdotes about famous personages, jokes about women, and tall tales from the West. First, he discussed *Nuts to Crack; or Quips, Quirks, Anecdote and Facete of Oxford and Cambridge Scholars,* terminating his remarks by "selecting one of its good things for the benefit of our own especial readers." Secondly, he liked the jokes he encountered in reviewing *Noble Deeds of Woman,* an anonymous work in two volumes. Thirdly, he was stirred by James Hall's lively recitals about the frontier in *Sketches of History, Life and Manners of the West.* But do these small concerns relate to his art importantly? In his work the awkward mixing of levity and seriousness constitutes one of the most glaring faults of his technique. A large number of his serio-comic tales are today appallingly dull. Their intended vivacity now seems wholly palsied. His brand of humor, imperfectly executed in imitation of the pseudo-classical styles, long ago became passé in America.

Poe's curiosity about genius exhibits another side of his personality. He was able to imitate the wit of La Rochefou-

cauld, whose works he had read, and to say in the twenty-
third entry under *Fifty Suggestions* (1845) that

> What the world calls "genius" is the state of mental
> disease arising from the undue prominence of some of the
> faculties. The works of such genius are never sound in
> themselves, and, in especial, always betray the general
> mental insanity.[102]

Poe's statement in the review of Cooper's *Wyandotté*,
reminiscent of De Quincey's remarks on the literature of
knowledge and the literature of power, is of sufficient import
to be included among his more vital literary interests. Poe
said:

> . . . thus there are two great classes of fictions—a popular
> and widely circulated class, read with pleasure, but without
> admiration—in which the author is lost or forgotten; or
> remembered, if at all, with something very nearly akin to
> contempt: and then, a class not so popular, nor so widely
> diffused, in which, at every paragraph, arises a distinctive
> and highly pleasurable interest, springing from our per-
> ception and appreciation of the skill employed, or the
> genius evinced in the composition. After perusal of the
> one class, we think solely of the book—after reading the
> other, chiefly the author. The former class leads to popu-
> larity—the latter to fame. In the former case, the books
> sometimes live, while the author usually dies; in the latter,
> even when the works perish, the man survives.[103]

It is from "Al Aaraaf"[104] that a yet more important idea
derives, one which pertains to both the American Imagists
and the French *Symbolistes*—indeed to poetry as a whole.
Poe made a forward stride considerably beyond Bryant's
communion with nature in her varied forms when he wrote:
"All nature speaks, and ev'n ideal things / Flap shadowy
sounds from visionary wings." The theory, an extension of
the Platonic system of ideas, has a touch of mysticism. It
recognizes that nature speaks a mysterious language of half-
hidden meanings, impressions that are at times conveyed
in unexpected, opposite, and contradictory images. The
system adopted by Baudelaire became famous as the theory
of "analogies." It sometimes is like a form of synesthesia, in
which Goethe, too, was interested. Baudelaire gave it particular application in two poems, "Correspondences" and
"Elevation." Though deriving from Plato, Plotinus, and

others, the new theory predicates that in the world of phenomena sounds may present themselves as shadows, perfumes as textures, and pictures as melody. Einstein's recent discovery that light has mass tends to verify the earlier suppositions of these poets. Hence the spectrum of poetry logically includes colors that are "blue like an orange." The poet capable of practicing this newest art approaches a superior Reality unknown to the average man or to the supine traditionalist. The theory perceives reality as immeasurable by the five physical senses and seeks to enlarge man's grasp of it. According to Baudelaire, the use of stimulants like opium was justifiable because these heightened a writer's apprehension of phenomena; but, so far as is known, Poe took the drug rarely and only for its medicinal properties in conformity with the practice of that day, not to gain mystical contacts. Poe's subscription to the metaphysical idea of the real existence of "analogies" is prepotently significant. It connects him with the advanced thinking of psychologists in our time and places him at the forefront among older authors who are influencing the mystical poetry being written today.

Poe's prose poem, *Eureka* (1848), brings together his dominant interests in poetry, religion, and science into one system.[105] This philosophy may be termed, for want of a better phrase, a religious estheticism. Poe himself corresponded with several persons about the meaning of his prose poem, his clearest exposition appearing in a letter to Eveleth, dated February 29, 1848. Since Poe's time, numerous learned men have attempted to elucidate the poet's intentions. The most famous commentator is Paul Valéry, who states that "The universe is formed on a plan the profound symmetry of which is present, as it were, in the inner structure of our mind. Hence, the poetic instinct will lead us blindly to the truth."[106] The sanctuary can be more speedily reached, I may add, by a cognition of the theory of "analogies." Both Valéry and others[107] are impressed with Poe's bold speculation as a forerunner of Einstein's theory. The symmetry of the universe is in the human mind. Valéry emphasizes the word symmetrical, declaring that "*it is in reality, a formal symmetry which is the essential characteristic of Einstein's universe.*" Like everybody else, Poe experienced difficulty in explaining the absolute beginning—the end of course is yet to be and hence is open to unbounded speculations.   Valéry disposes of the beginning by observing that "it is necessarily a myth."

As a specimen of literature, *Eureka* employs near its outset a manuscript, in this case a letter, "found corked in a bottle and floating on the *Mare Tenebrarum*"—so that one again encounters the device Poe featured in "MS Found in a Bottle" and "Mellonta Tauta."   Interesting as it is to observe this repetition in technique, *Eureka* offers more to the reader in the materials it contains on literary theory. In *Eureka* Poe compares the artist and God, his first sentence being reminiscent of his review of Bulwer's *Night and Morning*:

> In the construction of *plot,* for example, in fictitous literature, we should aim at so arranging the incidents that we shall not be able to determine, of any one of them, whether it depends from any one other or upholds it.   In this sense, of course, *perfection of plot* is really, or practically, unattainable—but only because it is a finite intelligence that constructs.   The plots of God are perfect.   The Universe is a plot of God.[108]

But Poe was always both theorist and technician.   It is instructive to see how he modified his abstract reasoning to conform with the requirements of verisimilitude even in his most fanciful narratives.   For example, later in *Eureka* he disposed of all human individuality with the predication that each soul combines with all other souls upon being absorbed into the single unity which is God, whereas in three of his tales—"The Conversation of Eiros and Charmion," "The Colloquy of Monos and Una," and "The Power of Words"—he represented his characters maintaining an individual life after death and discoursing on matters pertaining to an aged world lately destroyed.   In addition, "The Power of Words" contains the scientific principle that there is a vibration of words: Agathos explains to Oinos that no thought can perish since all motion is creative and originates as the volition of God.   "Poe here extended the principle of conservation of energy to the power of a word once spoken. The story is, in a sense, a forecast of the radio waves."[109] It is clear that the philosophy incorporated in *Eureka* was the culmination and efflorescence of much of his earlier thinking. Many of his profoundest thoughts are foreshadowed in the ideas appearing not only in the tales but also in the essays and especially in the poems.

In the "Philosophy of Composition" Poe sought to prove his theories with mathematical precision; in "The Poetic Principle," to identify Poetry with Truth. This procedure and this idea are encountered once more in *Eureka,* a further indication that his practical ideas about creative writing were often ultimately grounded on theories austere in their abstractness. Here Poe said that "the sense of the symmetrical is the poetical essence of the Universe . . . . Thus Poetry and Truth are one . . . ."[110]

The closest tie between Poe's philosophy and his poetry occurs in *Eureka* and "Sonnet—Silence" (1840). I refer to Poe's idea of "No More"— the inevitable end of matter and so of the human body. According to *Eureka* there will be eventually a death of Matter, at which time it will become Ether which is in turn expelled upon its homecoming into absolute Unity—with the result that there will be *"Matter no more."* In "Sonnet—Silence" Poe explained that "There is a two-fold Silence . . ./Body and Soul" and that the corporate body finally will relinquish its material existence and be named "No More." To Poe these words "No More," thought to be the germinal form of the "Nevermore" of "The Raven" (1845), pealed out funereally the requiem of all cosmic matter and the final and complete annihilation of Man.

This stupendously painful conclusion, at which Poe's mathematical mind arrived with relentless logic, would be appalling were it not for the abstractness of the idea. Perhaps in order to allay the fears of his worried readers he subjoined at the very end a note reiterating his main tenet respecting the conversion of the soul into God. Poe said: "The pain of the consideration that we shall lose our own individual identity ceases at once when we further reflect that the process, as above described, is, neither more nor less than that of absorption, by each individual intelligence of all other intelligences (that is, of the Universe) into its own. That God may be all in all, each must become God."[112]

7. His Stature as an Essayist

How shall one estimate Poe's standing among the essayists? Was he a learned man? In reply, one could say "Yes" and quote his references to several profound thinkers not hitherto mentioned: men like the mathematician Euclid, the scientist Humboldt, the historian David Hume, the political philosopher Machiavelli, and the theosophist Swedenborg. Or one could argue that his learning was a pose, a veneer, and cite James O. Bailey's recent disclosure that Poe's erudite comment on "Some Account of Stonehenge" was drawn almost *verbatim* from the thirty-fifth volume of A. Rees's *Cyclopaedia*.[113] What one can say finally is that the evidence reviewed here suggests that Poe was a good deal more learned than has been hitherto supposed.

Was Poe a stylist? If so, he displayed a lack of taste in reviewing such books as *Bubbles from the Brunnens of Nassau,* a volume discussing the medicinal properties of mineral water. Poe's mixture of seriousness and levity is a stylistic flaw of his more ambitious essays like "The Rationale of Verse." His attempts at humor reveal the strain of misplacement and lack the indispensable requisite of true wit, a sense of proportion. His penchant for vitriol is less open to objection, although it often is wasted in attacks on very small fry. The caustic strain in Poe may be defended on the basis that it rendered his style more lively. It is this spirit of rebellion, so notable in even his utilitarian compositions, that composes the romantic aspect of Poe's genius.

What was Poe's contribution to literary criticism? There is not elsewhere in the whole body of nineteenth-century American essays so resolute, so original, and so constructive a treatment of practical criticism as is offered by the mature theories of Poe. His three most famous essays—the practical

"Philosophy of Composition," the technical "Rationale of
Verse," and the theoretical "Poetic Principle"—entitle him
to a place alongside the leading critics of the world.   Indeed
one or more of these compositions inevitably reside in the
anthologies selected to illustrate the finest ideas of literary
men from Aristotle to T. S. Eliot.   It is Eliot who admires
Poe's cultivation of the quality of suspense.[114]   A small body
of essays joins with a slight volume of verse and a larger
collection of tales to form the tripod of Poe's contributions.
Poe is remarkable for the quantity of his critical writings,
as contrasted with the smaller numbers of either poems or
tales.   But he is memorable, as before, for the high quality
of only a limited few of his critical writings.

A scientific side of Poe is revealed in his mechanistic interpretation of art and also in his espousal of originality.   "In
some ways Poe resembled the half-crazed inventors of his
time . . . much more than he resembled any other American
writer.   His hatred of plagiarism . . . was exactly the attitude
of an inventor toward those who infringe his patents."[115]
Poe also was a proponent of a theory of coherence; his large
discovery, as in *Eureka,* was the theory of integration, of
unity—which he thereafter everywhere vigorously espoused.
H. L. Mencken is enthusiastic about Poe, but states that his
influence was slow to manifest itself: "Immediately he was
dead, the shadows of the Irving tradition closed around his
tomb, and for nearly thirty years thereafter all of his chief
ideas went disregarded in his own country.[116]   Mencken's
utterance, valuable as literary appreciation, is historically
inaccurate so far as it relates to Poe's fiction.   Henry James,
for one, took up the gothic manner used by Poe and continued by Hawthorne, for James published his story, "The
Ghostly Rental," in 1876.

The intense modernity of Poe's ideas, especially his
connecting literature with science [117] and with mysticism,
is one of his main contributions as a critic.   His practical
recommendations will assure him respectful homage long
past our time.   His fame as an essayist today is making a bid
to surpass his achievements as poet and short-story writer.

Chapter Three

Renown and Recognition

1. Precursor of Decadence

Poe's artistry is one of the richest literary heritages claimed by the United States. The position he occupies today, both at home and abroad, is a delayed payment to a genius. He cleared the way for future generations of professional writers, and he did so with small financial return. The fame of Poe, whose works hold uppermost the principle of art for art's sake, has established him as a permanent figure in world literature.

Edgar Allan Poe made his first weighty impression in France. He made it, not as a poet of the dark tradition, not as a writer of tales of ratiocination, and not as a critic of the practical school. He made it as the precursor of decadence.

"Decadence" is an outgrowth of art for art's sake. Its partisans believe that literature need have no purpose beyond the cultivation of the beautiful for the pleasure it conveys. Man has a natural hunger for beauty and, in moments of exaltation, a longing for ideal loveliness. More-

98

over, undue emphasis on technique sometimes resulted in a merely decorative estheticism, wherein the artist has no real passion and disbelieves in positive values. He is then pre-eminently the absolute stylist. Concerned principally with external form, he remains above questions of morality, the significance of his theme, the proportion of his design, or the commercial value of his work. Philistine malice attached "decadent" as an epithet of opprobrium to daring young esthetes and impressionists. In their revolt from bourgeois insipidity, the rebels welcomed it as a badge of distinction. They were unconcerned with existing middle-class institutions and mores; their aristocratic tastes preoccupied them with art. Villiers de l'Isle Adam's prescription, "As for living, our servants will do that for us,"[113] explains the movements of the decadents from life to art. Poe's famed unsociability links him with this group of writers. Indeed, at the mid-nineteenth century the three main sources of decadence were John Keats, the German romantic philosophers, and Edgar Allan Poe.[119]

Poe's striving for perfection made him a natural symbol of the accurate technician, the stylist supreme. The fact that he earned little money for his compositions further illustrated his decadence. His preoccupation with morbidity, with death, and with decay also fittingly associated him with a genre of literature neither didactic nor moral in its purpose. His disregard for such topics as war and patriotism, love and honor, industrialization and material progress characterize the disinterest of any author motivated by the consideration of art for art's sake.

Arthur Symons and Oscar Wilde were the exponents of the new school in England. In 1893 Symons wrote his famous study, *The Decadent Movement in Literature* (reprinted in 1929 in his *Dramatis Personnae*). Oscar Wilde's definition, included in his volume *Intentions* (1891), was given also in an essay, "The Critic as Artist" (1891).[120] Wilde declared that "what one has to destroy is vulgarity and stupidity" and that to effect improvement "we must turn to the decorative arts: to the arts that touch us, not to the arts that teach us." Wilde expressed here Poe's disdain for

the didactic and Poe's determination to touch the reader—
in fact, to excite his nervous system. Poe also defended
the principles represented in Wilde's further statements
that "the art that is frankly decorative is the art to live with"
and that "To be natural is to be obvious, and to be obvious
is to be inartistic." The new school of literature was at
times called *"maladie de fin du siécle."* To Walter Pater
it was "strangeness added to beauty." The grand aim of
the decadents was to avoid a complete innovation, to keep
within the limits of the old tradition at the same time that
they made it extraordinary.[121]

In France the movement was due to the works of Poe; the
translations of his French defender, Charles Baudelaire; and
the contribution of Laforgue. When Baudelaire's versions
of Poe first began to appear, Barbey d'Aurevilly wrote that
"Poe was the king of Bohemians and Baudelaire has translated him twice: in his work and in his life."[122] The
influence of Poe was felt by Verlaine and by Rimbaud, whom
the Englishman John Gray translated. Laforgue's *Moralités
légendaires*, which became the model for Beardsley's *Under
the Hill* (1896), was also influential. Laforgue's mixture of
the bizarre, the precious, the humorous had its early parallel
in Poe's extravaganzas on nosology, his humorous sallies in
tales and epigrams, and his efforts to appear superciliously
witty.

It was Baudelaire, "probably the greatest poet of the
nineteenth century,"[123] who combined decadence with
dandyism, a fad which Poe had earlier adopted in his youth,
possibly in imitation of Lord Byron. The new dandyism
had been called a return to the politeness of the past,
another expression of decorum. Francois Porche, a biographer of Baudelaire, says that "Dandyism was only a
reaction against bad manners."[124] It was also a mask for
concealing the abnormality of such figures as Baudelaire and
Rimbaud. Baudelaire's egotism was unbounded. He wrote
letters "at exactly the same time" to both Mme. Marie and
Mme. Sabatier "in exactly the same terms,"[125] which is what
Poe had done in the two love epistles he addressed, respectively, to Mrs. Whitman and Mrs. Richmond. As a dandy,

the Frenchman was more "beau" than Brummel. Max White's novel, *The Midnight Gardener* (1948), recounts Baudelaire's excessive attention to clothes. Poe was in no economic position to lavish money on his attire. Yet Baudelaire conceived of him as a solitary aristocrat among multitudes of unfashionable bourgeois. The champions of decadence, who professed to be imitating Poe, bound themselves in their life as in their art in a conspiracy to catch the eye and to startle the beholder.

The twentieth-century impression of Poe, at least in the United States, is far different from that of Baudelaire. Today successful American writers prize Poe, whom they know chiefly for his yarns, as the first discoverer of the secret of effective narration, which "is to make a good story out of a man performing a feat of reasoning." According to the detective-story writer Rex Stout, "That is the pattern set by Poe, and no one has ever deviated from it without making a mess."[126] Christopher Morley praises another aspect of Poe's genius, his modern spirit. In commenting on the obscure history of allergic distress, Morley cites the malady of the hero in *The Fall of the House of Usher,* "Where with his usual clairvoyance Poe lists . . . what are now recognized as classic symptoms of allergy."[127] Poe's close ties with today demonstrate that his influence was not restricted to the decadents or, to mention a related school, the symbolists of nineteenth-century France.

It is as the spiritual embodiment of decadence, however, that Poe is presented in Oscar Cargill's *Intellectual America.* Cargill's book is the best treatment of the subject, except that he assigns Poe a mother complex to prevent the normal gratification of his eroticism.[128] Edgar Allan Poe was certainly neither the first nor the last American poet to be in love with more than one woman. The fact is evident. Poe was both forgetful of Virginia and cognizant of his own capacities when he wrote Mrs. Clemm (August 28-29 (?), 1849) that he wished to live near Mrs. Richmond and advised "Muddie" that he cared to hear nothing concerning the lady "unless you can tell me that Mr. R[ichmond] is dead."[129]

The interpretation of Poe as a decadent rests on conflicting testimony.   According to legend, he was an outcast from
society, a depraved roué who had married a child of thirteen
years, a profligate whose irresponsibility kept his family
constantly on the verge of starvation.   In Europe false
reports circulated regarding his drunken, wayward life, his
death by suicide, and even Griswold's ugly allegation of his
criminal relations with Mrs. Clemm.   Rumor painted him
a satanist; and in his role of decadent he becomes the
poète maudit, America's despised poet.[130]   There is, however, a brighter side to Poe's estheticism.   In *Holiday and
Other Poems* (1906), the Englishman John Davidson explained that rhyme was originally a "property of decadence" and
that when fresh decay demanded expression a new order
of rhyme was certainly evolved.   The new order, Davidson
said, was re-echoing rhyme, "the equisite invention of the
most original genius in words the world has ever known—
Edgar Allan Poe."   In the journal *Colophon* (1930) the
American scholar Carl F. Schreiber reverted to the earlier
view, saying that Poe "represents for American literature the
supreme type of the starving poet."   T. S. Eliot, in *Notes
Toward a Definition of Culture* (1949), referred to the
French tradition as the greatest contribution to European
poetry in the second half of the nineteenth century.   It
inspired, Eliot stated, the work of three poets in other
languages—his own, Rainer Maria Rilke's, and that of W.B.
Yeats.   "And," he continued, "so complicated are these
literary influences, we must remember that this French
movement itself owed a good deal to an American of Irish
extraction: Edgar Allan Poe."

Decadence, however, is only one part of the poetic record;
and it is now time to examine how writers in different lands
have variously interpreted other aspects of Poe's genius.
A factual survey of their opinions of his achievement should
prove or disprove his claims to world renown.

2. Poe's Vogue in France

During his own lifetime Poe had the satisfaction of knowing that his fame had reached Paris. In a letter to Evert A. Duyckinck of December 30, 1846, he wrote: "Dear Duyckinck,—Mrs. Clemm mentioned to me, this morning, that some of the Parisian papers had been speaking about my 'Murders in the Rue Morgue.' "

Poe first became known in France in November, 1845. It was then that his celebrated tale "The Gold Bug" appeared as "Le Scarabée d'or," by A. B. [Alphonse Borghers], in *La Revue Brittanique*. Alphonse Borghers, who credited the story to Poe, was therefore his first French translator. Some six months later *La Quotidienne* ran (June 11, 12, and 13, 1846) a free transcription of "The Murders in the Rue Morgue" under the title "Un Meurtre sans exemple dans les Fastes de la Justice." This version, which involved a few verbal changes—including the substitution of the name Bernier for that of Dupin—was signed "G. B." [?], and Poe's authorship went unmentioned. In September, 1846, *La Revue Brittanique* printed another Poe tale and attributed it to him. The story was "Une Descente au Maelstrom," signed "O. N." ("Old Nick"), the pseudonym of E. D. Forgues. On the following October 12 this same Forgues, without referring to Poe, published in the newspaper *Le Commerce* a version of "The Murders in the Rue Morgue" entitled "Une Sanglante Enigme." Promptly *La Presse,* recently angered by Forgues, charged him with mistreatment of Poe in basing his French story on the version that had appeared in *La Quotidienne*.

Forgues immediately acknowledged Poe's authorship in his reply, which *La Presse* refused to print. Thereupon the Frenchman sued the journal but lost the suit at the trial in December, 1846. The notoriety of the lawsuit had good effects for Poe: it brought his name prominently before the French public three years prior to his death and gave him in his last years pride and gratification in the knowledge that his talents were appreciated abroad.[131]

Forgues's "Les Contes d'Edgar A. Poe" (*La Revue des Deux Mondes,* October 15, 1846) is important on two scores. First, Forgues demonstrated that Poe was ignorant of Paris and assembled evidence of his errors in localities to disprove the report of Alexander Dumas the elder, repeated by Hervey Allen in the *Dictionary of American Biography,* that Poe "in the summer of 1832" was at the French capital. Secondly, in treating the *Tales* of 1845 seriously, Forgues aroused sufficient interest in Poe among readers for Frenchmen to feel justified in translating, not merely a selection or so as heretofore, but comprehensive collections of the American's stories. Apparently unaware of Poe's poetry and criticism, Forgues analyzed such tales as "Monos and Una," "Eiros and Charmion," "A Descent into the Maelström," "The Purloined Letter," "The Gold Bug," "The Mystery of Marie Rogêt," "The Black Cat," and "The Man in the Crowd." Enthusiastic about the brevity of Poe's prose, Forgues declared that *"Le diamant n'est jamais bien gros, l'essence n'emplit jamais des vastes foudres; et un conte comme ceux de M. Poe offre plus de substance à l'esprit . . . que vingt volumes comme ceux que fabriquaient naguére, et par centaines, les Sandraz de Courties, les Darnand-Baculard, les de Lussain, précurseurs et prototypes de beaucoup des feuilletonistes contemporains."*[132] Forgues knew some American literature, for he pointed out that in the exploitation of the gothic Poe was related to Brockden Brown.[133]

It was Alphonse Borghers who published, at Paris, the first collected volume of Poe's stories—*Nouvelles choisies d'Edgar Poe* (1853). Translations of small groups of tales had preceded this. In 1847 Madame Isabelle Meunier translated "The Black Cat," "The Murders in the Rue Morgue," "Eiros and Charmion," and "A Descent into the Maelström"; in 1848 she translated "The Gold Bug"—and all these appeared in *La Démocratie Pacifique.* After that, numerous versions of Poe fed the literary markets of France. According to Émile Lauvrière, there were thirty-four book-length translations by the year 1897. In more recent times, Frenchmen have widened their study of Poe to include his letters and even his little known poetic drama, as may be

seen from Georges-Bazile's transcription of *Lettres d'Amour
à Helen* (1924) and H. R. Woestyn's translation, *Politien*
(1926).

With Poe's works readily accessible, French prose writers
soon became acquainted with Poe and commenced to draw
upon his tales for inspiration. The celebrated Guy de
Maupassant sometimes mentioned Poe and Poe's characters.
Maupassant's narrative about Schopenhauer's false teeth may
have been influenced by the episode on false teeth in Poe's
"Berenice." Émile Gaboriau, the famous French writer of
detective fiction, studied Poe's methods so closely that the
critic Marius Topin has averred that "Son maître, son
génératur est incontestablement Edgar Poe." The popular
French author Jules Verne also read Poe with care. In his
Sphinx des Glaces, which is dedicated "A la mémoire d'Edgar
Poe," Verne borrowed from "The Narrative of Arthur
Gordon Pym." *Sphinx des Glaces* continued Poe's novelette
and utilized a number of the same characters. The fourth
chapter of Verne's novel is called "Le Roman d'Edgar Poe,"
where Verne lauds the "célèbre ouvrage de notre romancier
américain."

Even the French stage was influenced by the plots of Poe's
better-known tales. Victorien Sardou based his drama *La
Perle Noire* on "The Murders in the Rue Morgue." When
this proved successful, he modelled his *Pattes de Mouche* on
"The Purloined Letter." Ernest Laumann employed Baudelaire's version of "The Tell-Tale Heart" in his play entitled
Le Coeur révélatur. After the turn of the century, André
de Lorde wrote a one-act drama (1903) in which he drew
upon the plot of "The System of Dr. Tarr and Professor
Fether." One of the greatest dramatist of the day, Maurice
Maeterlinck, whose *Pelléas et Mélisande* reflected the atmosphere created in Poe's stories, when once asked if he liked
the works of Poe, replied: "Oui, Edgar Poe; ses *Poèmes*
surtout, et, dans ses *Contes*: La Chute de la Maison Usher."

Poe's wizardry as a narrator left an indelible impression
on modern French prose. The extent of his influence may
be inferred from C. P. Cambiaire's study, where thirty or
more French novelists and tellers of tales are mentioned as

followers of Poe. The list includes such well-remembered names as Emile Gaboriau, Gautier, the Goncourt brothers, Gaston Leroux, Eugene Sue, and Jules Verne. But the fame of Poe in France is knit eternally, not with any of these authors, but with Charles Pierre Baudelaire.

From his earliest knowledge of Poe in 1846 or 1847, through the translations of Félix Tournachon ("Nadar") and Isabelle Meunier, Baudelaire (1821-1867) was enthusiastic about Poe's works. He remained so for the last two decades of his life, which he largely devoted to the study of this man who had become his favorite author. The art of Poe was the gospel of Baudelaire. He preached the doctrine so widely that, according to *La Revue Internationale* for August 1, 1859, the young people of France referred pell-mell to "Plato the Greek, Goethe the German, Shakespeare the Englishman, Poe the American, and Dante the Florentine."

Baudelaire understood Poe's contribution in its three-fold aspects of poetry, prose fiction, and literary criticsm. When he wrote his essay, "Conseils aux jeunes littérateurs" for *Art Romantique* in April, 1846, Baudelaire incorporated some of the ideas Poe had expressed in "The Philosophy of Composition." In his "Notes nouvelles sur Edgar Poe," printed in 1857, he objected, as Poe had done before him, to the inclusion of morality in poetry. That Baudelaire read even Poe's miscellaneous criticism attentively is testified by the fact that he wrote a confession piece, "Mon Coeur mis à nu," which title is a translation of the one mentioned in *Pinakidia*—"My Heart Laid Bare."

Baudelaire's command of Poe's works in prose is amply illustrated in the series of famous translations which were issued between 1856 and 1865. These are, in chronological order, *Histoires extraordinaires* (1856), *Nouvelles Histoires extraordinaires* (1857), *Aventures d'Arthur Gordon Pym* (1858), *Eurêka* (1863), and *Histoires grotesques et sérieuses* (1865). Baudelaire had composed a version of "Mesmeric Revelation" as early as 1848, so that the period of his activity as a translator of Poe comprises exactly seventeen years.

The repute of the French version has almost eclipsed that

of the American original. In 1934 Hazael S. Williams, author at Southern Methodist University of the Master's thesis *Baudelaire, Translator of Poe,* made an important discovery: namely, that Baudelaire had a definite style of his own which gave the French translation a greater brilliance than the original. This circumstance may explain why Walter Pater preferred to read Poe in the language of Baudelaire. The preference of Spanish people for the French form rests obviously on the kinship of the two languages. As for Baudelaire the translator, he sought to report Poe's text faithfully. Sometimes he understandably slipped, as when he rendered "pâle comme une oie" (white as a goose) the negro Jupiter's statement in "The Gold Bug" that his master was "as white as a gose" (*i. e.,* ghost). But Baudelaire, perceiving in the strange tales precisely the new effect that Poe was striving for, correctly pronounced him "the writer of the nerves."

That Poe's bequest to Baudelaire's poetry has been over-estimated is the opinion of Benjamin Inabnit Harrison, who at the University of Viriginia in 1938 wrote an impressive Doctoral dissertation, *A Chronological Concordance to the "Fleurs du Mal" of Baudelaire together with Baudelairian Studies.* A number of the twenty-five French poems supposedly indebted to Poe Harrison ruled out on chrono-logical grounds. Thus "Incompatabilité," which reeks with the Poe atmosphere, was composed when Baudelaire was aged sixteen—ten years before he even heard of Poe. Many of the similarities in style are due to the two poets' possess-ing an identity of temperament. This fact doubtless explains Baudelaire's confession that he saw in Poe's works "not only subjects I had dreamed of, but *sentences* that I had thought of and that he had written twenty years before." Though not greatly dependent on Poe's poetry, Baudelaire, who prayed to Poe as an intercessor for his soul, used the words *corbeau* and *jamais.* In March, 1853, he published his prose translation of "The Raven."

To Baudelaire, obsessed as he was with the idea of evil and his own sinfulness, Poe became a saint. It is as such that Baudelaire named him in 1856 in the "Préface" to

Histoires extraordinaires: "J'ajoute un saint nouveau au martyrologe." For a last reference, in *La Fanfarlo* the thumb-nail sketch of Samuel Cramer, beginning "Nature ténébreuse, bariolée de vifs éclairs," bears a strong resemblance to Poe.

The French poet who most admired the art of Poe's verse was Stéphane Mallarmé, What Baudelaire did for the tales, Mallarmé accomplished for the poems.[135] The one important difference is that Poe's wide recognition as a poet came a good deal later, for it was not until the year 1874 that Mallarmé published, with five illustrations from Manet's drawings, a prose version of "The Raven." This publication was followed in 1888 by a more imposing collection of twenty pieces, *Les Poèmes d'Edgar Poe, traduction de Stéphane Mallarmé, avec portrait et fleuron par Edouard Deman.* The remarkable feature of Mallarmé's French translation is that he presented Poe's poetry in the form of prose. In doing so, the translator, at least in the eyes of Frenchmen, established Edgar Poe alongside Walt Whitman as a founder of *vers libre*.

The first complete French collection of Poe's verses came in 1889, the translator being Gabriel Mourey. This ambitious version was succeeded in 1908 by Victor Orban's *Poésies complètes d' Edgar Poe.* In 1933 there appeared *La Réhabilitation d'Edgar Poe,* by Suzanne d'Olivera Jackowska. The volume by Jackowska makes two noteworthy contributions. First, it includes a laudatory sketch of Poe's life; secondly, it contains twelve of his poems transcribed into rhyming French verse. The most recent popular French version to intrigue Parisians was the work, in 1942, of Pierre Pascal, *Poèmes d'Edgar Poe.*

Mallarmé's famous translations of Poe's poetry outrank all others, whether in prose or verse, because this French professor of English was then the leader of the new generation of poets arising in France. In 1941 Jeanne Rosselet, in her survey of Poe's French vogue, said that "If Baudelaire was Poe's prophet, Stéphane Mallarmé became his high priest . . . he soon attracted a group of young poets who made his modest apartment of the Rue de Rome their Mecca and who had became known in 1886 under the name of the 'Symbolists.' "[136] Among the French poets who have imitated Poe, one may mention Théophile Ducasse, Max Jacob, Francis Jammes, Charles Van Lerberghe, Jean Rameau, Adolphe Retté, George Rodenbach, Maurice Rollinat, Albert Semain, Paul Verlaine, and Viélé-Griffin.

The Symbolist poets of France did not restrict their attention to Poe's verses. In his *Bateau Ivre* (1871) Rimbaud apparently referred to "A Descent into the Maelström" when he wrote: "Moi qui tremblais sentant geindre à cinquante lieues/Le rut des Behemots et des Maelström épais." The suggestion of Rimbaud's editors, Ramon Guthrie and George E. Diller, is that Rimbaud drew from either Jules Verne's *Vingt mille lieues sous les mers* (1870) or Baudelaire's translation "Une Descente au Maelström." In similar manner, Théophile Gautier, another French author, did not limit his attention to Poe's tales. When describing the death of Gérard de Nerval (1855) in *Portraits et souvenirs littéraires,* Gautier quoted the words of Poe's raven: "Never, oh! never more![137] Further illustrations may be seen in the work in 1923 by L. Seylaz, *E. Poe et les premiers symbolistes français,* which remains the authoritative study on Poe's relations to Mallarmé and his disciples.

Of all recent French poets, it was Paul Valéry who studied Poe most devotedly. Like Baudelaire, Valéry regarded Poe as a "grande homme." In 1927 his book *Variété* appeared in an American translation. It contains Valéry's penetrating exposition of *Eureka*. Poe's *Eureka, A Prose Poem* had already elicited comment in France as early as the year 1864 in an article by Judith Gautier, daughter of the distinguished French author just mentioned. Valéry's analysis, however, has become by far the most celebrated in comparative letters. In 1948, shortly after Valéry's death, his *Reflections on the World Today* was posthumously published in New York. Here Valéry, in the chapter on "Our Destiny and Literature," mentioned the fantasies of Jules Verne and H. G. Wells and then referred to Poe as "the greatest and most profound of the authors of that kind."[138]

There are similar indications among French biographers and critics of continued interest in Poe and his ideas. To the past century belong such "classic" studies as A. Barine's *Nevroses* (1898), E. Hennequins's *Écrivains françaisés* (1899), and T. de Wyzewa's *Écrivains étrangers*: Poe (1896). In the first decades of the twentieth came A. Fontainais' *La Vie d'Edgar Poe* (1919), R. de Gourmont's *Promenades littéraires* (1904), E. Lauvrière's *Edgar Poe, sa vie et son oeuvre* (1904) and his *Edgar Poe* (1911), C. Mauclair's *L'Art en silence* (1901) and his *La Génie d'Edgar Poe* (1925), and A. S. Patterson's *L'Influence d'Edgar Poe sur Baudelaire* (1903). In 1932 Claire-Ellaine Engel reported in *Modern Philology* on "L'État des Travaux sur Edgar Allen [*sic*] Poe en France." French books on Poe have continued to appear. Léon Lemonnier, author of earlier studies on French critics and translators of Poe, completed a third book in 1933, *Edgar Poe et les poètes français*. Marie Bonaparte's biography of *Edgar Poe* was issued in 1933, to compete with the earlier work of M. de Casanove, *Edgar Allan Poe* (1920); and her article on "The Black Cat" appeared in *Partisan Review* in 1950.

It is the French, more than any other nation, who have sought out Poe for romantic treatment. And they are yet doing so. In 1942 he was discussed imaginatively by G. Bachelard in his volume entitled *L'Eau et les rêves*. In 1945 Jacques Castelnau published his biography on *Edgar Poe*, a book of sympathetic interpretations conforming to the tradition of French criticisms of Poe.

What lies behind the persistent French veneration of the American poet? The answer may have been suggested as early as 1909 by Curtis Hidden Page. Poe's art appeals to the French, Page said, from the circumstance that its essence is pure logic—a logic wholly separated from the reality demanded by Americans. "The French of the Parnassian epoch especially, found in him a kindred spirit because of his devotion to art for art's sake. The lesser, or lower Parnassians and Decadents loved him for his perversity and grotesque horrors. The Symbolists found in him their ideal, because his work so often seems to have much greater significance than it really possesses."[139] The flavor of *art pour l'art* animated the esthetic of André Gide (1869-1951), who in youth espoused the ideals of the revolutionary decadents.

Poe's debt to France is more considerable than that of any other major American author, for it was French enthusiasm which first made him famous throughout the literary world. Gallic admiration often reached the peaks of eulogy, as in C. P. Cambiaire's report of André Fontainais' exasperated questioning of an American correspondent on July 22, 1922: "Why the devil won't your fellow-country-men admit once and for all that Edgar Poe was one of the most wonderful, *most influential* and most profound poets who ever lived?"

The obligation of Poe to France, which throughout its history has harbored exiles, has been met in the rich contributions which Poe made to the decadents and symbolists. Today "existentialism" is the mode in Paris, its modern founder being Jean Paul Sartre. The three abnormal characters inhabiting the Hell depicted in Sartre's play *No Exit* are from the same family tree that produced William Wilson and Roderick Usher. The argument of "existentialism" that the identity of the individual soul is preserved after death only as the "existence" *seen* by other people here in life is not unlike the theory in *Eureka* that man's soul loses its individual quality after death in merging with the sum of all knowledge which, to Poe, is God.

The future fate of Poe's works in France may never again attract a champion like Baudelaire. Yet it is worth remembering that his art won the later admiration of Valéry and that Poe's "darkness" has today a bearing on the horrors evoked in Sartre's plays and short stories. There are no signs on the literary horizon that Poe's vogue in France has ended.

3. Imitations in Spanish

In both the Old and New Worlds, people of Spanish descent have long regarded Poe as one of the greatest writers of the United States. Poe's renown was won originally in Spain and then spread to South America, where his poetry was more broadly acclaimed. By the beginning of the twentieth century Poe's fame had reached Mexico, a street in Mexico City being named Edgar Poe to honor the poet in 1937.

On July 9, 1856, an anonymous article in the "Sección de variedades—Correspondencia de Paris" of *La Iberia,* introduced Poe to Spain, exactly one decade after the notoriety he received in Forgues' famous French lawsuit. The unknown Spanish author referred to Poe in French translation: "M. Carlos Baudelaire ha elegido entre las novelas y artículos que ha dejado Poe; mezcla extraña de imaginación, de delirios, de sagacidad científica; provocación violenta e una curiosidad llevada hasta la fiebre." The next year, on February 15, 1857, another anonymous Iberian author presented in *El Museo Universal* a version of "Three Sundays in a Week" as "La semana de los tres domingos." An interesting fact about this tale is that since Baudelaire omitted it, the unknown Iberian translator must have worked from an English original. The customary procedure in Spain was to turn to the *Histoires extraordinaires,* which in the account of September 1, 1858 (by Pedro Antonio de Alarcón· in *La Época*) was thought to reproduce the American title exactly—"traducción francesa de la que escribió con el mismo título el anglo-americano *Edgar Allan Poe.*" The appearance in Madrid during the winter season of 1857-1858 of the first volumes in Baudelaire's French prose inspired three separate Spanish versions of Poe's tales prior to 1860.

According to John Englekirk, most early Spaniards relied wholly on the translation by Baudelaire.[140] When writers in Spain employed English versions, they expressly noted the fact. Pedro de Prado y Torres on June 17, 1860, in *El Mundo pintoresco* declared that "La verdad de lo que pasó en casa del Señor Valdemar" is "una traducción directa" from English. The Spanish versions of A. Chocomeli Codina's "The Conqueror Worm," printed at Valencia in 1883, were based on American editions. Other translators of Poe's verses from American editions include Eduardo Marquina, N. A. Cortés, and the collaborators Aguilar y Tejera and Ortega y Frías. Several book editions of the prose likewise express their English derivation: Juderías Bender's "Metzengerstein" in the *Biblioteca de cuentos y leyendas* (1883) and Luis A. Santillano's two publications: *Cultura popular, Obras de Edgardo Poe* (1908?) and *Cuentos fantásticos* (1930?). But the so-called *Obras completas* (1918-1919), the work of several collaborators, comprises in six volumes a tale-by-tale translation of Baudelaire's *Histoires extraordinaires, Nouvelles Histoires extraordinaires*, and *Euréka*. Thus Baudelaire, whose French versions are in Spain unsupplanted even by native renderings, has remained the classic source for Spanish translations of Poe.

The Spanish critics, on the other hand, have displayed a spirited, independent interest in Poe's life and works. Besides Alarcón, to whose efforts are due the formal introduction of Poe in Spain, the more serious Iberian students are Manuel Cano y Cueta, Ángel Guerra, Miguel S. Oliver, Juan Prieto, and especially Nicasio Landa. Landa anticipated modern psychologists on Poe in stating that "The origin of his unhappiness must be sought in the peculiar constitution of his own character and not in democracy." Excepting Manuel de Montoliu, a Catalán, Spanish critics of Poe are rather limited in outlook: Emilio Carrere stressed the legendary Poe of Baudelaire's preface; Rafael Lasso de la Vega represented him as persecuted in his native land ("la miseria de Norte América!") José Pablo Rivas exclaimed that the poet was not of America; and José Deleito y Pinuela saw in Poe only the "estético del dolor."

Poe's tales were prized for form as well as content by Pedro Antonio de Alarcon and others. Vicente Barrante's tale "?Quién es él?" is an abbreviated adaptation of "The Murders in the Rue Morgue." Poe was linked with Hoffmann in 1860 by "F." in a story called "Ellen." The Poe technique was cultivated in an anonymous tale, "Un recién nacido de ciento setenta años," and also in Luis Alfonso's *Cuentos raros*. In 1883 "La canción de Holland" was issued

as an *inedited tale of Edgar Poe,* but it now is ascribed to
Aurelian Scholl, author of "Un sueño de Edgardo Poe."[141]

The Spanish theatre likewise paid tribute to Poe. In 1867
Adolfo Llanos y Álvarez transformed "The System of Dr.
Tarr and Professor Fether" into "¿Quién es el loco?" A
more appealing imaginative drama is Manuel Genaro
Rentero's *Edgard Poe* (1875), which recounts the last hours
of the poet's life: The setting is a tavern in Baltimore on
Sunday, October 7, 1849. The principal characters are Poe,
the *debauché* William Wilson, and a young girl named
Virginia. Poe is described as a poet addicted to rum and
ominously dressed in black. In the tavern he gives the girl
Virginia his watch when she enters asking alms. Then he
defends her from the approaches of Wilson. He staggers from
the place to expire, reverting in his last thoughts to his wife
Virginia, whom the girl's name had called to his besotted
mind.

Poe's poetry had several imitators among the *Modernistas.*
Emilio Carrere, the chief imitator, employed Poe's theme of
the return of the "pálido enlutado" in *El caballero de la
muerte* (1909), in which collection it is "El bardo maldito"
which presents the Spaniard's vivid word-picture of the
American's life and introduces his comments on "The
Raven," "The Bells," and "The Doomed City" (*i. e.,* "The
City in the Sea"). In the poem "Tristeza galante" Carrere
recalled Poe's shriek in "The Raven": "Take thy beak from
out my heart":

> Cuando miro hacia el pasado,
> junde un fatídico cuervo
> su pico en mi corazón.

Among many other poems indebted to Poe, Carrere's "El
romance de la princesa muerta" echoes "Annabel Lee." The
work of Carrere is permeated with the Poe spirit, his "El
campanario de las brujas" being a metrical version of the
story "The Devil in the Belfry." Sometimes he retained
the same prose medium, as when he based his tale "El
espectro de la rosa" on "Ligeia." Of all Poe's works,
Carrere preferred the poem "The Raven" and the tale
"Ligeia."

Francisco Villaespesa's mournful elegies on his departed Elisa reflect the inspiration he received from Poe's dolorous ballads. Both "Ulalume" and "Ligeia" were consulted before Villaespesa composed his book *In Memoriam* (1910). "La elegía de las compañas" imitates the meter of "The Bells" and reworks the vision-motive of "The Raven." Villaespesa at times drew inspiration from Poe's prose, the verses in *El libro del amor y de la muerte* containing reminiscences of both "Ligeia" and "Berenice." The most comprehensive indebtedness to Poe occurs in Villaespesa's volume *Paz*.

Juan Ramón Jiménez was another student of Poe. For his small collection expressing "Memorias tristes," he chose the title *Nevermore*. After visiting the United States, Jiménez experienced an increased interest in Poe. In his *Diario de un poeta recién casado* he wrote a visionary sketch of his reactions upon observing the Poe cottage. He further recorded that one of the compositions in his *Eternidades* (1916-1917) derived from Poe's "Silence." In conclusion, there is a striking parallel between the opening verses of "The City in the Sea" and three lines in *Piedra y cielo* (1919):

> Lo! Death has reared himself a throne
> In a strange city lying alone.
> Far down within the dim West.

> Mi ciudad interior tambien se extiende
> hacia el ocaso, persiguiendo
> el caer del sol triste.

Poe's verses have left their stamp on yet other Spanish poems. Ramón Peréz de Ayala chose for the argument of *La paz del sendero* the lines on "supernal Loveliness" in "The Poetic Principle." The brothers Manuel and Antonio Machado expressed indebtedness to Poe's technique. Ramón Goy de Silva composed several poems imitative of "The Bells." A. Torres-Ruiz dedicated stanzas to "El cuervo" that derive from "The Raven."

Poe's prose won the admiration of the recently deceased and world-renowned dramatist Gregoria Martinez Sierra, whose tale "Almas ausentes" was suggested by "The System of Dr. Tarr and Professor Fether." In 1907 Sierra named the poets of his choice: "Basta, Heine es uno de mis tres poetas: Poe y Verlaine son los otros dos," and on another occasion remarked: "Claro es que el *Poeta,* por serlo ama el arte por el arte y para la Belleza—! Oh Edgar Allan Poe!—"

The Basque novelist Pio Baroja has long venerated Poe. His pronouncement in favor of the short composition reveals knowledge of Poe's critical writings: "Yo creo que no debe haber ni puede haber unidad en la obra literaria más que en un trabajo corto. Me refiero a la unidad natural, a la unidad de impressión y de efecto." One may add that Poe's tales of fantasy influenced Baroja's "Medium," "Parábola," "La sombra," "El reloj," and "De la fiebre"; Poe's stories of the psychic and pseudo-scientific, his "Marichu," "Agueda," "El trasgo," "La sima," "La vida de los átomos," "Grito en el mar," and "Nihil"; and "The Gold Bug," his "Yan-Si-Pao, o La esvástica de Oro." Baroja's new novel, *El Hotel del Cisne* (1946), shows in its surrealistic treatment of an old man's nightmares his modification of the dark tradition cultivated by Poe.

W. Fernández Flórez, Joan Santamaria Monné, Miguel de Unamuno, and in particular V. Blasco Ibáñez are four other Spanish writers who have paid homage to Poe's prose. In November, 1919, during a visit to the Poe cottage, Ibáñez remarked: "Poe is my spiritual and literary father."

This much can be said, in summary, about Poe in Spain. His fame there owes a good deal to the work of Nicasio Landa, who deserves credit for his penetrating observation that Poe is a pioneer in the discovery of the romance of science. The recent statement in 1941 of Pedro Salinas, that "the work of Poe has had scarcely any influence on the writers of Spain,"[142] is an extreme view of the matter and is hardly in accord with even such selected data as I have reviewed here. But, as Ferguson noted in 1916, Poe met some opposition in Spain.[143] He nonetheless exercised from the start a healthy reaction on its literature. His standing today as a writer of prose is high on the roster of Iberian readers who are fond of detective tales and bizarre narratives.

In South America, about a decade after Poe's vogue in the Iberian Peninsula, translations of his tales from texts in both French and English began to appear. In Buenos Aires the early anonymous version of Poe's "The System of Dr. Tarr and Professor Fether," issued in the *Revista Argentina* for 1860, was a translation into English from the French of Baudelaire. The Chilean Eduardo de la Barra translated "Lenore" into Spanish in 1874 from an English original. There was no warm enthusiasm for Poe in South America until 1887, when Pérez Bonalde translated "The Raven."

Unlike the Spaniards, South Americans evidenced a preference for Poe's lyrics, though his prose was translated by Carlos Olivera in 1884 and by Carmen Torres Calderón de Pinillos in 1920. The poet-translators of South America were in general ably versed in the English tongue. Their number includes F. J. Amy, Pérez Bonalde, A. Bolaños Cacho, Domingo Estrada, Rafael Lozano, J. P. Rivas, R. Mayorga Rivas, and C. A. Torres. The work of Bonalde in 1887 is the best, a close second being the little-known translation in 1892 of "The Raven" by Guillermo F. Hall. Those of Rafael Lozano in 1922 and of Francisco Soto y Calvo in 1927 are likewise said to possess merit. Poems favored by Spanish translators in South America are "The Raven," "Eldorado," "The Conqueror Worm," "To Helen," "Annabel Lee," "Ulalume," and especially "The Bells." One of the standard complete editions is Carlos Obligado's *Los Poemas de Edgar Poe,* which was printed at Buenos Aires in 1932.

In Brazil there was a group of poets in the last quarter of the nineteenth century known as the "geracâo perdida" ("lost generation"). Two of these Brazilian poets, Alvares de Azevedo and Machado de Assis, were disciples of Poe. One of Azevedo's sonnets was inspired, it is said, by Poe's "The Sleeper." A third Brazilian writer, Manoel Antonio, became addicted to a form of necrophilia reminiscent of that depicted by Poe in his "Ligeia."[144]

Among South American critics, Enrique Pineyro was the first to recognize Poe. His article in "El primer siglo de la literatura norte-americana," appearing in 1877 in *La Patria,* though not wholly laudatory (probably because it was influenced by Griswold's "Memoir"), stated that outside the United States Poe was better known than Longfellow and that he was "un talento realmente original y un temperamento desgraciado." Far more famous is the "Introducción" to Bonalde's 1877 version of "The Raven," by Santiago Pérez Triana, a Colombian poet whose acceptance of Poe's errors and failings set the sympathetic tone of critical thought in South America.

Poe did not gain wide attention until 1893, when Rubén Darío's article in *La Nación* was republished as a leading essay in his celebrated collection entitled *Los Raros*. The Nicaraguan Dario's study of the man Poe was based entirely on Ingram's biography and omitted an evaluation of the American's attainments. Of less value was the Cuban Enrique José Varona's essay in 1895, which attacked shortcomings of the portrait of Poe drawn by Max Nordau and Baudelaire. Domingo B. Castillo's study in 1902 was unusual in its reference to Poe as a dramatist. F. Salcedo Ochoa's article in 1905 paid a generous tribute to the American's genius. There were no other significant essays until the appearance of Blanche Z. Baralt's *Estudios de arte y de vida* (1914?), a serious attempt to evaluate Poe apart from the legends reported by Griswold. In 1915 Justo de Lara in his *Historia y literatura* regarded Poe as a worthy rival of Hugo and Tennyson. In 1922 Esteban M. Cavazutti printed in *Nosotros* an article with the self-explanatory title "Del epistolario de Edgardo Poe y de sus amores."

For Poe's prose South America has shown little taste. The fantastic stories of Carlos Olivera, who translated Poe's tales in 1884, reflect his influence, as do the grotesque productions of Eduardo Wilde (1844-1898), especially "La primera noche de cementero." A few individual tales have been translated, as "El sistema de Doctor Alquitrán y del Professor Pluma" (1869), "Adventura inaudita del llamado Hans Pfaal" (1887), "El retrato" (1909), "Metzengerstein" (1910), "El alce (una mañana en el wissahiccon)" (1911), "El hombre que perdió el aliento" (1911), "El espectro" (1911), "La máscara de la muerte roja" (1926), and "La sombra" (1929).

These indications are too scanty to suggest that Poe is widely known as a narrator in South America. The publication in 1944 of Armando Bazan's *Obras completas de Edgardo Poe* at Buenos Aires was therefore a literary event of real significance, as its full texts of poems and tales alike offered wide opportunities for the South American study of Poe.

The poems have made a better showing. Pedro Salinas observed in 1941 that as "they studied and came to known French symbolism, the young writers of Spanish America discovered that a poet of the northern American continent, of the English tongue, Edgar Allan Poe, was the idol of the French Symbolists and the great initiator of the modern tendencies of French poetry."

Leopoldo Díaz's devotion to Poe, whom he read in Mallarmé's translations, comprised a period of over twenty years. Poe's influence is evident in Díaz's first poems of 1885 and in the later *Atlántida conquistada* of 1907. One of his *Sonetos* of 1888 was dedicated to Poe's memory, whereas two others, "Media noche" and "Baile de máscaras," respectively echo "The Raven" and "Eleanora." Following the publication in 1897 of his *Traducciones* of Poe, Díaz became fully absorbed with Poe's symbolism, his "La selva de los sueños" and other poems in the volume *Las sombras de Hellas* recreating in Spanish the eerie atmosphere of "The Dreamer," "The City in the Sea, "Dreamland," and especially "Ulalume." In "Tierra de sueño" Díaz invoked the weird atmosphere of "Dreamland" and for his argument chose these lines:

> . . . From an ultimate dim Thule,
> From a wild weird clime that lieth sublime
> Out of Space, out of Time.

In "A un poeta," published in 1914 in *La Revista de América,* he mentioned both Poe and Mallarmé. Díaz's "La leyenda de los lirios" bases its theme on a verse from "To Helen": "Ah! bear in mind this garden was enchanted!" His "El Palacio del dolor" recalls both "The City in the Sea" and "The Haunted Palace"; his "El sueño de una noche de invierno" echoes "Ulalume." Finally, the Poe air is detectable in Díaz's later collection of sonnets, *Las ánforas y las urnas* (1923).

Rubén Darío (1867-1910) was another admirer of Poe's technique. In fact, the two poets are alleged to have shared such qualities as "love for the strange, fear of death, abuse of alcohol, sensitiveness to auditory sensations, and this even in theoretical as well as applied poetics." In Darío's prose, references are found to such tales as "MS. Found in a Bottle" and "Narrative of A. Gordon Pym"; but it is his poetry, like the "Epístola a la señora de Lugones," that better expresses his affinity with Poe's themes of resignation and misery. The poetic prose of *Azul,* in which Darío commented that he understood philosophy upon hearing the music "de los astros," may borrow the idea from "Al Aaraaf";

> A sound of silence on the startled ear
> Which dreamy poets name 'the music of the sphere.'

As early as 1889, Darío was acquainted with "The Bells," for he used the word "tintinabular." Like "The Bells," Darío's poems abound in repetitions of a single word for effect, as testified by a quotation from *Prosas profanas:*

> La divina Eulalia, rié, rié, rié.
> Rié, rié, rié la divina Eulalia.

Through practice Dario became a master of the Poe technique in his employment of inner rhyme, alliteration, and the repetend. In his elegiac prose poem "Stella," he waxed biographical, picturing the heroine as returning in the night with the "liliales vírgenes" of "el celeste Edgardo." Other poems indebted to Poe include "Divina Psiquis," "El reino interior," "La isla de los muertos," and "Nocturnos." The great popularity in Central America of Poe's technique among the *Modernistas* is principally due to the work of Darío, a Nicaraguan.

The "audacious meters" of the Columbian poet José Asunción Silva, whom Muna Lee calls the "Brother of Poe," derived from the American, the Spanish verses of the *Nocturnos* re-echoing the primitive rhythms of "The Raven."[145] Silva's "Día de difuntos," in turn, developed from "The Bells." In the incomplete novel *De Sobremesa* Silva affiliated himself with Poe in his sense of loneliness.

The melancholy pictures of his dead beloved in the novel look like descriptions repainted from "The Fall of the House of Usher" and "Ligeia." Silva's famous "Un poema" reiterates Poe's poetical theories; his "Estrellas fijas" imitates the passage on eyes in "To Helen"; and his "Serenata" borrows technical devices from "Ulalume." It was in his "unusual combination of known meters" that Silva displayed his close knowledge of Poe the technician.

The Cuban poet Julian del Casal (1863-1893) probably became attached to Poe through his friendship with Darío. Casal's own temperament, influenced by ill-health and psychological maladjustment, would have led him inevitably to appreciate Poe. It is the exotic and supernatural which most deeply affected Casal. His shadowy, chaste heroines in "Cuerpo y alma" belong to the same genre as Poe's romantic princesses. The apparition of "Eleonora" haunts the mysterious settings of "Laus noctis" and "Tardes de lluvia"; "Pax Animae" reproduces the mournful marching cadence of "The Raven"; "Las Alamedas" and "Aegri somnia" recreate from "Ulalume" the vague "misty mid region of Weir—." Because Casal felt the misery and terror of life keenly, he naturally was drawn to 'For Annie," and his "Tras una enfermedad" unmistakably displays his reliance on Poe's verses:

> Y la fiebre domada no consume
> El ardor de la sangre de mis venas.

The elegies "Ausencia" and "Del libro negro" received stimulation respectively from "Lenore" and "Annabel Lee." A line in "The Black Cat," about there existing no infirmity comparable to alcoholism, gave Casal the motive for his tale "La tristeza del alcohol."

Poe's gifts to South American literature were distributed among several other authors. Three tales by Amado Nervo (1870-1919), "Amnesia," "Un Sueño," and "Las cases," have for their respective models "Berenice," "Ligeia," and "A Tale of the Ragged Mountains." Several of Nervo's poems in *Rondos vagos* utilize material from "The Raven," "Ulalume," and "Dreamland." Literary kinship is further established in the recurring references in Nervo, who read

"The Philosophy of Composition," to the most important themes of Poe's works. Leopoldo Lugones (or Gil Paz) was also a keen student of Poe. The weird alcoholic vision of his poem on "metempsicosis" derives its plot from "Metzengerstein." His prose poems on "Las vacas" and "El viento" develop from the fable "Silence" and the allegory "The Masque of the Red Death." His later *Los crepúsculos del jardín* (1905) relies less on Poe, the resemblances being confined to vague echoes of the melancholy atmosphere of "The Raven." Poe's influence on Julio Herrera y Reissig (1875-1910) is impressive, for the South American purposely accentuated Poe's spirit of evocativeness and indefiniteness. Lastly, additional reminiscenses of Poe have been detected in the works of, among others, such notable figures as José Santos Chocano, Léon de Greiff, José María Eguren, Rafael Arévalo Martínez, Horacio Quiroga, Froylan Turcios, and Alváro Armando Vasseur.

In order to distinguish the attitude of South America from that of Spain, a few salient facts should be mentioned. Poe's translators in the Southern countries of the New World have not relied as extensively on the French versions of Baudelaire as the Spainards did, but often have consulted Poe in his own tongue. It also is memorable that in Spain people desiring to read Poe's lyrics in the Spanish language have been obliged to consult, not their own infrequent translators, but the better-known versions of their South American kin. It is also a matter of literary history that Spanish Americans installed Poe as the founder in the New World of the poetic ideals of the *Modernistas*. They saw in him, said Pedro Salinas in 1941, "the great figure of a revolutionary poet, of an innovator—perhaps the first new and original poet of the continent; the first spiritual conqueror of Europe, the first American poet to teach the Old World a lesson in poetry."[146]

The poet Poe has a small but loyal following in Mexico, where today he is most revered as the author of "The Raven." The most celebrated version of Poe's "bird" poem is that by the Mexican poet Ignacio Mariscal, which was initially published as the work of an anonymous translator in *La Patria* for January, 1880. The art of Gutiérrez Nájera (1859-1895) owed much to Poe's poetry of love and death, whereas his last poem, "A la corregidora," experimented with Poe's achievements in sound effects. In 1902 "Mi pesadilla," probably written by F. Z. Ruiz, was printed as a hoax, being described as the "last tale by Edgar Poe." The name of Mariscal appeared as the translator when "The Raven" was subsequently re-issued in *Ateneo* for April, 1907. A greater Poe event at the opening of the twentieth-century in Mexico City was the public address by the poet Balbino Dávalos in 1901. In his eulogy of the American, Dávalos judged Poe greater than Whitman, placing him "entre los poetas universales y de todos los tiempos, bañados perpetuamente por la luz de la luz de la immortalidad."

Poe's prose is of easiest access to Mexicans in South American translations published at Buenos Aires. Among those available, there are Vicente Algarra's *La máscara de la muerte roja* (1943) and his *Doble asesinato en la calle morgue* (1943), Roberto D'Elio's *Aventuras de Arturo Gordon Pym* (1940; 2nd edition, 1944), L. N.'s *El escarabajo de oro* (1943), and A. Jimenez Orderiz's *Historias Extraordinarias* (1940; 2nd edition, 1944). Orderiz's title proves that Baudelaire's version remains the chief medium in which Poe is consulted by these translators.

If one may judge by Carlos Dávila's article for *América* in 1947, Poe is highly prized in Mexico as the orginator of the "police novel." Dávila regarded the publication of "The Murders in the Rue Morgue" in April, 1847, as the historical beginning of the detective story. In his essay entitled "Poe y el centenario de la novela policíaca," published in April, 1947, the Mexican critic explained the tremendous popularity in the United States of "Whodunit" fiction, commented on the literary output of American "mass production factories" of mystery tales, and observed that newspaper reviewers like Will Cuppy worked solely in the branch of detective yarns. Dávila concluded that the "police" narrative invented by Poe had only one rival encroaching upon its sales records—the comic strips, which, he said, "are selling in the United States at the rate of 45,000,000 copies per month."[147]

The close relationship of two romance tongues, French and Spanish, which had promoted the first discovery of Poe in Madrid, effected the spread of his fame to the new World. The proximity of the United States to Mexico counted very little in the early recognition of Poe, for the barrier of language was more formidable than one might suppose. Reproductions in Spanish of Baudelaire's versions have at last made Poe's contributions famous. Dear to Spanish-speaking people is the contrast in Poe between fact and fancy, a kind of dualism in the American's personality which links him with the basic idea in one main current of Spanish thought. The psychology I refer to is the preference among this Latin race for literary plots with wildly imaginative subject matter presented in a realistic manner. Poe's wide renown today as an innovator is reasonable assurance that his art will continue to intrigue readers in the Spanish-speaking world.

4. His Position in Russia

In 1848 an anonymous Russian compilation, whose English title is *An American Hunter for Treasures,* contained a free and barely discernible paraphrase of "The Gold Bug." This publication marked the first known appearance of any work by Poe in Russia, and his individual artistry attracted an enthusiastic following in the half century which followed. His fame showed some indications of waning upon the advent of Communism, but today reports attest that Poe is continuing to occupy an enviably high position in Russian literary circles.

C. Alphonso Smith's flattering statement in 1921 about the Russian role in the spread of Poe's prestige rests upon a misunderstanding. Smith declared: "It was Russia, not France, that took the initiative in Europeanizing Poe's fame."[148] Smith's authority for this declaration was Abraham Yarmolinsky, who in 1916 claimed that translations by Poe had been printed in Russian periodicals during the late 1830's.[149]   According to Lubov Breit Keefer, whose essay was printed in 1941, Yarmolinsky based his assertion upon the poet Andreevsky's "Preface" to his translation in 1878 of Poe's "The Raven"—where, continues Keefer, "the biography of the American poet to which Andreevsky alludes is lacking and instead there appears in the *Pantheon* for 1851 a life-sketch of Margaret Fuller."[150]   Keefer, in his authoritative statement, further observed that two early Russian works similarly entitled were almost certainly unknown to Poe, these being a poem "The Raven" by A. Timofeev (*Reader's Library*, VII) in 1835 and a novel *The Ravens* by Mrs. Charles Rebeau (*ibid*, XXXI) in 1839.   It is accordingly necessary to return to the paraphrase in 1848 of "The Gold Bug" for the first authentic record of Poe's earliest fame in Russia.   One is likewise on firm ground when turning to the critical notice of Poe which appeared in the magazine *The Russian Word* in 1861.   Here the American's works are described as "fantastic realism."

The notable Poe event in Russia occurred after the beginning of the present century.   I refer to Konstantin Balmont's translation of Poe's complete works, begun in 1906, which is said to be admirably executed.   It made available to Russian readers the full texts of a genius from the New World whose unconventionality the Russians heartily endorsed.

The apogee of enthusiasm was reached by Yarmolinsky himself, who erred in assigning Poe's initial fame to the 1830's but whose appreciation of Poe's merits was unlimited. He said that he could not breathe, and thousands of Russians with him, "if there were not Poe's *Raven,* with its unforgettable burden of 'Nevermore'?"   Fond of the characters Annabel-Lee, Morella, and Ligeia, he added: "And how could the evening and morning bells chime if there were no 'Bells' of the mad Edgar?   And was I not among the masks of the Red Death?   And have I not fled in frenzied terror from the falling house of Usher?"   On the authority of Yarmolinsky, "The first name a Russian is most likely to mention when the conversation turns to American literature is that of

'mad Edgar.' It is Poe that has come to be popularly identified in Russia with the American literary genius in its highest
achievements." The words may compose an extreme view of
Poe's popularity among the Slavs, but there is evidence that
Yarmolinsky was well acquainted with his subject. He
mentioned, in particular, that "Stéphane Mallarmé's
celebrated prose version of 'The Raven' and other pieces
utterly fails to render the lilt and the manifold sonorities of
Poe's verse." Balmont's Russian renditions Yarmolinsky
pronounced "the most adequate transposition of Poe's poetry
yet produced in any language."

Presumably it was Balmont who introduced Poe to the
Russian *literati*. Poe's style is said to have influenced
Leonid Andreyev and Fedor Sologub, whose subscription
to the gothic mode is reflected in their respective well-known
narratives *The Seven that Were Hanged* and *The Sorcery
of Death*. The art of Poe stirred the imagination of the poet
and translator Merezhkovsky. Golikov's *Night-Thoughts*
(1902) and his *Novels* (1904) both reflect the influence of
Poe. Slavic Symbolists, as seen in *A Treasury of Russian
Verse,* edited in 1949 by A. Yarmolinsky, included a number
of poets indirectly influenced by Poe, such as Belyi, Blok,
Ivanov, Sologub, and Solovyov. In addition, the rare ex-
oticism of such poems as "The Conqueror Worm," "The
Bells," "Elorado," and "Silence" impressed Rachmaninoff
and Gmiessen, Miaskovsky and Podgoretzky. Rachmaninoff's
choral symphony "The Bells" is, in fact, based on a Russian
version of Poe's poem.

From their initial acquaintance with Poe, the Russian
critics displayed an attitude both appreciative and analytical.
In 1862 E. Lopushinsky acclaimed him in *Edgar Poe (an
American Poet)*, stating that "he dwells simultaneously in
two spheres, one of fancy and one of fact." In 1874 the
author of *Edgar Poe as Psychologist,* who signed his contributions with the initials N. Sh., included abbreviated
versions of nine of Poe's tales to illustrate his analysis of their
technique. In 1900 A. Krasnoselsky ranked Poe alongside
De Quincey, E. T. A. Hoffmann, and Gérard de Nerval. The
criticism by E. Anichkov in 1909 possessed special interest.

Anichkov reported that he preferred Poe to Baudelaire. He then described Poe as a "calculating detached Yankee, at once a frenzied lunatic and a journalist with a flair for the popular."

The year 1878 marks the first appearance of "The Raven" in a Russian translation. This was a work which S. A. Andreevsky contributed to *The Messenger of Europe* (II, 108-127.) In 1881 an anonymous translator presented versions of three of Poe's tales to *The Russian Wealth*. In 1882 a writer who signed himself O. P. translated the opening eleven chapters of "Pym" for *The Messenger of Europe* (III). In 1885-1895 the celebrated Balmont issued Poe's *Ballads and Fancies, Introduction,* and in this he said: "No artist is capable of conveying so forcefully and tensely the atmosphere of hallucination, premonition, supernatural fascination, the static landscape." Also in 1885 there simultaneously appeared separate translations of Poe's verses by A. S. Suvorin and V. N. Marakuev. In 1888 L. E. Obolensky composed a prose exposition of "The Raven." This version, however, was superseded by that of the symbolist poet Merezhovsky in 1892. The famous translator Andreevsky, who had earlier published his version of "The Raven," translated "Dreamland" in 1898. An anonymous anthology, printed in 1908 as a ten-volume supplement to the periodical *Around the World,* contained a large number of translations from Poe. In 1917 a writer with the signature V. I. T. translated "The Oval Portrait" and "William Wilson." In 1923 Vasili Federov published *Poe—Poems and Verses.* In 1926 Valery Bruisov, author of *Edgar Poe—Full Collection of Poems and Verses,* paid Poe a fine tribute: "The lyrics of Poe are one of the most marvelous phenomena of the world literature."

Not all Russian criticsm has been favorable to Poe. Two antagonistic early studies are Brasol's *Critical Contours* in 1910 and V. L. Friche's *The Poetry of Nightmares and Horrors* in 1912. The strongest attack on Poe by a Communist writer was launched in 1931 by S. Dinamov in *The Scientifico-Fantastic Novels of E. Poe: Literature and Marxism.* Dinamov visualized Poe as a decadent product of capitalism. Later on, in *The Novels of E. Poe* (1933) and *Edgar Poe—the Artist of Death and Decay* (1934), the Communist Dinamov continued to dismantle the reputation of Poe.

The rise of a Marxist school of criticsm among the Slavs may have a bad effect on the repute of various American writers. The evidence regarding Poe is not conclusive. In 1941 Keefer, whom I have previously cited, expressed the view that "Today in the Russia of the Soviets the star of Edgar Allan Poe is setting with meteoric swiftness." On the other hand, in 1945 Malcolm Cowley reported that the Georgian poets in Tiflis repeatedly asked George Soule, a correspondent, one question: "The poets want to know why Americans don't appreciate their own great poet Aidgarpo?"[151]

Whatever be Poe's fortunes in the Russia of tomorrow, he has already exerted an influence on such great Slavic figures of yesterday as Leonid Andreyev, Anton Chekov, and Feodor Mikhailovich Dostoievsky. Andreyev and Chekhov, Russian masters of the short story, are said to have attained skill in their art from studying Poe's technique. In his own periodical *Wremia* (January and March, 1861), Dostoievsky reprinted three of Poe's stories ("The Tell-Tale Heart," "The Black Cat," and "The Devil in the Belfry") parallel with his own work "Low in Spirit," while Poe's "Narrative of A. Gordon Pym" shared space with his *Diary from the Dead House.*

Dostoievsky has further connections with Poe.[152] *His Crime and Punishment* as well as *The Brothers Karamazov* were partly fertilized by "Ligeia" and "Berenice." Moreover, in discussing Poe in the above-mentioned *Wremia* in 1861, he remarked: "What a strange, though enormously talented writer, that Edgar Poe!" Dostoievsky claimed that Poe was individual as a writer in adopting for the treatment of the fantastic the methods of a realist. He observed that the American was gifted with a rich faculty for details: "his imagination is endowed with a quality which in such magnitude we have not met anywhere else, namely the power of details." It was Poe's ability to make the fantastic seem real, as in "The Balloon Hoax," which most impressed the Russian. This quality Dostoievsky interpreted as typical of the genius nurtured in the New World: "Even his most unbounded imagination betrays the true American."

The position which Poe holds today in Russia is too secure to be easily dislodged by Marxists. In 1949 Robert Magidoff, author of *In Anger and Pity,* stated that "It is impossible to overestimate the influence of Edgar Allan Poe on Russian poetry of the late nineteenth and early twentieth centuries." Magidoff then cited the words of the celebrated translator Konstantin Balmont that Poe was the "first Symbolist of the nineteenth century" and "my adored singer of songs, the most starlike of all troubadours of eternity, lost wandering on our planet." Magidoff further quoted Balmont's penetrating statement that "Poe's poetry is closer than any other to our complicated sick souls; it is the very embodiment of majestic consciousness that stares in horror at the inevitability of the wild chaos encompassing it at every side." Poe's prose, particularly its influence on Andreyev and Dostoievsky, is next praised by the author of *In Anger and Pity.* Andreyev pronounced Poe the world's "greatest madman, who is at the same time the most perfect logician." To Dostoievsky, Poe was, in the language of the poet Valery Bruisov, the "precursor and teacher in the field of subtle psychology."[153]

How is Poe's popularity among the Russians to be explained? Certainly there is nothing in common with Marxism in Poe's criticism of democracy, for Poe tended to believe in an aristocratic, not a proletarian society. His appeal to the Russians therefore must be based on his accomplishments in art forms, not in the promulgation of political doctrines. At any rate, he is greatly admired in the land of the Slavs, where, according to United States press reports, Stalin has included Poe high on his list of favorite American authors.

Poe's preoccupation with details is probably the feature of his technique best liked by Slavonic stylists, while his use of the themes of death, dissolution, and decay probably has perhaps most impressed the Russians.

5. The German School

In Germany the exact status of Poe's reputation today is unknown. His standing there in the recent past, as well as the future, is difficult to speculate about because of the troubled conditions prevailing in that country.[154] Yet as a part of the report on him in world letters, attention must be directed to Poe's preeminent position in Germany as a romantic author. According to Herbert Schaumann in 1941, in contemporary Germany "the spirit of Poe is a living force."[155]

The influence of Poe on the great classics of Germany was slight. His writings there attracted no devotee like Baudelaire in France, no series of translations like those in Spain and South America, and no imitators like the gothic novelists and symbolist poets of Russia. Teutonic appreciation of Poe, except in the realm of literary research, has lagged behind that of the other major countries of Europe. Moreover, his impress on German fiction occurred in the works of minor or mediocre writers whose productions are now seldom read by the literate German public. In a few instances Poe's technique was adopted by outstanding Teutonic authors, and the continuing good repute of their works has helped to keep his name alive. Proofs of specific literary borrowings exist principally in the styles of lesser Germanic authors, so that his largest bequests to the literature of the Teutons lie emtombed amid the defunct reputations of these now virtually forgotten practitioners of the gothic style.

To be more explicit, I may report that two or three lesser German authors worked under Poe's spell. One of these men was Gustav Meyrink, although not even he followed Poe slavishly. Really gifted novelists like Thomas Mann, of Lübeck, and Franz Werfel, of Prague, withdrew automatically from the fields cultivated by Poe, perhaps in recognition that the American's genius already had exploited the possibilities fully. The preoccupation of the modern Austrian Franz Kafka with the grotesque, as in his tale "Metamor-

phosis," associates his writings with the Poe who wrote "Hop
Frog."

Schaumann believed that the prestige of Poe was due
chiefly to the partisanship of Rainer Maria Rilke (1875-
1926). It is apparent, says Schaumann, why Rilke when
"speaking about loneliness, uncerainty, and fear in modern
man" should quote the American "as the oustanding expert
on these timely subjects."[156] T. S. Eliot, who was cited
earlier, also recognized that Rilke was indebted to Poe.

Perhaps another factor in Poe's renown among educated
Germans was his influence on their music. "The Masque
of the Red Death" is said to have inspired Franz Schreker
in his outline for an opera.

The poetry of Poe was known in Germany prior to 1885,
for in this year the Englishman John F. Ingram called
attention to a German translation of "The Raven,"[157] and as
recently as 1938 Otto F. Babler listed several more translations of the same poem.[158] It is of historical interest that
in 1909 the German Theodore Etzel prepared a centennial
version of "The Raven." The translator Etzel rendered the
raven's "Nevermore" as "Nie du Thor" ("Never, you fool"),
where sense is sacrificed for sound. The Germans early had
curiosity about even Poe's minor works, and in 1895 G.
Edmund Gundel, in his Freiburg publication *Edgar Allan
Poe,* regretted that portions of *Politian* were yet unpublished.

For a long time now, German readers have had access to
reputable treatments of Poe's texts in both prose and verse.
In 1908 Bodo Mildberg translated "Pym" as *Die denk-
würdigen Erlebnisse des Artur Gordon Pym.* This book,
printed in Berlin, was illustrated by Ernst Stern. In 1913
an anonymous translator assembled a book of selected tales,
Ausgewählte Erzählungen. Another anonymous collection
of Poe's stories, printed without date, bears the title *Der
Brief ihrer Majestät.* Yet more attractive are the two
volumes by Hans Lebede printed in Berlin at a date unknown, because these books, entitled *Der Goldkäfer
(Schluss),* have the texts in both English and German on
parallel pages. Probably the most famous German translation was made in 1911-1914 in the gatherum of three volumes

by Hedda Moeller-Bruck and Hedwig Lachmann, *Edgar Poes Werke*. So far as I am informed, it remains the definitive full German rendition of Poe. Selected short stories from the works of Poe have been available for a longer period among the popular collections of world authors edited by Reclam, Hendel, Cotta, Speman, Meyer, and other compilers.

The Teutons, who have long excelled at research in literature, early selected Poe as a worthy subject for scholarly investigation. If their regard for Poe, said C. Alphonso Smith in 1921, "has been less devotional than that of either France or Russia it at least has been more dissertational, the number of special studies that appeared in 1909 far surpassing those that appeared in any other country."[159] All of the important German studies were by no means doctoral dissertations, however.

As early as 1860 Friedrich Spielhagen published a notable memoir on Poe in *Europa*. Whereas most Germans were captivated by Poe's prose, Spielhagen was ecstatic about his poetry. He declared that Poe was "the greatest lyric singer that America has produced." Such praise promoted the spread of Poe's fame in Central Europe, though C. Alphonso Smith exaggerated the facts in terming Spielhagen "the German Balmont as Balmont was the Russian Baudelaire and Baudelaire the French Ingram."[160] What one safely may assert is that Friedrich Spielhagen was the first Teutonic scholar to appraise Poe correctly as the outstanding lyricist of the United States. An earlier writer, in a leading German review in 1854, had declared only that Poe's name "was bound to live in the annals of American literature."[161]

A fuller view of Poe's vogue among German scholars may be seen in a chronological review of several important publications. One of the initial scholarly studies of Poe was composed in 1902 by Louis P. Betz. His *Edgar Poe in der französischen Literatur* treated Poe's literary relations with Baudelaire as well as with later French authors. In 1905 there appeared H. H. Ewers' book, *Edgar Allan Poe*. In this Ewers analyzed representative works of Poe, traced his influence on French literature, and compared him with Hoffmann and Heine. The memoirs by Ewers closed with a

glowing tribute to Poe as the greatest American writer, a
poet whose soul lives eternally in an immortal alhambra:

> Die Vereinigten Staaten *ihrem*
> grossen Dichter.
> Mögen sie die Knochen behalten, die da drüben!
> Wir aber wollen des Dichters Seele lauschen, die in den
> Nachtigallenkehlen der Alhambra lebt.[162]

In 1907 Karl Hans Strobl issued his volume, *Worte Poes,* to
which was appended an excellent bibliography by the
German scholar Moris Grolig.   In 1908 Alfred Lichtenstein
composed an historical study called *Der Kriminalroman,* in
which Poe was recognized as the originator of this "police"
type of popular fiction.   Lichtenstein said: "Der moderne
Kriminalroman ist der Analytische und E. A. Poe hat ihn
geschaffen."[163]   For *The Book of the Poe Centenary* (1909),
the distinguished German poet and critic Doctor Georg
Edward contributed, as a general summarization, the provocative statement that Poe "is regarded in Germany as the
typical and characteristic American author."[164]

Since the centennial of 1909, virtually uninterrupted
interest in Poe has continued to be manifested in German
literary circles.   The two periods of relative silence were
comprised by the unproductive eras of the two World Wars
(1914-1918, 1939-1945).   Thus in 1910 Karl Walter Just
selected Poe as one of the three major American authors
representing the spirit of romanticism.   He subjected Poe,
Brockden Brown, and Hawthorne to a rather detailed examination in his study, *Die romantische Bewegung in der
amerikanischen Literatur.*   In 1911 Poe's further affinities
with the romantic school, particularly his predecessors in
Germany, was discussed in Paul Wachter's Leipzig doctoral
dissertation, *Edgar Allan Poe und die deutsche Romantik.*
In 1913 Fritz Hippe's *Edgar Allan Poes Lyrik in Deutschland*
commended the American's poetry to the Teutonic world.
In 1914 Friedrich Depken wrote a penetrating monograph
on *Sherlock Holmes, Raffles und ihre Vorbilder.* In his study
Depken named Poe the forerunner of "detective" fiction and
for his exhibition at deciphering in "The Gold Bug" render-

ed homage to him as "the king of secret-readers of secret writings."[165]

Most importantly, in 1934 Marie Bonaparte's four imposing volumes, to which Sigmund Freud fixed a "Vorwort," were issued at Vienna under the title *Edgar Poe, eine psychoanalytique Studie.* The German titles of the four parts of this collection are as follows: 1. Das Leben Edgar Poes. II. Die Geschichten: Der Zyklus Mutter. III. Die Geschichten: Der Zyklus Vater. IV. Poe und die menschliche Seele. This initial psychological approach to Poe on a grand scale followed in 1937 by Anne Lise Wolff's monograph, *Tod und Unterblichkeit: das Leitmotiv von E. A. Poes Werk.* In this manner the German school of criticism has run its course from the historical approach—first represented by Betz's book on Poe in France—to the psychological —most completely illustrated by Bonaparte's work.

The other salient discovery made by Germany was its apprehension that Poe's art epitomizes the spirit of America. The Teutons were the first to detect, and later conclusively to trace in his works, a predominant note of Americanism. This fresh interpretation of Poe won in the United States a strong champion in the observant F. M. Darnall, who in 1927 contributed a convincing paper to the *English Journal* entitled "The Americanism of Edgar Allan Poe." Darnall noted that Poe's contemporaries were often likened to English writers, whereas Poe was not: Cooper was called the American Scott; Irving, the American Addison; and Bryant, the American Wordsworth. It is perfectly clear that C. Alphonso Smith's observation in 1921 was unquestionably farsighted: "the German contention that Poe is representatively American rather than un-American seems to me one of the most valid contributions to Poe criticism yet made."

The German women also knew Poe's heroines. This is illustrated by one of C. Alphonso Smith's experiences at the University of Berlin in the winter of 1910-1911. A German lady in his Poe Seminar asked Smith, "Whom do you consider the most famous woman born in America?" Smith answered that his choice would lie between Pocahontas and

Dolly Madison. Then he queried, "But what would your answer be?" The lady promptly replied, "Why, I should have said Annabel Lee."[166]

The association of Poe with the German language in America is a further manifestation of German-American culture. Leland Schubert has shown that Poe was read by the Pennsylvania "Dutch" as early as 1869, for in that year a German edition of "The Raven" was issued at Philadelphia.[167]

The lasting renown which Poe's name achieved in Germany resulted from the labors of that country's talented critics. Even in France, the land in which Poe became a literary saint, there was no cult of scholarly devotees comparable to the Germans. No matter what materials might be assembled to show that Poe was much translated into German or that his art influenced innumerable authors unmentioned here, one fact would not be altered. The Teutonic mind, with its flair for original investigation, contributed as its gift to Poe criticism two brilliant deductions: first, these scholars opened the door to a psychological understanding of Poe; and, secondly, they rightly evaluated the mood of Poe's modern art as essentially American.

F. O. Matthiessen, who lectured in Prague during 1947, reported in *From the Heart of Europe* (1948) that in Central Europe Poe was today being read and that his works were available "in a couple of more or less complete editions."

6. British Receptions

At the beginning the English critics were quick to detect promise and even genius in Poe's writings, but they also were inclined to censure his immorality. The British reaction to Poe differed from that of other foreign countries in bringing the moral question to the forefront and showed that Englishmen were ignorant of the facts concerning his life.

During Poe's lifetime a number of his works were available in British reprints. In the year 1846 there appeared in London a "pirated" edition of *Mesmerism "in Articulo Mortis,"* Poe's volume *The Raven and Other Poems,* and "The Facts in the Case of M. Valdemar" (the last in the London *Popular Record of Modern Science* as "The Last Conversation of a Somnambule"). These reprints, together with the absence of a language difficulty, justify the expectation that Poe should receive his heartiest welcome from Great Britain.

On May 17, 1845, Poe received a note from Elizabeth Barrett, whose poems in an American reprint of 1844 he had reviewed for the *Broadway Journal* in January. Miss Barrett, appreciative of Poe's praise, sent the note by R. H. Horne and referred to Poe as "a wonder among critics," saying: "Will you tell Mr. Poe this, or to this effect, dear Mr. Horne." But in her letter proper to Horne, dated May 12, Miss Barrett was critical of "The Raven" when she wrote: "There is certainly a power—but it does not appear to me the natural expression of a sane intellect in whatever mood . . . ."

Poe had dedicated *The Raven and Other Poems* (New York, 1845; London, 1846) to "Elizabeth Barrett Barrett"; and in her letter of reply (April, 1846), the future Mrs. Browning restricted her comment principally to "The Raven," saying that Mr. Browning also "was much struck by the rhythm of that poem." The lady then briefly alluded to his story about Valdemar, "which is going the rounds of the newspapers." She commended Poe's gifts, "and the faculty he has of making horrible improbabilities seem near and familiar."[168] What she really felt about Poe's reference to her is shown in her letter of 1845 to John Kenyon:

> Today Mr. Poe sent me a volume containing his poems and tales collected, so now I *must* write and thank him for his dedication. What is to be said, I wonder, when a man calls you the 'noblest of your sex'? 'Sir, you are the most discerning of yours.'[169]

Miss Barrett's favorable attitude towards the Valdemar story represented the contemporary tone of British criticism, for both the *London Literary Gazette* (March 14, 1846) and the *London Athenaeum* gave Poe's poems scanty notice and praised his *Tales*. That Poe was aware of his repute abroad is shown in his epistle of December 30, 1846, to Evert Duyckinck:

> By the enclosed letter from Stonehaven, Scotland, you will see that the "Valdemar Case" still makes a talk, and that a pamphlet edition of it has been published by Short & Co. of London under the title of "Mesmerism in Articulo Mortis." It has fairly gone the rounds of the London Press, commencing with "The Morning Post." "The Monthly Record of Science" &c gives it with the title "The Last Days of M. Valdemar. By the author of the Last Conversation of a Somnambule"—(Mesmeric Revelation).

Unfavorable evaluations of Poe, ostensibly influenced by Griswold's reports, began to appear in 1852. An anonymous reviewer regretted that in Poe's works "so much intellectual power may coexist with so much moral weakness." *The National Magazine,* also in 1852, narrated the story of a young man who was wrecked by bad habits and then stated that the person was none other than Edgar Allan Poe. In 1853 *Chambers' Journal* appraised Poe's talents as those of "genius joined with vice." In 1854 George Gilfillan italicized his objections to Poe by calling him "probably *the* most worthless and wicked of his fraternity." This early school of invective reached a climax in 1858, when the distinguished *Edinburgh Review* averred that Poe was "incontestably one of the most worthless persons." During the period there was one laudatory voice, that of W. Moy Thomas, who during April, 1857, launched a bitter attack against Griswold's unreliable portrait in the London periodical *Train.*[170]

Two great Englishmen who early gave credit to Poe were the poet Swinburne and the biographer Ingram. Swinburne's eulogy appeared in *Under the Microscope* in 1872:

> Once as yet, and only once, has there sounded out of it all [America] one pure note of original song— worth singing, and echoed from the singing of no other man; a note of song neither wide nor deep, but utterly true, rich, clear, and native to the singer; the short exquisite

music, subtle and simple and sombre and sweet, of Edgar
Poe.[171]

Ingram's collection of the works came in 1874 and 1875,
being prefaced by a biographical sketch of ninety pages.
His scholarly labors wrung immediate encomiums, not from
R. L. Stevenson, who dissented from the general tide of
praise, but from such critics as William Hand Browne and
Richard Holt Hutton. At this period Swinburne was
corresponding with Ingram, and some of the British poet's
letters are quite revealing. A letter dated March 6, 1874,
disparged Griswold and sympathized with Rosalie Poe,
whereas another of April 10 stated that the poison on Poe's
grave should be removed. Four later letters (December 31,
1874—December 28, 1876) thanked Ingram for copies of his
edition of Poe, his remarks on *Politian,* and information
about the Baltimore Memorial. Swinburne was not a man
to mince words, and his letter of March 10, 1874, bore
directly on Poe's erotic life. He said that a "nymphomaniac
habit of body or mind . . . seems to have regulated the relations of the literary ladies with Poe."[172]

The early opinion of one other eminent British poet may
be cited. In 1883 Tennyson drew his cue from Swinburne
and lauded Poe. "I know several striking poems by American
poets," he said, "but I think that Edgar Poe is (taking his
poetry and prose together) the most original American
genius."[173]

The attitudes of a number of lesser English writers belong
in this review. In 1856 Andrew Lang compiled an edition
of the poems, to which he prefixed an essay complimentary
to Poe. In either 1872 or 1873 John Camden Hotten,
notorious London "pirate" printer, issued an edition of Poe's
works. Hotten's publication contained Baudelaire's comments on Poe as translated by Henry Curwen. In 1893 Sir
Edmund Gosse, who wondered at the American neglect of
Poe, extolled his contributions to the fields of fancy and
romance. Poe's contributions were also praised in 1909
by Norman Douglas, author of the famous novel *South Wind.*
Joseph Conrad admired Poe's sea stories, particularly "MS.

Found in a Bottle," which he termed "E. A. Poe's impressive version of the Flying Dutchman."

It was in 1909, the hundredth anniversary of Poe's birth, that R. Brimley Johnson issued *The Complete Poetical Works of Edgar Allan Poe.* At the London celebration of the Poe centennial, which occurred a trifle belatedly on March 1, 1909, the two principal speakers were Whitelaw Reid and Sir Arthur Conan Doyle.[174] For the centenary J. M. Robertson wrote in the *Contemporary Review* that "He has left a body of widely various criticism which, as such, will better stand critical examination today than any similar work produced in England and America in his time."[175]

The gifts of Poe early received favorable notice in England from painters and musicians. In 1890 the American artist James McNeill Whistler, who had settled in England in 1863, mentioned him twice in *The Gentle Art of Making Enemies.* In one place he referred to "the horrible 'Case of M. Waldemar,'" but in the other reference he praised Poe and Baudelaire as artists superior to painters and musicians:

> The poet is the supreme Artist, for he is the master of colour and of form, and the real musician besides, and is lord over all life and all arts; and so to the poet beyond all others are these mysteries known; to Edgar Allan Poe and Baudelaire, not to Benjamin West and Paul Delaroche . . .
> [176]

Furthermore, Poe captured the attention of the painter and esthete Aubrey Beardsley, who in 1901 printed *Four Illustrations for the Tales of Edgar Allan Poe.* And then there is the musician, Sir Arthur Somervell, whose *Kingdom by the Sea* drew its lyrics from "Annabel Lee."

The Pre-Raphaelites, interested as they were in both poetry and painting, were of course fond of Poe. According to an entry in the *Pre-Raphaelite Journal* (November 8, 1849), William Michael Rossetti had heard a false report concerning Poe's death. He wrote: "At Patmore's we heard of the reported death of Edgar Poe, concerning which some suspicions of suicide exist."[177] A later entry in the same *Journal* (December 13, 1849) concerns Coventry Patmore and Thomas Woolner: "Patmore was at Woolner's last night,

and read him Poe's tales to his own great satisfaction. He
considers Poe the best writer that America has produced."
"The Raven," as testified by the *Journal,* is another of Poe's
works which was read and recited at these literary parties.[178]
Dante Gabriel Rossetti composed a parody of "Ulalume,"
though it unfortunately does not survive. In the *Pre-
Raphaelite Diaries and Letters,* edited by Dante's brother
William Michael Rossetti, an entry (December 20, 1850)
states: "Gabriel finished, all but the last verse, his parody
on Ulalume." William Rossetti's note to this adds: "Now
lost, I am sorry to say. I forget what may have been the
subject of this parody of Poe's strangely haunting poem."[179]
That Poe's poetry, especially "The Raven," inspired "The
Blessed Damozel" is known from Dante Gabriel Rossetti's
statement to Hall Caine: "I saw that Poe had done the
utmost that it was possible to do with the grief of the lover
on earth, and so I determined to reverse the conditions
and give utterance to the yearning of the loved one in
Heaven."[180]

Later criticism of Poe in England has been mixed in tone.
As Walter De La Mare said in *Early One Morning* (1935),
"Concerning no man of genius or of fudge are the critics even
of our own days more acridly at odds." Thus George Bernard
Shaw's high praise of him as "This finest of finest of artists"
is counterbalanced by Middleton Murry's ignorant stricture
in *Discoveries* (1930) that "He was not by temper a meti-
culous artist." The opinion of George Saintsbury is entitled
to respectful notice. Saintsbury's essay, originally printed in
The Dial (1927) and later in *Prefaces and Essays* (1933),
affords a careful, detached estimate of Poe. Saintsbury discussed Poe's principal compositions, commended Mabbott's
editing of *Politian,* and ended by declaring the American
a poet of the first order.[181] Poe criticism in England, it is
clear, manifests considerable variations in opinion.

The most vigorous recent critic of Poe is Aldous Huxley.
In 1930 he asked if Edgar Allan Poe was a major poet and
answered that it would not occur to a Britisher to believe so.
Huxley avowed that Poe's substance was refined and his form
vulgar. He called the American "one of Nature's Gentle-

men, unhappily cursed with incorrigible bad taste." Huxley
explained that no "high-souled man" would be forgiven for
sporting a diamond ring on every finger and that Poe did
precisely the equivalent of this in his poems. According to
the Englishman, foreigners are blind to this, for their ears
do not detect Poe's vulgarity "in the details of execution."
There is a brassy and mechanically expressionistic air about
"The Raven," but Huxley is too severe in his concluding
remarks: "It is when Poe tries to make it too poetical that
his poetry takes on its peculiar tinge of badness. Protesting
too much that he is a gentleman, and opulent into the
bargain, he falls into vulgarity. Diamond rings on every
hand proclaim the parvenu."[182]

The fullest recent endorsement of Poe's principles is that
of D. H. Lawrence. A keen student of the works of Poe,
Lawrence anticipated the opinions of such Americans as
Malcolm Cowley, who regards Poe as a scientific author,
when in *Studies in Classic American Literature* (1923) he
wrote: "Poe has only one [vibration], the disintegrative
vibration. This makes him almost more a scientist than an
artist." Lawrence's observation is particularly applicable
to Poe's critical theories and to his later compositions written
in accordance with those theories. Lawrence was likewise
acute in analyzing *Ligeia* and *The Fall of the House of Usher*
as really love stories. He further declared that "Poe knew
only love, love, love, intense vibrations and heightened
consciousness." Lawrence noted that Poe was entranced by
psychological explorations, that he "was an adventurer into
vaults and cellars and horrible underground passages of the
human soul." The British writer was correct, too, in perceiving that Poe's creations were a type of self-destruction,
in realizing that there is a relation between disease and
literature, and in understanding that the tragedies of Poe's
life culminated in a triumph:

> He sounds the horror and the warning of his own
> doom.
> Doomed he was. He died wanting more love, and love
> killed him. A ghastly disease, love. Poe telling us of his
> disease; trying even to make his disease fair and attractive.
> Even succeeding.[183]

In the literary history of Britain the spirit of Poe has lived in the estheticism of Oscar Wilde and Ernest Dowson and in the adventures of Conan Doyle's detective Sherlock Holmes. Today it animates the soul of some of T. S. Eliot's best criticsm. In 1926 Eliot wrote "Note sur Mallarmé et Poe" for *La Nouvelle Revue Française,* in which he classified Poe with Donne and the Metaphysical poets. Eliot likewise has endorsed a number of Poe's critical principles, such as the use of economy in art, the necessity of producing a unified effect, and the advantage of the element of surprise in poetry. The support of a critic of T. S. Eliot's stature is good security that Poe's reputation in England will be preserved for the future. According to F. O. Matthiessen, the rules of poetry passed from Ezra Pound to Eliot sound like Poe's.[184] Among English critics Poe's repute is high and bids fair to remain so.[185]

7. American Attitudes

American periodicals indicate a lively interest in Poe today. References to him in magazines like the *Saturday Review of Literature* are of frequent occurrence, and publications like *American Literature* annually feature at least a note or a paper on Poe. Biographies and critical studies naturally appear more rarely—and within the last decade there has been no ambitious volume to supersede Quinn's in 1941. Books continue to be written and published, however, so that obviously considerable attention is directed towards Poe at the present time.

Contrary to the general notion that Poe's age neglected him, there was never a time that he did not receive praise or blame, commendation or censure. Yet Killis Campbell misconstrued the matter when describing Poe's early reputation. Campbell said that

1. Poe as poet was not esteemed by his contemporaries and was virtually ignored until after the appearance of "The Raven" in 1845.
2. He early achieved local fame with his tales and before

his death was regarded as a leading writer of short
stories in the United States.

3. He was best known in his own time in America as a
fearless though sometimes unjust critic.[186]

The facts are quite the contrary. From the start Poe had
his admirers and supporters. As early as December, 1829,
Poe received his first encouragement as a poet in a review
entitled "Unpublished Poetry," from *The Yankee and
Boston Literary Gazette.* On April 13, 1835, John Pendleton
Kennedy wrote the editor J. W. White that "This young
fellow is highly imaginative, and a little given to the
terrific."[187]   On August 11, 1838, L. A. Wilmer published
a favorable criticsm of him in "Ode XXX—To Edgar A.
Poe." On May 19, 1841, Longfellow wrote that "all that I
have read from your pen has inspired me with a high idea
of your power; and I think that you are destined to stand
among the first romance-writers of the country, if such be
your aim."[188]   On May 8, 1843, Lowell said in his letter to
Poe that "Your early poems display a maturity that astonish-
ed me & I recollect no individual . . . whose poems were
anything like as good." In 1844 Lowell stated that Poe
combined two faculties " . . . a power of influencing the mind
of the reader by the impalpable shadows of mystery, and
a minuteness of detail which does not leave a pin or a button
unnoticed."[189]   In 1849 Margaret Fuller reported to Mrs.
Browning that "Several women loved him, but it seemed
more with passionate illusion which he amused himself by
inducing than with sympathy. I think he really had no
friend. I did not know him, though I saw and talked with
him often, but he always seemed to me shrouded in an
assumed character."[190]   In *The Restoration, A Metrical
Romance* (Chicago, 1881), L. A. Norton's discussion of the
poet is "interesting as evidence of widespread admiration of
Poe in the West." Washington Irving passingly mentioned
in a letter of July 18, 1859, that he had received "two or
three letter from Poe. One asked permission to use certain
materials of mine for a story. I gave it."[191]   There is certainly not the slightest evidence from these early American
writers that Poe suffered from a lack of appreciation.

Moreover, on November 22, 1845, Poe compiled an editorial miscellany, "Boston and the Bostonians," for the *Broadway Journal.* In this he quoted a complimentary account of himself which had just appeared in the *Charleston Southern Patriot* and which showed the favorable attitude taken by his early critics in the South:

> Poe's Poetry.—Mr. Edgar A. Poe is one of the most remarkable, in many respects, among our men of letters. With singular endowments of imagination, he is at the same time largely possessed of many of the qualities that go to make an admirable critic . . . . As a Poet, Mr. Poe's imagination becomes remarkably conspicuous, and to surrender himself freely to his own moods, would be to make all his writings in verse, efforts of pure imagination only. He seems to dislike the merely practical, and to shrink from the concrete. His fancy takes the ascendant in his Poetry, and wings his thoughts to such superior elevations, as to render it too intensely spiritual for the ordinary reader.[192]

This passage from the *Charleston Patriot* leaves no doubt that both Poe and his poetry were known and warmly discussed in his own lifetime.

Killis Campbell's summations of Poe's contemporary stature are unacceptable. In fact, Campbell was also incorrect about Poe's high repute as a critic. Writing about the year 1851, John Esten Cooke said: "In this character—that of a literary critic—Mr. Poe seems not to have attracted proportionate attention. His wonderful genius as a weird poet, and storyteller, has dazzled everybody."

Later on, such writers as Whittier, Holmes, Lafcadio Hearn, and Whitman gave their homage to Poe's accomplishments. On September 21, 1875, Whittier's letter for the Baltimore Poe Memorial contained the pronouncement that "The extraordinary genius of Edgar Poe is acknowledged the world over."[193] On the same occasion in that year Holmes paid his respects to the poet's memory. On October 22, 1879, Lafcadio Hearn stated in the New Orleans *Item* that "Poe was a writer who understood the color-power of words and the most delicate subtleties of language as very few English or American writers have ever done."[194] In 1882 Whitman composed a paper for *The Critic* entitled

"Edgar Poe's Significance," and in this he claimed that one midnight he had a nightmare about a storm at sea. He said that the "figure of my lurid dream might stand for Edgar Poe, his spirit, his fortunes, and his poems—themselves all lurid dreams." Six years later, in 1888, Whitman expressed to Traubel a beginning passion for Poe:

> Do I like Poe? At the start for many years, not: but three or four years ago I got to reading him again, reading and liking, until at last—yes, now—I feel almost convinced that he is a star of considerable magnitude, if not a sun, in the literary firmament.[195]

Another group of writers censured Poe, both his writings and his character.[196] It was Bryant who most unreservedly reflected the Yankee reaction to the rebel Poe. On September 14, 1846, he wrote his wife that "I have been run down with beggar women," particularly "Mr. Poe's mother-in-law, who says her son-in-law is crazy, his wife dying, and the whole family starving."[197] Bryant's severest display of animosity occurred on November 6, 1865, when he answered Miss S. S. Rice's solicitations for the Baltimore Memorial:

> I am very unwilling to do anything which may seem disobliging, yet I cannot comply with the request in your note . . . My difficulty arises from the personal character of Edgar A. Poe, of which I have in my time heard too much to be able to join in paying especial honor to his memory. Persons younger than myself who have heard less of the conduct to which I refer may take a different view of the matter, and, certainly, I do not intend to censure them for doing so. I think, however, that there should be some decided element of goodness in the character of those to whom a public monument directs the attention of the world.[198]

Later on, in 1864, John P. Frankenstein joined the skeptics with an abusive attack on Poe in *American Art: its awful altitude.*[199] When similarly requested to aid the Baltimore Memorial, both John Burroughs and Barrett Wendell exhibited an unforgiving attitude towards Poe. Likewise, in *Recollections of a Busy Life* (1868), Horace Greeley remembered that a young man once wrote him to ask for several Poe autographs and that he had responded by saying that he owned "exactly one . . . It is his note for fifty dollars, with my endorsement across the back." Then Greeley concluded: "That autograph, I regret to say, remains on my hands, and is still for sale at first cost, despite the lapse of time, and the depreciation of our currency."[200] Even Emerson failed to realize that Poe was a genius. To him the poet was the "jingle man." Thus in 1874 Emerson omitted Poe's name from his *American Parnassus*. On December 2, 1899, an unknown author disparaged Poe's ability as an editor by saying that "The Southern Literary Messenger . . . seemed to promise definite encouragement to Southern writers and to offer a kind of leadership to Southern literary development; but Poe . . . was not fitted by temperament to do such a work."[201]

Censure of Poe, much of which has been borrowed from Griswold's early opinions, has continued into the twentieth century. Some of it occurs in literary criticism; much of it in fictional portraits of the man. Paul Elmer More in 1923 blasted both the poet and his admirers: "Health is above disease in art as it is in life. Poe remains chiefly the poet of unripe boys and unsound men."[202] Yvor Winters is another disparager of the poet.[203] It is in popular fiction that the false Poe more frequently occurs. In Edith Wharton's novel *False Dawn* (1924) Poe appeared as a man given over to dark moods and atheism. In Sophia Treadwell's drama *Plumes in the Dust* (1936) the actor Henry Hull presented Poe as the broken habitué of a "tristful tavern." Anya Seton's recent novel *Dragonwyck* (1944) showed Poe as a decayed creature conquered by dope.[204]

There are of course the Poe defenders.[205] On January 19, 1909, New York University held a Poe centennial celebrabation of one day. At the same period the University of Virginia held a centenary of three days and published *The Book of the Poe Centenary*, edited by Charles W. Kent and John S. Patton. Eugene L. Didier's *The Poe Cult* also was issued in 1909. David K. Jackson's *Poe and the Southern Literary Messenger*, a book correct in its praise of Poe's policies as an editor, was printed in 1934. John W. Robertson's two volumes, *A Bibliography and Commentary of the*

Writings of Edgar A. Poe, also published in 1934, showed that Poe was a literary figure of far-reaching significance.

Through the years various scholarly studies, such as Joy Bayless's on Rufus White Griswold of Hartford, another critic of Poe with the name Griswold (in *American Literature* [1934]), have appeared. In 1939 May G. Evans made a contribution to American scholarship in her *Music and Edgar Allan Poe.* In 1939 Henry R. Evans delivered an address (printed afterwards) before the Poe society in Baltimore on *Edgar Allan Poe and Baron von Kempelen's Chess-Playing Automaton.* Charles F. Heartman and James R. Canny's *A Bibliography of First Printings of the Writings of Edgar Allan Poe* appeared in 1940 and was revised in 1943. The year 1941 was the date of publication for B. A. Booth and C. E. Jones's valuable work, *A Concordance of the Poetical Works of Edgar Allan Poe.* In 1943 Horace Gregory observed, with pertinence, that Poe's *Literati* created a precedent for Mencken's *Prejudices.* In 1946 George Snell in the *Quarterly Review of Literature,* convincingly demonstrated that Poe's widening fame is fixed on secure foundations. Snell further remarked that "There are . . . numerous foreshadowings" in Poe's works of Proust and Joyce. The recent statement in the first volume of the editors R. E. Spiller, W. Thorp, T. H. Johnson, and H. S. Canby's *Literary History of the United States* (1948), a title reminiscent of Poe's own unfinished *Literary America* (1848), affords an apt summary of the poet's contribution: "He stands as one of the very few great innovators in American literature. Like Henry James and T. S. Eliot, he took his place, almost from the start, in international culture as an original creative force in contrast to the more superficial vogue of Cooper and Irving."[206] It is a little remarkable that Henry James in 1878 expressed an antipathy for the poet and more in harmony with the circumstances that in 1949 T. S. Eliot should indicate the kinship he felt with Poe. The present list of studies was fittingly capped by the publication of *English Studies in Honor of James Southall Wilson* (Charlottesville, Virginia, 1951), which contained three strong papers on Poe.

8. Poe Triumphant

In 1950, one year following the hundredth anniversary of the poet's death, there appeared *The Centenary Poe,* Montagu Slater's edition of the tales, poems, criticism, *Marginalia,* and *Eureka.* At the mid-century in the United States Poe was the outstanding literary "great" of the past. An exhaustive treatment of Poe in America cannot be attempted here. One must simply note scattered references to him, like the mention of him in the Foreword of James Branch Cabell's *Jurgen* (1919), the memorial poems to him by John Erskine and others (1909 *et seq.*), the travesty of his style in James Whitcomb Riley's "Leonainie" (1883), and the serious remarks on his art in James Huneker's *Ivory Apes and Peacocks* (1915). As observed earlier, Poe's prose influenced Ambrose Bierce and H. P. Lovecraft; his poetry, Amy Lowell and her program for the Imagists. "The Raven," it now may be added, inspired James William Carling to produce his finest expressionistic illustrations. The fame of Poe in the United States has likewise been kept alive by scholars and reviewers. Recently, George Arms discussed Quinn and O'Neill's edition (1946) in the *New Mexico Quarterly Review* (Spring, 1948). Homage to Poe is paid in yet another quarter, for each year Mystery Writers of America, Inc., makes to the best detective novel the Edgar Allan Poe Award. Poe's popularity, it is clear, extends in manifold directions and touches many people.

The nine Titans of American letters presumably are Emily Dickinson, Emerson, Hawthorne, Henry James, Melville, Poe, Thoreau, Mark Twain, and Whitman. In this list Edgar Allan Poe is a strong challenger for the foremost position. For none among them can match his achievements in the triple fields of poetry, prose narrative, and critical essay. One American attitude toward Poe was voiced by his friend J. P. Kennedy three days after the poet's death in Baltimore. No later author in the United States has improved on the quiet, genuine, and sympathetic remarks which Kennedy entered in his journal on Wednesday, October 10, 1849:

> Poor Poe! He was an original and exquisite poet, and one of the best prose writers in this country. His works are among the very best of their kind. His taste was replete with classical flavor, and he wrote in the spirit of an old Greek philosopher.[207]

To trace further the spread of Poe's worldwide fame would result in an extensive exploration of comparative literature. Interest in him has extended around the world. He is well known in China and Japan. In Europe he is discussed in several countries unmentioned in the present survey, these including Czechoslovakia, Hungary, Jugoslavia, and Sweden. The title of Remigio U. Pane's recent doctoral dissertation at Columbia is *Poe: His Critics and Translators in Italy.* Senator Elbert D. Thomas, of Utah, who recommended on August 25, 1949, the issue of a centennial stamp for Poe, has remarked on Poe's influence on a number of important European authors. In the *Congressional Record,* Thomas said that Poe "was the forerunner of Kipling and Masefield, William Butler Yeats, and many French and German bards."

Today Poe's far-flung renown is proof that he has passed the tests of time, to occupy a lasting place in world literature.

Chapter Four

Fable and Fact

1. Legend of a Poet

The brief life of Edgar Allan Poe constitutes the most disputed biography in American literary annals. The bases of the dispute—his drinking proclivities, his alleged addiction to opium, his struggle against poverty, his forced withdrawal from the University of Viginia, his expulsion from West Point, his unhappiness as an orphaned boy rejected by his foster father, and, perhaps this above all, his attachment to more than a score of women—are pivotal in his biography.

In breaking a number of the conventions of what in his day was still a staidly moral United States, Poe was possibly the first great literary exponent in America of a way of life for the artist in opposition to Puritan tradition. Much of the original misinterpretation of his character was due to the prevailing conservatism that then dominated American manners.

With so individualistic a literary man, it is small wonder that various biographers of differing age and nationality have either eulogized or censured Poe. The peculiar quality of Poe's writings has also played its role in moving critics and biographers alike to try their hands at explaining his genius. The Poe bibliography is accordingly extensive. Since his death on October 7, 1849, in a dismal hospital in Baltimore, not a year has passed that someone in this country or another has not written a book or a paper on aspects of the life or works of Poe. Why has no definite picture of the author resulted from this continuing stream of biographical compositions? The answer is extremely involved.

One cause for the incompleteness of the portrait has already been implied; namely, the natural inability of a biographer to remain dispassionate when dealing with a figure whose personal life and habits have been made an issue of his biography. Poe's unsavory literary subjects are also likely to induce a feeling of revulsion in any biographer, even one who acknowledges the brilliance of his literary technique. Yet still another reason for the biographer's inability to present the complete Poe is that some of the relevant materials, especially the author's letters, have been suppressed. What, for example, was the true cause of the rift between Poe and his foster father, Mr. Allan?

Mabbott contends that while Poe was attending the University of Virginia he wrote a letter which forever estranged him from his foster father. In this letter Poe accused Allan, who is known on other counts to have been a libertine, of having infected his wife, Frances Valentine Allan, with a venereal disease. According to Mabbott, who had the story at first hand from Mr. Stanard, a relative of the family, this letter came into the later possession of the Valentines and was destroyed by them.

The major facts of Poe's life are well known and can be recapitulated briefly.

On January 19, 1809, Edgar Poe was born in Boston. The next year, in July, his father, David Poe, Jr., disappeared and his mother moved to Richmond. On December 8, 1811, Poe's mother died; and he then entered the household of his protectors, John and Frances Keeling Valentine Allan. With this family the boy Edgar made a trip to England (June 23—

July 28, 1815), where he was enrolled during 1816-1817 in the London school of the Misses Dubourg and during 1818-1819 in the Manor House at Stoke Newington, near London, of the Reverend John Bransby. In 1820 the family returned to America, and Poe shortly was enrolled in the Richmond school of Joseph H. Clarke, where he stayed for some two years. In the fall of 1824 Poe saw Lafayette, who visited Richmond and the grave of Poe's grandfather. The next year he was removed from William Burke's academy to be tutored for entrance at the University of Virginia, where he actually matriculated on February 14, 1826. The day before Christmas of that year he returned home in debt and disgrace. He became completely estranged from John Allan in the ensuing year and left home, appearing soon in Boston as Henri Le Rennet. A little later he enlisted in the army under yet another *alias,* Edgar A. Perry; but in the year 1831 he used his own name at West Point, where he was dismissed. For some time he had paid more attention to poetry than the army or schooling, so that after marrying his cousin, Virginia Clemm, on May 16, 1836, he led a literary life. In 1843 he failed to secure, in Washington, a government appointment which he had sought since 1841. Then in 1844-1845 he supplemented his meager literary income by lecturing. In July, 1845, however, he did not appear for his lecture at New York University. Exactly four years afterward he was detained overnight in Moyamensing Prison, Philadelphia. Three months later he died at Washington College Hospital, Baltimore.

Mystery suffuses several gaps indicated in the record above. Much more information about Poe's father, David Poe, Jr., is needed before he can be pronounced a penniless, drunken neglecter of his family. Similarly, Edgar Poe's occasional insobriety has never been established as the result of heredity. The elder Poe, it is true, drank, and he did permanently disappear in July, 1810, precisely when his wife was enduring the extremities of ill-fortune. But it must be remembered that his reasons for disappearing are not known. These matters, so often emphasized by motive-hunting biographers, are not the whole, unvarnished story.

After their marriage in Richmond on March 14, 1806, there is proof that the poet's father sought to protect his wife from slurs levelled at her acting. J. T. Buckingham, editor of the influential Boston journal *Polyanthos,* recalled in 1852 that "Mr. Poe—the father of the late Edgar A. Poe—took offense at a remark on his wife's acting, and called at my house to chastise my impertinence . . ."[208] This testimony that the elder Poe endeavored to shelter his wife from slander is enough to discredit the jeers about his ungentlemanly behavior and the reasons for his disappearance in 1810. The inferences, shakily based, but often stated, as to David Poe's character and motives illustrate a tendency among some biographers to fill a gap in knowledge with detail of their own manufacture. With the scant data at hand, one cannot objectively condemn the character of David Poe. A large feature of the Poe legend makes the poet a facsimile descendant of his father with the latter's propensities for drinking and borrowing money. But these isolated conjectures on David's actions, without valid reference to his general behavior or indeed to the circumstances explaining them, cannot be accepted as relevant in a factual biography of his son.

Poe's means of livelihood in Boston after his break with John Allan form another lacuna in the chronology. At that period did he work as a seaman and travel out of Boston harbor for a second visit to Europe? Did he change his name and work with a theatrical troupe in the same profession which his mother and father had followed? The record at this point is so nearly blank that one is tracing faint leads in even posing these questions. The facts about Poe's activities in Boston in 1827 stand incomplete.

Over the years the accumulation of Poe material has become so large that today it affords enough new documentation to correct many misleading impressions created in the "standard" biographies. In view of the great wealth of materials now open to the Poe student, he should be able to separate the man from the myth if the conflicting interpretations in the biography are reviewed.

2. Poe's Own Fabrications

Poe's own falsifications about himself, in statements made to many different people, markedly differentiate the record of his career from that of most other authors. His sole responsibility for the fabrications must be admitted in full and the consequent impression of him squarely met. Why did he issue misstatements about his age, his peregrinations abroad, his expectation of a vast inheritance, and his training at the University of Virginia? The correct resolution of these queries would supply a most important clue to the true character of Edgar Allan Poe. Perhaps the answer is near at hand.

If any explanation of the matter may be said to have gained general acceptance today, the view is that personal vanity dictated Poe's actions. He earnestly wished to present his interests in the best light, to establish everywhere a reaction sympathetic to him in his predicament, and to suggest to the public at large that he was an important personage, aristocratic, cultured, experienced, widely traveled, and a man of the world whom fate prevented from becoming a rich and influential Southern gentleman. Self-admiration has a bearing on the mystery. It is not, however, a wholly adequate solution; nor is it by any means the only possible one.

First of all, there is the matter of age at the time of his enlistment in the Army (May 26, 1827) under the assumed name of Edgar A. Perry. A little over eighteen, he gave his age as twenty-two years. Since minors were then accepted into the service, Poe's declaration is a perplexing misrepresentation. Possibly he hit upon this only as an added ruse in his attempts to lose his original identity. Perhaps he considered his chances for advancement greater if he appeared on the records as a soldier one year past his majority. He certainly had made an altogether creditable showing in both South Carolina and Virginia when on January 1, 1829, after less than two years of service, he was promoted to Sergeant Major, the highest non-commissioned grade. On entering the Army, he listed his occupation as clerk. This, too, may have been a fabrication. Although it could disclose his means of livelihood in Boston earlier in 1827, the theory is doubtful, for at that period anyone who could write intelligibly or add a string of figures was arbitrarily listed as being a clerk.

When Poe took up quarters at West Point (July 1, 1830), he took delight in regaling his fellow cadets with tall tales about his imaginary adventures in South America and elsewhere.[209] There is no evidence that Poe misrepresented his age at West Point as he had done earlier upon his enlistment at Boston. The reasons for the yarns about South America may have been his eagerness to create interest in his poems, towards the publication of which he extracted subscriptions from his admirers among the cadets. Later in life the poet wished to appear younger than he actually was: in the "Memorandum" replying to Griswold's request of January 14, 1845, he declared, for publication in Griswold's *Prose Writers of America,* that he was born in 1811. No woman was ever more inconsistent about her age than Edgar Allan Poe.

At an earlier date (August 20, 1835) an inexact statement about his expected inheritance occurs in Poe's letter to William Poe, Jr., the poet's second cousin.[210] In this he claims that he was "educated in the expectation of an immense fortune"—a declaration baldly contrary to fact inasmuch as John Allan never adopted Edgar legally and at no time is known to have given him cause to entertain the great expectations which he thus so grandly describes. The danger of attributing Poe's false remarks to downright lying or an unnatural display of exaggerated egotism is illustrated forcefully later in the same letter when he asks William for "whatever aid you may have it in your power to bestow upon Mrs. Clemm," his mother-in-law whom he deeply loved. Poe was making it clear to a relative that he had no money of his own and had not inherited a fortune as uninformed people might think. In writing thus, he was motivated by a wholly understandable solicitude for the pitiful Mrs.

Clemm. The interpretation of this letter demonstrates how
cautious one should be in judging a piece of evidence so
apparently dependable as the author's own words. His
name should be delayed on the docket until sufficient proof
is found for haling him into court, for irreparable damage
can be inflicted upon the author's reputation when relevant
circumstances are ignored. The citation of this letter by
Harrison, compiler of the Virginia edition, amid other
examples of obvious inaccuracies is therefore seriously misleading. The extenuating motive in Poe's lengthy explanation of Maria Clemm's need of succor is his warm and human
concern for her welfare. In this letter to William Poe, the
poet was, then, seeking to aid Mrs. Clemm, and his exaggera-
tion about his "expectation of an immense fortune" was a
simple effort to convince William that his loan at this time
would be a safe risk.

The document of prepotent significance in giving a large
public a false portrait of the poet is the "Memorandum"
which Poe sent to Griswold for his use in writing a biographical sketch. Poe's issuing the "Memorandum," unless
mere bravado, is an act demanding an explanation. Perhaps
it was simply a puff; but the main inaccuracies of the brief
sketch, reprinted by Harrison in an Appendix,[211] should be
listed in a corrective review before any attempt is made to
establish the poet's motives for an action so puzzling.

Poe states here, first, that he was born in 1811, whereas
the correct date of 1809 is fully certified. Secondly, he
alleges that his mother died of pneumonia. Actually, her
illness was "consumption." Thirdly, he affirms that John
Allan adopted him, whereas that gentleman only gave him
a home. He says, too, that he attended the University of
Virginia for three years, though he actually remained at
Charlottesville only one year (1826). Finally, he attests that
in being prevented from joining the Greek rebels he made
his way to Russia and returned in 1829. In truth, during
that year he was in Virginia in the Army all the time and
was discharged on April 15. The "Memorandum" does
contain a number of correct statements, these perhaps being
included in order to lend an air of authenticity to the sketch

as a whole. The poet rightly declares that his paternal grandfather, David Poe, was a quartermaster general and a friend of Lafayette. He is truthful in reporting that he went with the Allan family to Great Britain, although the year was 1815, not 1816 as he here recalled. He is accurate in recording that he entered West Point as a cadet and that he left there abruptly to pursue a literary career. Also he correctly describes the circumstances of his winning literary recognition in Baltimore through *The Visitor* as well as his work in Richmond under T. W. White on the *Southern Literary Messenger*. Although other matters are mentioned—for instance, his doubtful contributions to two unnamed British journals—it is clear that the "Memorandum" was prepared skillfully enough to mislead the average reader.

Why did Poe thus mingle so much fiction with fact in a chronicle that purported to be accurate? Can it not be dismissed as a hoax, a type of mystification of which Poe was fond, or as a shallow travesty whose complete falsity would immediately be recognized? Probably the motive behind Poe's perpetration of this astoundingly fanciful biography was, more than anything else, his passionate longing for recognition. Nothing is so dominant among the impressions received of Poe, his conversations with friends, his pretentious comments in and on his own works, as his abiding and agonized hunger for literary fame. When being transferred from South Carolina to Virginia, the youthful Poe, in a letter to John Allan of December 22, 1828, bragged that "the world shall hear of the son whom you have thought unworthy of your notice."[212]

Something else to remember is that Poe was among America's first professional writers, a man who was determined to make his own way by the sale of his compositions at a time when such was all but impossible. Having no sinecure from either his family or the government and unable to gain regular employment in any profession or trade, he somehow managed to drag out a living from journalistic work and from the occasional sale of a poem, a tale, or an essay. Hard work had not won him readers; no portion of the literate public demanded to see his words in print. Indeed, all legitimate means of bringing his name to favorable notice had failed. After years of privation and unremitting toil he was yet, in a real sense, unknown. It was under these conditions that he now made his bids for celebrity.

To become famous, Poe resorted to the most blatant tricks of sensationalism. By legitimate means or otherwise, he was determined to arrive at lasting fame. The fabrications in the "Memorandum" are the largest cases in point, but his determination to achieve renown is always implicit in references to himself which he included in letters addressed to famous personages. His underlying motive is discernible, too, in the autobiographical allusions in his works—in the suggestive portrayal of his foster father, John Allan, in "The Business Man"; in the glowing, rebellious spirit he draws as his own in scattered passages of the essays; and in the highly fevered lines of his passionate lyrics. The purpose behind his misstatements is easier to perceive in the "Memorandum" than in his letters or his isolated works, that is all.

No matter how unattractive the picture may be, the "Memorandum" is at one with the other evidence in revealing Poe as a writer irrevocably determined to creep and crawl, to climb and crowd, into the ranks of the immortals. If to do so meant that he must exaggerate, he was capable of precisely this. There is no need to interpret his passion for fame—his shrewd lying with self-aggrandizement as its object —in terms of paranoia; for to one extent or another "author-advertising" like Poe's is today a commonplace of the commercial book business. His intent is unmistakable in his statements about his drinking. Poe declares that for three years at the University of Virginia he "led a very dissipated life." In other words, he trebles the time and accents the manner with a more intensive adverb than the facts warranted—"a very dissipated life," says he. As he would have desired, biographers and critics have fallen for Poe's subterfuge.

Is it possible to study the man as a craftsman and relate his behavior to his output? Of the forty years that Poe lived, approximately half were devoted to writing. He wrote enough for Harrison to compile in 1902 an edition of seventeen volumes, sixteen of which comprise the complete works of Edgar Allan Poe. What a stupendous labor packed into some twenty years! To have written and rewritten so much in uncomfortable surroundings, with insecure prospects for the morrow, and with never an abundance of food for his family is an incredible accomplishment. The very fact of this achievement should be sufficient testimony that he had preciously few hours to spend on drunken sprees.

It is an essential part of the record that Poe was a hard-working young man trying to establish writing as a legitimate profession, as a means of livelihood, as an advance commitment to fellowship with the immortals. Edgar A. Poe was industrious, determined, publicity-seeking, an egoist bent on achieving the limelight. He was willing to fabricate incidents in order to appear in a good light, though in doing so he might bring down raillery upon his head. At least discussion would be aroused; notice would be called to him. Any comment, favorable or otherwise, would be better than no notice at all. Poe is, from one point of view, the *poète maudit*—the accursed poet of American literature. The child of parents who acted, Poe tended to strut as well. In this he was not alone, for the same was done by writers before and after him. Shakespeare in his sonnets extolled himself and was inebriated with the certainty of his lasting fame. In the twentieth century the most famous proclaimer of his own imperishable genius was Shaw. Poe was his own press agent, initiated fabrications about himself after the fashion of other authors, and acted out his role to the point of overplaying it. In Elizabethan times or in the Hollywood of today, Poe's peacock pose would be *à la mode*. In the puritanism of his own era, his exhibitionism was regarded as abnormal and therefore subject to vilification.

Poe's various fictions about himself contain a key to his character. This key was his unquenchable thirst for fame, the grand ambition which he confessed to his friend Mrs. Mary Gove Nichols:

> I love fame—I dote on it—I idolize it—I would drink to the very dregs the glorious intoxication. I would have

incense ascend in my honour from every hill and hamlet, from every town and city on this earth. Fame! Glory!— they are life-giving breath, and living blood. No man lives unless he is famous![213]

3. Gossip of the Times

The gossip of Poe's acquaintances, sometimes trustworthy and sometimes not, is a chief source of information about him. At times one seems finally to approach the real man when reading the opinions of him expressed by his contemporaries. Poe was a man who so often aroused strong feeling among his associates that even the report of a "friend" must frequently be weighed before it is accepted as an unbiased personal observation. His true character is accordingly most difficult to appraise from such evidence.

About one clouded aspect of his early life there yet remains some question; namely the paternity of Edgar's sister Rosalie. Campbell, Hervey Allen, and Mabbott have not been hesitant to declare her illegitimate. Mrs. Clemm seems to have possessed knowledge of a "family secret" damaging to the Poes. The "family secret" may relate to the waywardness of Poe's mother or to his father's wildness. Since the secret was never divulged and went with Mrs. Clemm to her grave, it may be objected that as evidence it has no utility at all. The illegitimacy charge against Rosalie, in any event, rests upon other, perhaps shaky, grounds: first, the prejudiced allegation of Mr. Allan and, secondly, the "veiled" reference to this charge in verses written by Edgar's brother, William Henry Leonard Poe. On November 1, 1824, John Allan's letter[214] to his brother refers to Rosalie as "half your sister" and then—as though "half" means not merely that the two brothers equally shared her love but specifically that Rosalie's parents were at fault—Mr. Allan adds, "and God forbid my dear Henry that we should visit upon the living the errors of the dead." In his poem for the *North American* (1827), published some three years after the date of the letter, William Henry alludes to his sister as "a falsity," saying,

" 'tis wrong to call thee mine." The final stanza, which concerns his father and mother, concludes as follows:

> But Love is like the pois'ning weed,
> That taints the air it lives upon.[215]

The letter and the derivative poem are sole pieces of evidence upon which rests the theory that Rosalie's father was not the same as that of Edgar and Henry. Such an inference may indeed be the logical one to draw; the words of John Allan and William Henry could be, however, quite differently interpreted.

Rosalie's mental growth was retarded, and her mind is said never to have fully developed. It is to this tragedy that Allan may refer in speaking of "the errors of the dead," especially since in that day mental instability was commonly held to be a hereditary fault. Similarly, the brother's mention of both "falsity" and "taint" could apply to Rosalie's weak mental condition. The purported instability of Rosalie, however, might be overestimated easily since she is stated to have supported herself, at least in part, by teaching. In Allan's letter the phrase, "half your sister," may mean only that both brothers shared her love equally; that is, Allan might have added the statement, "and half yours." Finally, the "secret" of the "taint" may allude simply to Mrs. David Poe's tuberculosis, a disease transferrable to her children. Poe's brother, in point of fact, did die of consumption, with complications of alcoholism. But Rosalie lived to a ripe old age, so her demise was hardly precipitated by tuberculosis. Perhaps the facts about his mother were suppressed because the disease could have been repugnantly associated with the "taint" of her promiscuity in having given birth to the illegitimate Rosalie. People were hasty at that period in criticizing actresses, anyway. In support of this reasoning, there is Poe's gloss in the "Memorandum," where he identified his mother's tuberculosis as the less despised disease of "pneumonia."

Poe's early school days, often alluded to as wasted, need to be mentioned again to recall the praise which his first teachers gave his efforts. The encomiums then addressed to him by his instructors in Richmond as well as in London testify that from the beginning he was an unusually apt student. Without entering into a discussion of his student days at Charlottesville, mention should be made of the excellent record which Poe made at the University of Virginia. Poe's personal troubles in Charlottesville with his creditors are another matter, and they do not alter the fact that as a student he was able to display superior ability in his classes. He appears to have shown real talent, if not genius, in his handling of linguistic subjects. Important features of Poe's character are revealed at Charlottesville on those occasions when he squandered too much of his own time and too much of Allan's money in drinking and gaming. But these derelictions should not cause one to forget that he was an excellent student who managed to achieve an altogether creditable showing in his classes. In his less than one year at Virginia, Poe assembled an impressive store of information, and his period at the University can not be cited as an example of unqualifiedly riotous and undisciplined behavior. Professor Blaetterman praised Poe's translation of Tasso,[216] testimony that even a severe old scholar approved the poet's habits of study, which were first solidly fostered at the University of Virginia.

The contemporary remarks about Poe's personal habits are of value since the people making them had opportunity to observe directly the exact circumstances of his behavior. After completing *Eureka* in 1848, Poe was at his lowest physical ebb; and it was at this time, according to his sister Rosalie, that he "begged for morphine" at Fordham. As for his alleged addiction to drugs, there is Poe's declaration that at Boston in 1848 he swallowed an ounce of laudanum and promptly "rejected" it.[217] Yet his inability to retain the laudanum, which was purchased at Providence and later consumed in Boston, may demonstrate that he was not accustomed habitually to use of the drug. As Poe states in his letter, dated November 16, 1848,[218] he actually intended to kill himself by this means. He could hardly have expected to do so if he had been, through custom, already inured to its effects. Furthermore, there remains the early testimony of Dr. Thomas Dunn English, who in 1845-1846 was in close though unfriendly association with Poe in New York City. As for the poet's addiction to drugs, the physician English explicitly declared: "I saw no signs of it and believe the charge to be a baseless slander."[219] Had there been grounds, certainly an enemy like Dr. English would have known and utilized the fact in answering the lawsuit Poe had brought against him for slander on July 23, 1846. There is also the frank statement of an unknown lady who declared in 1847 that "I never saw him excited by liquor or any other stimulant."[220]

Are the allusions to opiates in Poe's works of any significance? Opiates are mentioned only a few times in sixteen volumes of Poe's writings, these references occurring often enough in versions that Poe later cancelled. Each time drugs figure in a fictional connection, not as a personal disclosure. Poe omitted allusions to opium in "Loss of Breath," "A Predicament," "Berenice," "The Oval Portrait," and retained them in "MS. Found in a Bottle," "The Duc de L'Omelette," "A Tale of the Ragged Mountains," "The Fall of the House of Usher," and the masterly "Ligeia." In 1951 Ruth Hudson said, in a volume honoring James Southall Wilson, that the author removed these allusions from "Ligeia" not because he was a "drug-addict concealing his secret" but because he was "the artist striving for unique effect in his masterpiece." An allusion in a note to "Al Aaraaf," added for explication, would appear patently editorial, not autobiographical. Finally, a reference to the subject in the text of "The Sleeper" should be studied in the light of a similar passage in both *Macbeth* (III. v, 20-24) and Thomas Moore.[221] None of the references to opiates connect positively with Poe's own life or are based on his personal experience. The statements are thus of a fictional nature; they have no value as self revelation and cannot be construed as proof that he was a drug addict.

What of the poet's drinking? Poe drank when he was a college boy and, with the exception of one or two periods, in his adult life. Moreover, drinking is frequently mentioned in both the poems and the tales. Contemporaries like the pious editor T. W. White, of the *Messenger,* and the envious editor Burton of the *Gentleman's Magazine*, expanded on his weakness for alcohol. He made little effort to conceal his drinking. He won the Thomas Dunn English lawsuit regarding his character, but the publicity of the affair, advertising his drinking to the world,[222] established him in the public eye as a confirmed addict. Some of his convivial friends remembered, after he had become a celebrity, that he drank heavily. Yet Captain Mayne Reid, the "boy" novelist, who visited the poet in 1843, testifies that Poe's actions were only those of the average man when intoxicated: "I have been his companion in one or two of his wildest frolics, and can certify that they never went beyond the innocent mirth in which we all indulge when Bacchus gets the better of us."[223] That Poe went for long periods without alcohol is attested by William Gowans. In 1837 Poe and Gowans for over eight months roomed and boarded at 113½ Carmen Street in New York, where Poe worked hard and where, according to Gowans, he was never "the least affected by liquor." In the autumn of 1849 he joined the Shockoe Hill Division of the Sons of Temperance.[224]

Poe's relations with romantically inclined women, many of whom figure importantly in his poetry, have a relevant bearing on his biography. Everyone is more or less acquainted with his abortive *amour* with Sarah Elmira Royster (later Mrs. Shelton), which furnished the subject for both his brother William's tale "The Pirates" *(North American,* November 27, 1827) and L. A. Wilmer's poetic three-act play *Merlin (North American,* August 18, 1827); and with his courtship of Mary Devereaux, who in December, 1889, remembered him in *Harper's New Monthly Magazine* as an irrepressibly ardent suitor. The poem "Annabel Lee" may have been directed to Poe's wife Virginia Clemm or to Mrs. Shelton.[225] Other early testimony links his name with Mrs. Sarah Helen Whitman, who on February 14, 1848, read before a meeting of *literati* her poem to him; with Mrs. Mary Louise Shew, at whose home in the spring of 1848 he started "The Bells"; and with Mrs. Annie Richmond, who was the inspiration of his "For Annie." Momentarily fascinated, Mrs. Elizabeth Frieze Lummis Ellet tried to replace Mrs.

Frances S. Osgood in the poet's affection and plagued Virginia Poe with anonymous letters about Poe's derelictions as a husband. This lady, the transcendentalist Margaret Fuller, and possibly the poetess Miss Anne C. Lynch once acted as a commission to call at Poe's home to ask the return of letters he had received from Mrs. Osgood, an emotional feminine admirer. Poe was a frequent visitor of such *literati* as the women in this group and also of Mrs. Seba (Elizabeth Oakes) Smith, a leader in the literary society of New York, and especially Sarah Anna Lewis, sentimentalist of the "starry sisterhood." In *Godey's* he was favored by Mrs. Sarah J. Hale, whose friendship he cultivated partly because she saw to it that his verses were presented to the feminine literary world which she dominated. The poetess Mrs. Mary E. Hewett befriended Poe's family and sought to keep track of the progress of his affair with Mrs. Whitman. Mrs. Jane Ermina Locke, a poetess of Lowell, Massachusetts, wished to be Poe's patroness; but when he spurned her for Mrs. Richmond, she became one of his most vocal detractors. Mrs. St. Leon Loud, the poetess of Philadelphia, was also captivated by Poe's reputation, though it was through her husband that she asked the poet to edit her verses. Another of his close feminine admirers was Mrs. Susan Archer Talley Weiss, author of *The Home Life of Poe* (1907). Even a cursory account of the poet's relations to women should include the names of Catherine Poitiaux, his first sweetheart; Elizabeth Herring, a cousin whom he loved; and possibly Mary Newman, a young lady of Baltimore who was enraptured by Poe's good looks as well as his skill as a poet.

Information about Poe's attachment to the score of women just mentioned comes from contemporaneous sources—from book notices, reported conversations, personal letters, and intimate diaries. From a newly-discovered letter written by Mrs. Annie Richmond's brother, a report comes of yet another young lady in the poet's life. Poe was sufficiently interested in her to hold a private conversation immediately after meeting her. The pretty young school teacher is not named in the letter but is said to have come from the interview with a blush on her cheeks.[226] There is, in addition, a newly-found Poe poem which was addressed to one of Mrs. Osgood's friends: Miss Louise Olivia Hunter, a school girl of nineteen years to whom the poet was attracted.[227]

Poe's acquaintance with women was obviously extensive. Whether or not these friendships were intimate is less certain. The poet W. H. Auden in the Rinehart edition of Poe (1950) jocosely observed that Poe "played house" with his lady friends. Captain Mayne Reid, who saw Poe in 1843, declared that he was not "a rake" and added that he was not attractive, physically, to women. Reid stated:

> His was a face purely intellectual. Women might admire it, thinking of this, but it is doubtful if many of them ever fell, or could have fallen in love with the man to whom it belonged. I don't think many of them ever did.[228]

If "many of them" did not love Poe, a number of them certainly seemed to. Poe, in his mimicry of Byron, was capable of having "affairs." Among these women were his early sweetheart Sarah Elmira Royster, his wife Virginia Clemm, and the poetess to whom he proposed marriage— Mrs. Whitman. One may add here the name of Mrs. Annie Richmond, to whom he was warmly attentive and whom he at one time invited to visit him in New York. The newly-discovered letter by her brother discloses that Mrs. Richmond complied with the request and actually did visit him. The testimony of Mary Devereaux, if not a farce, leaves no doubt as to Poe's vitality since she charges him with seeking to assault her. Better evidence of what the world calls an *amour* is afforded by his attendance upon Mrs. Osgood, wife of the painter of Poe's portrait. To her he poured out his heart in letters and in poems, and she replied in kind with equal ardor. What makes their relationship appear an affair of passion is that she alone of all the women he knew left the city for safety in Albany. Apparently her emotions had carried her so far that she had to flee. That Poe was by then fully captivated by the pretty Mrs. Osgood is shown by his continuing the chase to Albany.

According to Mabbott, at whose suggestion these details are included, Mrs. Osgood in "Ida Grey" (August, 1845) may represent her own feelings and actions in the person

of the fictional heroine. Like Mrs. Osgood, Ida had been
married; but her husband had died, whereas Osgood was
still living. Like Mrs. Osgood, she attended literary parties.
And just as Mrs. Osgood met Poe at such a gathering, so
did Ida among the visiting *literati* fall for a strange man
whose face was "wonderfully spiritual." Extracts from Ida's
journal furnish details about her idol, whose counterpart in
actual life was supposedly Poe.

> "I have seen him at last!—him of whom I have read
> and heard so much! For several days before our introduc-
> tion there had been a presentiment at my heart that stilled
> and awed it . . . and when we met I was so strangely
> affected that I could hardly speak."[229]

Another extract may remind one that Poe, too, was married,
that his Virginia is said to have been cold, and that he was
an outstanding man of intellectual appearance:

> "He is married. His wife, they say, is cold and does not
> love him . . . How purely intellectual and spiritual is the
> beauty of his face and head! He thinks, he talks, he writes,
> he looks as never did man before!"[230]

A passage recalls, further, the exchange of letters between
Poe and Mrs. Osgood:

> "He has written to me words of almost divine passion . . . .
> it is sweet to read those thrilling words. He feels, as I
> knew he felt—that God has sent him to me—to calm my
> heart—to spiritualize my being—to wean me from the
> world. How perfectly already he sees into my soul."[231]

The story ends with a long poem, in which Mrs. Osgood,
the partner in the *amour* in real life, is the heroine, Ida Grey.
Three important adjectives used to describe Ida are "ardent,"
"guileless," "impetuous"; and Mrs. Osgood's acquaintances
report that she was "ardent, sensitive, impulsive." In the
fictional narrative Ida "was the veriest sunbeam that ever
gladdened the weary, weary world with beauty and with
light" and "then entered the convent"; a friend said of Mrs.
Osgood that "she sparkled, exhaled and went to Heaven."
The identification is brought to focus when one remembers
that E. T. S. Grey was a name used by Poe to receive letters
confidentially.

The discussion of early reports about Poe could be
indefinitely extended. One finds in Captain Reid's account

the statement that in 1843 the poet "on his crown" was "then prematurely bald."[232]   Since he has been found trustworthy in many instances (*e.g.*, the matter of Poe's familiarity with Scandinavian literature), his description of Poe's baldness has the value of an eye-witness reporter known to be reliable where it is possible to check him.   Perhaps Poe wore a wig. Reid's observation contrasts sharply with indications in spurious photographs that Poe possessed a wealth of luxuriant, flowing hair and acts as a stringent antidote to romantic portraits of him as a Byronic dandy.

Gossip of the times was not infrequently contradictory. Poe's eyes are referred to by separate witnesses as of three different colors: blue, gray, and hazel.[233]

Fotunately, a substantial part of contemporary testimony is helpful.   "Ida Grey" suggests an interpretation of the poet's love life that biographers have overlooked: Poe's fondness for women reveals more colorful sidelights of his character than do his weaknesses for wine and song.   Poe's *amour* with Mrs. Osgood should scout thoroughly the notions entertained today, largely as a result of Joseph Wood Krutch's wild suppositions, that intemperance left him without normal sexual vitality.   More attention to the early reports would have prevented other grievous errors about Poe's character, such as the psychologist O. Hobart Mowrer's probably presumptive declaration, in *Learning Theory and Personality Dynamics* (1950), that "we can only say with confidence that his heterosexual adjustment was at best tenuous."

According to a short biography by Poe's friend T. H. Chivers, written about 1852 but unpublished until 1952, the poet made a most revealing confession while he was drinking.   He said to Chivers: "I am in the d——dst amour you ever knew a fellow to be in in all your life . . . "In Providence," [*sic*] by G—d!   I have just received a letter from her, in which she requests me to come on there this afternoon on the four o'clock Boat." [*sic*]   Her husband is a Painter—always from home—and a d——d fool at that!"   Richard Beale Davis, editor of *Chivers' Life of Poe* (1952), states that "Poe's ungallant remark points to Mrs. Osgood, whose husband fits the occupation and situation. And with the lady herself Poe made an excursion to Providence about this time, a journey Chivers probably knew nothing of. Almost surely this record would have supplied more ammunition for the mudslingers who were besmirching Poe and the poetess in the late forties. Even now it is additional serious evidence that the relationship may not have been on as high a plane as many biographers have tried to make it. Or it may merely indicate an inebriated Poe boasting of an imaginary conquest."

4. Griswold's Poe

> Edgar Allan Poe is dead. He died at Baltimore the day before yesterday. This announcement will startle many, *but few will be grieved by it.*
> —RUFUS WILMOT GRISWOLD[234]

The foregoing sentences by the Reverend Griswold, the biographer responsible for the incredible Poe legend, appeared only two days following the poet's death. He had been deputized by Poe to act as his literary executor, but he came closer to being a literary executioner. It is not fully known why he elected to impale Poe's reputation. Both he and the poet had courted the favor of Mrs. Whitman, so that Griswold, the biographer, may have been swayed, in part, by Griswold, the jealous rival. Possibly he still rankled with ill-feeling because of an earlier business misunderstanding with Poe. Whatever the causes, Griswold as the official biographer chose the role of castigator of his subject's character.

On the death of Poe, Rufus W. Griswold wrote an obituary signed "Ludwig" for the New York *Tribune* (Evening Edition), October 9, 1849. Many of the details derived from the autobiographical "Memorandum" (Harrison I, 344-345) which Poe had furnished him years before. This explains the inaccuracy of certain biographical statements in the obituary, since it already has been made clear that Poe deliberately falsified the record. But the remarkable feature of Griswold's biography is that the author's tone is openly hostile. In attempting to vilify what he considered the darker elements in Poe's nature, Griswold quoted a passage from Bulwer-Lytton's novel *The Caxtons* (VIII, 3) describing the character of Francis Vivian, a man dominated by cynicism and pride.

The "Ludwig" sketch became the basis for the more notorious "Memoir" in the third volume of Poe's *Works,* published in September, 1850. Griswold's slurs, his desire to vilify Poe's character, now became more than ever apparent. In the "Preface" to the "Memoir" he printed letters which Poe had written him, and which it is now generally known that Griswold had either forged or tampered with—letters obviously quoted to reflect unpleasantly on Poe. In the "Memoir" proper Griswold employed as sources not only the "Memorandum," but a sketch of Poe which had appeared in the Philadelphia *Saturday Museum* for February 25, 1843, and for which Poe himself must have furnished the major part of the data. Griswold further relied upon unauthentic anecdotes and malicious gossip. He closed the "Memoir" by presenting, this time without quotation marks, the passage from *The Caxtons,* which he had used in the "Ludwig" sketch.

> He was in many respects like Francis Vivian in Bulwer's novel of the "Caxtons." Passion, in him, comprehended many of the worst emotions which militate against human happiness. You could not contradict him, but you raised quick choler; you could not speak of wealth, but his cheek paled with gnawing envy. The astonishing natural advantage of this poor boy—his beauty, his readiness, the daring spirit that breathed around him like a fiery atmosphere—had raised his constitutional self-confidence into an arrogance that turned his very claims to admiration into prejudice against him. Irascible, envious—bad enough, but not the worst, for these salient angles were all varnished over with a cold repellent cynicism while his passions vented themselves in sneers. There seemed to him no moral susceptibility; and what was more remarkable in a proud nature, little or nothing of the true point of honor. He had, to a morbid excess, that desire to rise which is vulgarly called ambition, but no wish for the esteem or

the love of his species; only the hard wish to succeed—
not shine, not serve—succeed, that he might have the right
to despise a world which galled his self-conceit.[235]

Griswold was patently concerned only with reprehensible
aspects of Poe's character, almost entirely ignoring those
finer traits of generosity, sympathy, and kindness which were
known to his family and to a small circle of acquaintances.

Sarah Helen Whitman's *Edgar Poe and His Critics* (1860,
reprinted 1949) is a short book in which the woman to
whom Poe had been engaged toward the close of his life
sought to defend the poet's reputation against the slanders
of Griswold and others. Although knowing as well as
anybody the moral weaknesses that were Poe's toward the
end of his life, Mrs. Whitman wished to remember her
former lover only by the grace and poetic sensibility which
she felt to be so much a part of the man. She especially
recalled the directness and sincerity of his conversation; and
she insisted that "in the artistic utterance of poetic emotion,
he was at all times passionately genuine." She declared that
there is much in his writings which "is altogether incompat-
ible with that cold sensualism with which he has been so
ignorantly charged." It was Mrs. Whitman who invented the
genealogical myth that Poe was descended from "the old
Norman family of Le Poer, a name conspicuous in Irish
annals." The facts are that the poet's progenitors on his
father's side were mainly of Irish descent and that Poe is a
nickname, being derived from the Anglo-Saxon *pawa,*
"peacock." An early English political song preserves the
word in the proverbial phrase "As proud as a po,"[236] and
with this derivation Poe's dandyism is entirely in keeping.
Mrs. Whitman's account is that of a partial, fallible observer;
but her description is always charming, if not always
convincing.

William F. Gill's *The Life of Edgar Allan Poe* (1877) was,
according to its author, "the first complete life" of Poe, and
was written in large part to discount the slanders of Griswold.
"It has been the aim of the writer," Gill said, "to give an
unpartisan transcript of the life and character of Edgar Allan
Poe." But Gill was incapable of performing this desirable

function of the biographer. It is true that he was among the
first to suggest that Griswold, in publishing Poe's letters, had
tampered with the documents. Moreover, he rejected the
story of Poe's second trip abroad which Ingram was later
to accept. From the start, however, Gill was so much
concerned with vindicating Poe's memory that he could not
examine impartially the harsher and more forbidding side
of the poet's true nature. Because of the biography's
rambling and disjointed style as well as its excessive use of
quotation, the work fails to leave with the reader an impression of thorough dependability.

The symbol of Poe which remained in the memory of
Americans was that of the dark and sorrowful bird to which
Griswold changed him:

> The remarkable poem of *The Raven* was probably much
> more nearly than has been supposed, even by those who
> were intimate with him, a reflection and an echo of his
> own history. He was the bird's
>
> > —unhappy master,
> > Whom unmerciful disaster
> > Followed fast and followed faster
> > Till his song the burden bore—
> > Melancholy burden bore
> > Of "Nevermore," of "Nevermore"[237]

Writers later than Griswold repeated the inapt metaphor.
In 1868 the anonymous editor of *The Poetical Works of
Edgar Allan Poe* declared that "Of all the poets whose lives
have been a puzzle and a mystery to the world, there is no
one more difficult to be understood . . . Like his own Raven,
he is, to his reader, 'bird or fiend,' they know not which."
In 1926 Hervey Allen, the author of *Israfel,* entitled his
twenty-second chapter "The Raven and His Shadow," which
title he retained in the revisions of 1934 and 1949. Griswold's baseless slanders were bruited everywhere.

5. British to the Defense

Endeavoring to counteract Griswold's vicious atttacks on
Poe, the Englishman John Ingram wrote numerous articles
during the 1870's. This effort to vindicate Poe's memory

culminated in Ingram's *Edgar Allan Poe: His Life, Letters, and Opinions,* published in two volumes, London, 1880. Ingram not only brought together the Poe material which had been accumulating since the poet's death, but gathered a considerable amount of fresh biographical data, especially derived from Poe's female acquaintances, such as Mrs. Helen Whitman and Mrs. Marie Louise Shew. Although he extensively corresponded with Americans who were in possession of Poe material and should thus have produced an authoritative biography of the poet, Ingram had neither the literary skill nor the scholarly objectivity to perform the task. His hatred of Griswold led Ingram to whitewash Poe's character and to present the poet, despite serious lapses, as essentially a man of "generous and charitable disposition." With all its failure to consider fully the shadows in Poe's nature, Ingram's biography, in its sympathetic and generally faithful portrayal of Poe, was the best yet to appear.

Una Pope-Hennessy's *Edgar Allan Poe. 1809-1849. A Critical Biography* (London, 1934) was written following the author's residence in the United States, where, she tells us, she visited the localities associated with Poe's name. Her purpose was the presenting of an objective portrait of Poe, sketching both the lights and the shades of his character. In a measure she achieved this aim. The biography is a re-telling of Poe's life based, for the most part, on readily available sources. The book is scantily documented, and the bibliography probably does not account for all the research which went into its making. Although the biography is largely a simple, straightforward narrative interspersed with criticism, the author did not hesitate occasionally to romanticize and color her story. Among other things, she endeavored to demonstrate, more fully than had critics here-tofore, what she regarded as the autobiographical origins of many of the tales and poems. A staunch British defender of the poet, she avoided popular psychological hypotheses. Una Pope-Hennessy wrote essentially for the general public, the book marking no perceptible advance in Poe scholarship.

6. Conflict and Correction

It was in the United States that a number of ambitious writers now sought to explain the mystery of the great American poet. Three of these biographers of Poe were men of notably different background and profession, one of them being a literary scholar, another a psychiatrist, and yet another a novelist. Wide variation in their opinions was a natural result.

George E. Woodberry's first biography of Poe appeared as part of the American Men of Letters series in 1885. This work, revised and expanded into two volumes, was republished in 1909. Woodberry, never sympathizing with Poe either as man or writer, was inclined to support Griswold's portrait of the author, and yet at Richmond in the 1920's, on the opening of a Poe shrine, he leaned over to Mabbott and whispered, "John Allan is damned." Possessed of far more biographical and critical discernment than Griswold, Woodberry found it possible to view Poe less partially and with more objectivity than any biographer of the author had yet shown. He added many new facts to the Poe biography. He also collected and published a large number of new letters which throw fresh light on the man's personality and works. Woodberry's discussion of Poe's poems and tales shows a critical discrimination which still makes his books standard works of reference in Poe scholarship. Perhaps Woodberry's finest virtue is that he "knew the value of exact scholarship."[238]

James A. Harrison's biography of Poe (the first volume of the Virginia Edition of *The Complete Works of Edgar Allan Poe,* 1902) followed the biographical tradition set by Gill and Ingram. To remove conflicting impressions, Harrison smoothed over the rougher traits in Poe's character and mitigated the aspersions which had been cast on his memory. Harrison quoted four pages by R. H. Stoddard, who described the famous gatherings of literary folk at the home of Anne C. Lynch. Only occasionally did Harrison present any new facts of significance or show any real insight into Poe's personality.

Dr. John W. Robertson, a specialist in mental disorders, subjected the poet to analysis in *Edgar A. Poe. A Psychopathic Study* (1922). According to this medical authority, Poe was not an opium addict, nor was he a confirmed drunkard. Rather he was a victim of dipsomania—a disease, Robertson contends, inherited from his father—and far from taking delight in alcohol, Poe between attacks had a strong aversion for liquor. His disease, the physician claims, finally developed into a serious brain disorder which is evidenced in the incoherent brilliance of *Eureka*. Insofar as Robertson confined himself to medical ground, he presented a thesis that is worthy of careful consideration; but he digressed so much in presenting his thesis that the book wearies the reader, and along with material that seems to have medical validity, there are many biographical and critical comments that cannot command serious attention. It is worthy of notice that the psychiatrist Dr. Robertson did not find evidence that Poe was a genuine "psychotic," though he did argue that his mind and senses were seriously impaired from alcoholic overindulgence.

Israfel: the Life and Times of Edgar Allan Poe (1926), by the novelist Hervey Allen, added little to the factual life of Poe, except for biographical detail in the *Ellis & Allen Papers,* which Allen was among the first to examine in the Library of Congress. Relying mainly on his biographical predecessors, especially Woodberry, Allen romanticized and fictionalized his subject. To him, the poet was the hero of "The Raven," the anonymous appearance of which Allen found significant. Allen attested that "With the revelation of the author's name, Poe found himself instantly famous, the object of curiosity, and the strange, romantic, diabolic, and tragic figure that he has ever since remained." He described Poe's long struggle with starvation, emphasizing the poet's "addiction" to alcohol and particularly to opium. Allen further traced the evidence in Poe of mental and physical decay which culminated in his death. Allen's

Israfel, which has been twice revised, possesses literary rather than scholarly merit.

Joseph W. Krutch's *Edgar Allan Poe, A Study in Genius* (1926) is a psychoanalytical examination of Poe. Highly speculative, it attempts to explore the hidden recesses of the poet's mind, and to account for the qualities which distinguish his work. Poe's idiosyncrasies are due in part, Krutch says, to sexual inhibition which may be attributed hypothetically to a morbid fascination for his mother's memory as well as to a feeling of inferiority which developed from his repressed life in Richmond. Poe, Krutch adds, was psychopathic, for in his literary work he sought to escape from his inhibitions. Usher and Dupin thus become projections of his inner self—Usher, the irrational, morbid neurotic who in essence Poe really was; Dupin, the cold, uncompromising analyst whom Poe created as a defense against a growing fear of insanity. Krutch's book is too much veined with psychological speculations, and conflict, not correction, was the contribution of this biography.

Two bulky volumes constitute Mary E. Phillips' *Edgar Allan Poe, the Man* (1926). The writing of this book was plainly a labor of love. It is essentially a defense of Poe in which Miss Phillips sought, on practical grounds, to prove that because Poe was a hard worker he was not a hard drinker. His moral lapses toward the close of his life, she believed, were due mainly to inherited nervous weakness. Miss Phillips's handling of her sources was often clumsy and amateurish; she quoted frequently from a secondary source when the primary source was at hand. The many illustrations, however, constituted a valuable feature of the biography.

Arthur Hobson Quinn's *Edgar Allan Poe, A Critical Biography* (1941) is a veritable compendium of facts on the author, often so interpreted as to constitute a defense. Quinn, however, has made a commendable attempt to sift conflicting rumor and evidence and to arrive at a true understanding of many aspects of Poe's character and disputed episodes of his life. As a specialist in the drama, Quinn dealt at greater length than other biographers with the theatrical careers of Poe's father and mother. He was among the first to treat Poe seriously as a thinker, especially analyzing evidence in *Eureka;* and he argued, with cause, that during the last two years of his life Poe was far from losing his mental vigor. Considerable space is devoted to a minute examination of the Griswold forgeries, which Quinn revealed as more extensive and far-reaching than had hitherto been suspected. For the first time, too, Quinn presented material relating to *Phantasy Pieces,* a projected volume of Poe's tales. Some readers find Quinn weak in his critical evaluation of Poe's work, and his countless details not always integrated. Yet the biography is an unquestionable—in fact, a major— contribution to Poe scholarship.

7. Triumph of Fact

Besides the biographies already referred to, there is the highly imaginative, if not purely fictional, narrative by Mary Newton Stanard. Her book, *The Dreamer,* appeared in 1909 and was frankly sub-titled "A Romantic Rendering of the Life-Story of Edgar Allan Poe." Miss Stanard allowed her imagination a free course, limning a sympathetic picture of the poet especially in the period of his Southern up-bringing. She was, though inaccurate in both, more successful at creating historical scenes than at describing the true character of Poe. Caroline Ticknor's *Poe's Helen,* which was published in 1916, is more limited in aim but is substantially a better explanation of Poe's poetry and also of the woman who helped to inspire him—Mrs. Sarah Helen Whitman.

About the only contribution made by C. Alphonso Smith's *Edgar Allan Poe* in 1921 occurs in Chapter One, entitled "The World-Author." For possibly the first time, significant documentation of this high claim was here argued persuasively. A less ambitious and shorter study is Sherwin Cody's *Poe—Man, Poet, and Creative Thinker,* published in 1924. In discussing Poe as a thinker, Cody touched on an important but neglected aspect of the poet's attainments.

In 1926, Jeannette Augustus Marks' *Genius and Disaster; Studies in Drugs and Genius* revived unfounded tales of the poet's depravity.

The legendary portrait was delivered a damaging blow in 1929, with the publication of Mabbott's *Doings in Gotham,* in which Mabbott, able to discount conclusively stories of Poe's unreliability, claimed that "he gave the best that was in him to whatever task was at hand."[239] While living in New York, Poe applied himself diligently to writing. In general he stayed sober. According to his friend William Gowans, he expended his spare time from work in cultivating the society of influential literary people. It was in New York in January, 1847, that he was assaulted by Thomas Dunn English over a loan. But a year later, in reply to a printed attack by Dr. English, Poe vindicated himself when he won his suit for libel against the New York *Mirror.*

Two relatively recent biographical sketches differ on important particulars in their interpretation. First, in the introduction to Philip Van Doren Stern's group of selections called *Edgar Allan Poe* (1945), Stern followed the well established path of the inaccurate legend. As for the numerous women in the poet's life, he said: "Poe's association with them all was probably on an asexual basis." As for alcohol, Poe is labelled an "irresponsible drunkard." Stern is on firm ground only in his analysis of Poe's literary achievement and observes that the poet "was one of the first to establish the dark tradition in American literature, a tradition carried on by Hawthorne, Melville, Bierce, and Faulkner among others."[240] The author of the second recent biographical sketch, Arthur Hobson Quinn, in 1946 wrote a provocative "Introduction" for the first two volumes entitled *The Complete Poems and Stories of Edgar Allan Poe.* This account is unquestionably the best short life of the poet to date. Eschewing gossip and sensationalism, Quinn demonstrated the known facts; namely, the principal data in the career of Poe compose here a straightforward credible story. On the basis of this offering together with his *Edgar Allan Poe, a Critical Biography,* Quinn has won the right to say that "The mystery so often associated with

Poe's life and nature is unjustified."[241] More than any other scholar, Quinn has adhered to facts, not surmises; in the history of Poe biography he will surely rank as the first giant among the legend breakers.

Papers and special studies, although too numerous to discuss fully, cast additional light on the life of Poe. This material, comprising the battleground for settlement of old debates and the field for presentation of fresh discoveries, is in significance second to none. The most important of these authors was Killis Campbell, who in 1916 communicated information about the poet's schooling in a *Dial* paper, "New Notes on Poe's Early Years." Sixteen years later, in 1932, he made a substantial contribution to scholarship in *The Mind of Poe, and Other Studies*. A paper in the *New Mexico Quarterly Review* (Autumn, 1949) praised *The Histrionic Mr. Poe* (1949) by N. Bryllion Fagin, for showing that Poe "had a less sombre side when he simulated the parts of a scholarly gentleman and of a courtly southern lover." The greatest Poe scholar today is Mabbott, who allows no year to slip by without unearthing new facts on the life or works of his favorite poet. Other prominent, major scholars include Mozelle S. Allen, James O. Bailey, Roy P. Basler, Carroll Laverty, D. M. McKeithan, Arlin Turner, John W. Ostrom, who completed a definitive edition of *The Letters of Edgar Allan Poe* (1948); and Richard Beale Davis, editor of *Chivers' Life of Poe* (1952).

8. Death of a Legend

The fables of Edgar Allan Poe's gay past started at the University of Virginia. Like the aristocratic students at Charlottesville, the poorer Poe had a "fling" during his youthful college days. When in the army in South Carolina and Virginia, he had made a creditable record, rising in a short span from the lowest to the highest non-commissioned grade. But at college? There he dismantled his earlier good reputation by his riotous behavior and by his reference to himself in the later "Memorandum" as a young hellion.

Undisciplined as he occasionally was, Poe actually was hardly a member of the wildest set at Charlottesville, where the students of the University of Virginia became famous as gay blades—pampered youths who indulged freely in drinking, gaming, and worse, who indeed pursued an almost unchecked course in their night life. The noise of their revelry spread everywhere, a number of the lads regularly conducting intimacies with the daughters of their Negro laundresses.[242] The real circumstances of Poe's irregular conduct at Charlottesville look pale beside the purple hues of the fastest set. Poe now and again must have felt a certain inadaquacy in himself, for in order to compete with these swashbucklers, he invented yarns about his trips to foreign lands and exaggerated his prowess as a drinker. Thus he built the foundation stone of his own legend.

In an excellent but unpublished study, *American Criticism of Poe since the Poe Centenary* (1931), Gay Wilson Allen made a firm contribution when he successfully maintained that the real Poe had little in common with the legendary figure. Allen showed that in the popular mind the man and his works have always been confused. Poe wrote weird stories; therefore he was weird himself. Poe wrote psychological fiction; therefore he was "psychological" himself. This sort of popular reasoning is difficult to eradicate and persists to a minor degree in some quarters today. Often the stories in question are based on literary sources or local happenings and therefore wholly unconnected with the author's own behavior, yet thoughtless readers sometimes read into them the very actions of Poe himself, his autobiographical confession to a fantastic act, to a dark deed of crime or degeneracy. Such a legend is not solidly founded and will not sustain a rigid examination.

As Allen further observed, Poe's madcap visit to Mrs. Whitman at Providence on November 7, 1848—together with the daguerrotype taken of him next morning when he looked his worst—"is perhaps responsible more than any other incident in the poet's life for the 'Poe Legend.'" The escapades of a man in love are hardly unique and are understandable enough to deserve no special comment. Where

Poe has suffered injury is in the Providence picture. In that daguerreotype his eyes are glazed, his face is bloated, and he is the incarnation of debauchery. The man in this daguerreotype scarcely resembles the person appearing in the Osgood portrait, which may have some relevance here. Yet the daguerreotype has been everywhere circulated, to create the lasting depiction of a poet physically debilitated. Actually the daguerreotype reflects only Poe's appearance after a single night of dissipation. The Osgood portrait, flattering though it may be, shows the face of an intellectual, of a sensitive man of refinement and some scholarship.

What, next, were the true factors in Poe's death? Three theories may be mentioned: one, Poe's untimely death was hastened by his addiction to drugs and alcohol; two, by a psychotic or neurotic personality; and three, by a combination of these factors, with the additional complication of a disease not hitherto prominently featured in the accounts of his demise.

First of all, alcoholism may have been a weakening element in him derived from his father David Poe. How his father died is unknown, although it is established that David sometimes drank to excess. Better evidence of this sort may come from his brother William, whose end, it is said, was in part precipitated by acute alcoholism. Drinking certainly never did the poet any good physically, so that it may well have been an attendant cause of his early decline. But there is not enough evidence to warrant the claim that alcoholism was either a major or the principal cause. Besides, as the aged sots of New York's Bowery amply testify, persons long inured to drink are not prone to die early. As for drugs, Poe clearly was not a confirmed dope addict. Moreover, drug addiction at times accompanies longevity and is not the impulse of sudden deaths. The dope-fiend Coleridge lived to be sixty-two and the opium-eater De Quincey died in his seventy-fifth year. In other words, this first proposal must be classified, at best, as a background element, and a diagnosis must be sought which is more consistent with and descriptive of what actually occurred to Poe.

The second possibility of Poe's having been psychotic hardly describes the conditions under which the poet died and is based on such shaky grounds that it constitutes, not a testimonial of proof, but a kind of stumbling block. If the hypothesis is to be dealt with, one might argue, on the basis of analogy, that since his sister Rosalie is stated to have been mentally unstable, Poe was perhaps so, too. The analogy is untrustworthy inasmuch as it could be applied with an opposite effect; that is, Rosalie lived to a fairly advanced age, whereas her brother died at forty. The lion in the path of the whole "psychotic theorizing" is precisely this: a genuine psychotic would be unlikely to accomplish the work that Poe did, and since he was productive until the end, he cannot be designated either a simpleton or the decrepit case that Ezra Pound finally became. Now, it is possible to entertain the idea that he was neurotic, that through worry over a disease that was destroying his health he developed, as people sometimes do, an indefinite kind of neurosis. Perhaps this happened; perhaps not. The large point in either eventuality, is that a neurosis ordinarily is not pernicious enough to precipitate or hasten a person's actual death.

It is the third possibility, that of a combination of factors involving at least one principal malady, which seems most likely to lead to the truth. A broad generalization like this has the advantage of showing the relation of minor ailments to each other before they culminate, as they usually do, in a final serious illness. Thus during more than one period of his life Poe was poorly fed—he mentions in his letters that he was obliged at times to subsist on "dandelion greens" picked by Mrs. Clemm—so that a mild form of malnutrition may have made it hard for him to resist disease and its ravaging consequences.

Poe sometimes doubtless suffered from exposure to the bitter Northern winters when, as often happened, he was thinly clad, for in the biographical records there are pointed references to his threadbare garments. It is certain that he exhausted his energies with long hours of hard work on the manifold problems of his manuscripts. It may be that

the bevy of women with whom he was often associated made
further inroads on his vitality. All of these factors had a
bearing on his health, and together they may have rendered
him an easy victim to a debilitating disease.

There is no question that he was ill during the last decade
of his life, and there is a patent lead on the nature of his
infirmity in the Poe letters. On December 30, 1846, he
wrote his friend N. P. Willis that "I myself have been long
and dangerously ill." He used here the word "long," a
statement in accord with his earlier collapse in 1839, so that
his illness of 1846 may have been with him for some seven
years.

What was wrong with Poe? Perhaps he had tuberculosis.
This disease was rampant in his family; its dread figure
overshadowed the end of his mother Elizabeth, his foster
mother Mrs. Allan, his brother William, and his wife
Virginia. Tuberculosis combined with alcoholism occasioned the demise of his brother William. Virginia Poe,
who died in 1847, is said in 1842 to have broken a blood
vessel in her throat while singing, but since a broken blood
vessel would likely have resulted in her immediate death,
the chances are that it was a pulmonary condition that swelled her throat with blood. To this condition Virginia refers
in her valentine poem to Edgar (1846), in which she says
that "Love shall heal my weakened lungs" (1. 8). The
inference of "consumption" seems obvious enough. When
this account was given to Ernest George Reuter, M. D., of
San Antonio, Texas, he diagnosed Virginia's ailment as
tuberculosis. He specified that, in his opinion, Poe's com-
plaint was the same.

Dr. Reuter cited poor weight and a weak stomach as
conducive to tuberculosis—symptoms characteristic of the
undernourished Poe, particularly the retching which,
according to his own declaration, he endured before the
Providence daguerreotype was taken. Dr. Reuter also
named extreme irritability as a symptom of tuberculosis and
mentioned, in this connection, Poe's well-known fits of bad
temper. For further evidence, there is the recently-unearth-
ed letter, dated December 24, 1848, of Amos Bardwell

Heywood, the brother of Poe's "Annie," which states that
the poet was "an inveterate fault finder" and calls this "the
predominant trait of his character."[243]

Another circumstance favoring tuberculosis as the major
complication is this, the stimulating nature of its toxemia
is widely recognized.[244] This disease, then, better accounts
for his fevered literary productivity than his immersion in
drugs and drink, which deaden a man's senses. Still another
point, though Dr. Reuter says it seldom appears in medical
texts, is that tuberculosis sometimes gives people heightened
sexual drive. Camille is the celebrated example in fictional
literature; Poe, if this diagnosis is accurate, would be a
famous example from life.

There is, frankly, little need to expand on the theory in
detail, for a piece of evidence contemporary with Poe may
now be cited as offering a reasonable solution to the matter.
On December 15, 1846, the New York *Morning Express*
carried the following notice about Poe's ailment:

> ILLNESS OF EDGAR A. POE—We regret to learn that
> this gentleman and his wife are both dangerously ill with
> consumption.[245]

Nothing is said of consumption in Philip Van Doren
Stern's account of Poe's death in the *Saturday Review of
of Literautre* for October 15, 1949. When Poe was found
unconscious at Ryan's Fourth Ward Polls on October 3,
1849, to die four days later in the hospital, he may· or may
not have been in this condition from the use of drugs or
stimulants. The two reports by Dr. J. E. Snodgrass and the
one by John Sartain came seven, eighteen, and thirty-four
years, respectively, after Poe's fatality,[246] so that there seems
now no way of knowing for certain if he was "drugged." Of
one thing, though, it appears possible to be sure. A man
of normal health probably would have survived Poe's
experience, and other men used as "repeaters" in the voting
on that election day unquestionably did.

Early notices of the death of Poe featured him as a casualty
of alcohol. Though Chivers reported that the poet left
Richmond suffering from "chilliness and exhaustion," he
tended to emphasize that it was "spirits" which induced in

him "a state of stupor."[247] About 1851 J. E. Cooke, in his *Poe as a Literary Critic* (first published in 1946), stated that his friend Poe's "lecture [Richmond, 1849] ended in the midst of general applause, and Poe disappeared soon afterwards, going northward—to fall a victim in Baltimore to a wild orgy and die suddenly."[248] This is the dark portrait of the poet which has remained in the minds of most people. But this is not all of the story. Reports of Poe's death, indicating disease as the cause, became known a little later. Cooke was convinced enough by these later reports to revise his earlier description: "The lecture ended in the midst of applause, and Poe disappeared soon afterwards, going northward—to fall a victim in Baltimore to disease and die suddenly."[249]

NOTES

1. T. O. Mabbott, "Poe's Tale, 'The Lighthouse,' " *Notes and Queries* (April 25, 1942), CLXXXII, 226-227; also excluded is "The Pirates," which appeared in the *North American* on October 27, 1827, with an introductory note by William Henry Poe, but in "Edgar Allan Poe: A Find," *Notes and Queries* (April 13, 1926), CL, 241, Mabbott says: "I believe that the tale is, at least in essence, by Edgar A. Poe." —On "The Atlantis, a Southern World," see A. H. Quinn, *Edgar Allan Poe, A Critical Biography* (New York, 1941), pp. 757-761; hereafter cited as Quinn.

2. T. O. Mabbott, "Newly Identified Verses by Poe," a reprint in the Henry E. Huntington Library from *Notes and Queries* for July 29, 1939. "A Lost Jingle by Poe," *Notes and Queries* (November 23, 1940), CLXXIX, 371; " 'Poe' on Intemperance," *Notes and Queries* (July 18, 1942), CLXXXIII, 34-35; and "Poe's 'Original Conundrums,' " *Notes and Queries* (June 5, 1943), CLXXXIV, 328-329.

3. Killis Campbell (editor), *The Poems of Edgar Allan Poe* (New York, 1917), pp. 302-303, especially xliv-liii; hereafter cited as Campbell's edition.

4. Quinn, p. 337. Poe's "Conversation" was revised to "The Destruction of the World" in 1843. Ernest Boll, "The Manuscript of *The Murders of the Rue Morgue,* and Poe's Revisions," *Modern Philology* (1943), XL, 302-315.

5. Campbell's edition, p. xxxv.

6. Enid Starkie, *Baudelaire* (New York, 1933), p. 170.

7. James A. Harrison (editor), *The Complete Works of Edgar Allan Poe* (New York, 1902), XIV, 273; hereafter cited as Harrison.

8. Quinn, p. 600.

9. Voltaire antedated Poe in the use of detective fiction; Mozelle S. Allen, "Poe's Debt to Voltaire," *University of Texas Studies in English* (1935), XV, 63-75; Percy G. Adams, "Poe, Critic of Voltaire," *Modern Language Notes* (1942), LVII, 273-275.

10. Horace Gregory, "Within the Private View," *Partisan Review* (1943), X, 267.

11. W. K. Wimsatt, Jr., "Poe and the Mystery of Mary Rogers," *Publications of the Modern Language Association* (March, 1941), LVI, 230-248; and Samuel C. Worthen, "A Strange Aftermath of the Mystery of 'Marie Rogêt' (Mary Rogers)," *Proceedings of the New Jersey Historical Society* 1942), LX, 116-123.

12. For other possible burlesques by Poe, see Thomas H. McNeal's paper, "Poe's *Zenobia*: An Early Satire on Margaret Fuller," *Modern Language Quarterly* (1950), XI, 205-216.

13. Edith S. Krappe, "A Possible Source for Poe's 'The Tell Tale Heart' and 'The Black Cat,'" *American Literature* (1940), XII, 84-88.

14. Walter F. Taylor, "Israfel in Motley, A Study of Poe's Humor," *Sewanee Review* (1934), XLII, 330-339.

15. Blanche Colton Williams (editor), "Introduction," *Tales by Edgar Allan Poe* (New York ,1929), p. xv.

16. Arlin Turner, "Sources of Poe's 'A Descent into the Maelström,'" *Journal of English and Germanic Philology* (1947), XLVI, 298-301.—On the source of "A Tale of the Ragged Mountains," see Henry Austin, "Poe as a Plagiarist and his Debt to Macaulay," *Literature* (1899), V, 82-84; J. H. Whitty, "Poe and Sources," *Literary Review* (August 18, 1923), III, 918; for further data on other tales, see Cornelia Varner, "Notes on Poe's Use of Contemporary

Materials in Certain of His Stories," *Journal of English and Germanic Philology* (1923), XXXII, 77-80.

17. Paull F. Baum, "Poe's 'To Helen,'" *Modern Language Notes* (1949), LXIV, 289-297.

18. Anonymous, "Valentine by Edgar Allan Poe Found Here; Poem in Morose Vein Hitherto Unpublished," *New York Times* (February 21, 1932), III, 2:7; and Sydney R. McLean, "A Valentine," *Colophon* (Autumn, 1935), I, 183-187.

19. Harrison, VII, xlvii.

20. Agnes M. Bondurant, *Poe's Richmond* (Richmond, 1942), p. 49.

21. T. O. Mabbott, "On Poe's 'Tales of the Folio Club,'" *Sewanee Review* (1928), XXXVI, 171-176.

22. For the view that Poe was "pretty deeply indebted to his age," see Killis Campbell *The Mind of Poe* (Cambridge, 1932), pp. 101-ff.

23. T. O. Mabbott (editor, "Introduction," *Politian: An Unfinished Tragedy* (Menasha, Wisconsin, 1923), pp. IV ff; "The Text of Poe's Play 'Politian,'" *Notes and Queries* (July 14, 1945), CLXXXIX, 14; and W. B. Gates, "Poe's *Politian* Again," *Modern Language Notes* (1934), XLIX, 561.

24. Killis Campbell, *The Mind of Poe* (Cambridge, Mass., 1932), p. 103.

25. Harold H. Scudder, "Poe's 'Balloon Hoax,'" *American Literature* (1949), XXI, 179-190; Sidney E. Lind, "Poe and Mesmerism," *Publications of the Modern Language Association* (1947), LXII, 1077-1094; and T. O. Mabbott, "English Publications of Poe's 'Valdemar Case,'" *Notes and Queries* (November 21, 1942), CLXXXIII, 311-312.

26. Ernest E. Leisy, "Folklore in American Literature," *College English* (1946), VIII, 124.

27. Floyd Stovall, "Poe's Debt to Coleridge," *University of Texas Studies in English* (1930), X, 70-128; George Kummer, "Another Poe-Coleridge Parallel?" *American Literature* (1936), VIII, 72; and Frank M. Durham, "A Possible Relationship Between Poe's 'To Helen' and Milton's *Paradise Lost*," *American Literature* (1945), XVI, 340-343.

[28.] Martin S. Shockley, *"Timour the Tartar* and Poe's *Tamerlane," Publications of the Modern Language Association* (1941), LVI, 1103-1106.

[29.] On Poe's debt to Byron, see the notes in Campbell's edition (pp. xliv-xlv) as well as Roy P. Basler, "Byronism in Poe's 'To One in Paradise,' " *American Literature* (1937), IX, 232-236.

[30.] Hoover H. Jordan, "Poe's Debt to Thomas Moore," *Publications of the Modern Language Association* (1948), LXIII, 753-757.

[31.] T. O. Mabbott, "Poe's 'Israfel,' " *Explicator* (1944), II, 57:8.

[32.] Harrison, VII, 168-171, 257; Campbell's edition, pp. 197-199.

[33.] James Routh, "Notes on the Sources of Poe's Poetry: Coleridge, Keats, Shelley," *Modern Language Notes* (1914), XXIX, 72-75; Marvin Laser, "The Growth and Structure of Poe's Concept of Beauty," *English Literary History* (1948), XV, 69-84.

[34.] Chateaubriand, *Génie du Christianisme* (Paris, 1836), III, 43. Other models have been suggested; Fred A. Dudley, "Tintinnabulation: And a Source of Poe's 'The Bells,' " *American Literature* (1932), IV, 296-300.

[35.] R. A. Law, "A Source for Annabel Lee," *Journal of English and Germanic Philology* (1922), XXI, 341-346.

[36.] Killis Campbell, "A Bit of Chiversian Mystification," *University of Texas Studies in English* (1930), X, 152-154. R. B. Davis seems to agree that Chivers wrote the poem himself; see *Chivers' Life of Poe* (New York, 1952), p. 116.

[37.] Nelson F. Adkins, "Poe's 'Ulalume,' " *Notes and Queries* (January 14, 1933), CLXIV, 30-31; and T. O. Mabbott, "Poe's 'Ulalume,' " *Notes and Queries* (February 25, 1933), CLXIV, 143; as well as Kenneth Leroy Daughrity, "A Source for a Line of Poe's 'Ulalume,' " *Notes and Queries* (July 11, 1931), CLXI, 27; Roy P. Basler, "Poe's 'Ulalume,' " *Explicator* (1944), II, 49:7; and J. O. Bailey, "The Geography of Poe's 'Dreamland' and 'Ulalume,' " *Studies in Philology* (1948), XLV, 512-523.

38. Oral S. Coad, "The Meaning of Poe's 'Eldorado,'"
Modern Language Notes (1944), LIX, 59-61; T. O. Mabbott,
"The Sources of Poe's 'Eldorado,'" *Modern Language Notes*
(1945), LX, 312-314; and Fred A. Dudley, "Tintinnabulation: And a Source of Poe's 'The Bells,'" *American Literature* (1932), IV, 296-300.

39. D. L. Clark, "The Sources of Poe's *The Pit and the
Pendulum*," *Modern Language Notes* (1929), XLIV, 349-
356; Ruth L. Hudson, "Poe and Disraeli," *American Literature* (1937), VIII, 402-416; and the doctoral dissertation at
Columbia in 1924 of D. L. Clark, *Charles Brockden Brown,
a Critical Biography* and Harry R. Warfel's study, published
by the University of Florida Press, 1950.

40. Lucille King, "Notes on Poe's Sources," *University of
Texas Studies in English* (1930), X, 128-134; Grace Smith,
Poe's "Metzengerstein," *Modern Language Notes* (1933),
XLVIII, 356-359; Celia Whitt, "Poe and *The Mysteries of
Udolpho*," *University of Texas Studies in English* (1937),
XVII, 124-131; Killis Campbell, "Three Notes on Poe,"
American Literature (1933), IV, 385-386; and Cortel
Holsappel, "Poe and Conradus," *American Literature*
(1932), IV, 62-65.

41. Palmer Cobb, "The Influence of E. T. A. Hoffmann
on the Tales of Edgar Allan Poe," *Studies in Philology*
(1908), III, 31, 49, 70, 81; and Gustav Gruener, "Notes on
the Influences of E. T. A. Hoffmann upon Edgar Allan Poe,"
Publications of the Modern Language Association (1940),
XIX, 1-25.

42. Franz Karl Mohr, "The Influence of Eichendorff's
'Ahnung und Gegenwart' on Poe's 'Masque of the Red
Death,'" *Modern Language Quarterly* (1949), X, 3-15;
Killis Campbell, *op. cit.*, pp. 167-171; Quinn, p. 395; Fannye
N. Cherry, "The Source of Poe's 'Three Sundays in a
Week,'" *American Literature* (1930), II, 232-235; T. O.
Mabbott, "Poe and Dr. Lardner," *American Notes and
Queries* (1943), III, 115; Archer Taylor, "Poe's Dr. Lardner,
and 'Three Sundays in a Week,'" *American Notes and
Queries* (1944), III, 153-155; Régis Messac, *Influences fran-
çaises dans l'oeuvre d'Edgar Allan Poe* (Paris, 1929), p. 111;

and Harry R. Warfel, "Poe's Dr. Percival; A Note on *The Fall of the House of Usher*," *Modern Language Notes* (1939), LIV, 129-131.

43. James O. Bailey, "Sources for Poe's *Arthur Gordon Pym*, 'Hans Pfaal,' and Other Pieces," *Publications of the Modern Language Association* (1942), LVII, 513-535; Arlin Turner, "A Note on Poe's Julius Rodman," *University of Texas Studies in English* (1930), X, 152-154; and "Another Source of Poe's 'Julius Rodman,'" *American Literature* (1936), VIII, 69-70.

44. John G. Varner, "Poe's *Tale of Jerusalem* and *The Talmud*," *American Book Collector* (1935), VI, 56-57. The quotation is from A. P. C. Griffin (editor), *Talmud* (London, 1901), folio 49, column 2. On Poe's tale as a burlesque of Horace Smith's *Zillah*, see James S. Wilson, "The Devil Was in It," *American Mercury* (1931), XXIV, 219.

45. Harrison, VII, xlvii.—For the belief that Poe is best known today for his short stories, see Darrell Abel, "Edgar Poe: A Centennial Estimate," *University of Kansas City Review* (1949), XVI, 77-96.

46. Harrison, XIII, 150.

47. *Ibid.*, XI, 107.—H. M. Belden, "Poe's Criticism of Hawthorne," *Anglica* (1901), XXIII, 376-405.

48. R. K. Root, *The Poetical Career of Alexander Pope* (Princeton, N. J., 1938), pp. 47-50.

49. Harrison, XIII, 37.

50. N. Bryllion Fagin, "Poe—Drama Critic," *The Theatre Annual* (1946), p. 28.

51. Harrison, VIII, 281; XI, 71; and XIV, 273.

52. *Ibid.*, XIV, 290.

53. P. E. More, "A Note on Poe's Method," *Studies in Philology* (1923), XX, 303-304.

54. J. J. Rubin, "John Neal's Poetics as an Influence on Whitman and Poe," *New England Quarterly* (1941), XIV, 359-362; Margaret Alterton, *Origins of Poe's Critical Theory*, *University of Iowa Humanistic Studies* (II, 3, 1925), Ch. IV.

55. Quinn and O'Neill, II, 1087.

56. W. L. Werner, "Poe's Theories and Practices of Poetic Technique," *American Literature* (1930), II, 162.

57. G. W. Allen, *American Prosody* (New York, 1935), pp. 56-90; Allen's full discussion of Poe's theories appeared in his doctoral dissertation, *A History of American Prosody from Bryant to Whitman* (Madison, Wis., 1934), pp. 95-158 esp. 157-158; Richard C. Pettigrew, "Poe's Rime," *American Literature* (1932), IV, 150-159.

58. Charles S. Sydnor, *The Development of Southern Sectionalism,* 1819-1848; W. H. Stevenson and E. M. Coulter (editors), *A History of the South* (Baton Rouge, La., 1948), V, 308.—Poe's attitude towards New England writers was thoroughly Southern, says Jay B. Hubbell, "Literary Nationalism in the Old South," *American Studies in Honor of W.K. Boyd* (Durham, N. C., Duke University Press, 1940), pp. 175-220.

59. E. E. Leisy, *Reinterpretation of American Literature* (New York, 1928), p. 106.

60. Clement Wood, *Poets of America* (New York, 1925), p. 25.

61. Napier Wilt, "Poe's Attitude Toward His *Tales: A New Document,*" *Modern Philology* (1927), XXV, 101-105.

62. Constance Rourke, *American Humor* (New York, 1931), pp. 185-186.—Poe's defects as a critic, his savagery and showmanship, were his virtues as a journalist, says Percy H. Boynton, "Poe and Journalism," *English Journal* (1932), XXI, 345-352.

63. J. W. Krutch, *Edgar Allan Poe, A Study in Genius* (New York, 1931), p. 84.

64. Samuel C. Worthen, "Poe and the Beautiful Cigar Girl," *American Literature* (1948), XX, 305-312.

65. H. B. Parkes, "Poe, Hawthorne, Melville: An Essay in Sociological Criticism," *Partisan Review* (1949), XVI, 162.

66. N. Bryllion Fagin (editor), *Poe as a Literary Critic* (Baltimore, 1946), p. 6.

67. Cullen B. Colton, "George Hooker Colton and the Publication of 'The Raven,' " *American Literature* (1938), X, 319-330.—Poe refers to G. H. Colton in *Autography.*

68. Angeline H. Lograsso, "Poe's Piero Maroncelli," *Publications of the Modern Language Association* (1943), LVIII, 780-789.

69. Don C. Seitz (editor), *A Chapter on Autography by Edgar Allan Poe* (New York, 1926).

70. E. L. Griggs, "Five Sources of Edgar Allan Poe's 'Pinakidia,'" *American Literature* (1929), I, 196-199.

71. Poe and Davis were friends; *The Magic Staff:An Autobiography of Andrew Jackson Davis* (New York, 1857), p. 317.

72. Edward Shanks, *Edgar Allan Poe* (New York, 1937), p. 102.

73. An able investigator was David K. Jackson, *Poe and The Southern Literary Messenger* (Richmond, 1934); "Poe and the 'Messenger,'" *Southern Literary Messenger* (1939), I, 5-11.

74. One branch of the subject has been studied by Nelson F. Adkins, "'Chapter on American Cribbage': Poe and Plagiarism," *Papers of the Bibliographical Society of America* (1948), XLII, 169-210.

75. Quinn, pp. 453-455; Harriet Monroe, "Poe and Longfellow," *Poetry* (1926), XXIX, 266-274.

76. Edmund Wilson, "Poe as a Literary Critic," *Nation* (October 31, 1942), CLV, 452.

77. T. S. Eliot, "The Metaphysical Poets," *Selected Essays* (New York, 1932), p. 244.

78. This list includes notices of Theodore Irving's translation of Hernando de Soto's *The Conquest of Florida,* Washington Irving's *The Crayon Miscellany,* No. II, Dr. F. L. Hawk's *Contributions to the Ecclesiastical History of the United States of America,* J. K. Paulding's *Slavery in the United States,* H. Manly's *The South Vindicated,* John Armstrong's *Notices of the War of* 1812, Frederick Von Raumer's *England in* 1835, G. W. Featherstonhaugh's translation of A. Manzoni's *I Promessi Sposi, or the Bethrothed Lovers,* E. S. Barrett's *The Heroine: or Adventures of Cherubina,* Calvin Colton's *Thoughts on the Religious State of the Country,* Bulwer's *Zanoni, a Novel,* and finally *The*

Poems of Alfred Tennyson, as well as *The Works of Lord Bolingbroke,* and *Corse de Leon; or The Brigand.*

79. Opposite the first part in his copy of Harrison's edition, Mabbott has written: "Doubted (Rejected by Campbell on what seem to be sure grounds *but* perhaps are not). I rather think Poe did it." Opposite the second part, Mabbott has added further: "Much dispute on authorship—but an academic question—Poe surely *had a hand* in this."

80. Frederick W. Coburn, "Poe as Seen by the Brother of 'Annie,'" *New England Quarterly* (1943), XVI, 468-476.

81. Killis Campbell, "Three Notes on Poe," *American Literature* (1933), IV, 385-386.

82. In an article in the *New York Mirror* entitled "The Successful Novel!!" Theodore S. Fay satirized Poe under the name of Mr. Bulldog. Frank Luther Mott, *A History of American Magazines,* 1741-1850 (New York, 1930), pp. 635-636. Thomas Dunn English satirized Poe as Marmaduke Hammerhead. L. B. Hurley, "A New Note in the War of the Literati," *American Literature* (1936), VII, 376-394.

83. J. L. Neu, "Rufus Wilmot Griswold," *University of Texas Studies in English* (1925), V, 101-165; Joy Bayless, *Rufus Wilmot Griswold: Poe's Literary Executor* (Nashville, 1943), pp. 51 ff., 163; and Edward H. O'Neill, "The Poe-Griswold-Harrison Texts of the 'Marginalia,'" *American Literature* (1943), XV, 238-250.

84. Quinn, p. 674.

85. May G. Evans, *Music and Edgar Allan Poe, A Bibliographical Study* (Baltimore, 1939); R. C. Archibald, "Music and Edgar Allan Poe," *Notes and Queries* (September 7, 1940), CLXXIX, 170-171; and, in another connection, Ernest Marchand, "Poe as Social Critic," *American Literature* (1934), VI, 28-43.

86. John P. Pritchard, "Horace and Edgar Allan Poe," *Classical Weekly* (1933), XXVI, 129-133; Emma Katherine Norman, "Poe's Knowledge of Latin," *American Literature* (1934), VI, 72-77; David K. Jackson, "Poe's Notes: 'Pinakidia' and 'Some Ancient Greek Authors,'" *American Literature* (1933), V, 258-267; and T. O. Mabbott, "Evidence

That Poe Knew Greek," *Notes and Queries* (July 17, 1943), CLXXXV, 39-40.

[87.] Mozelle S. Allen, "Poe's Debt to Voltaire," *op. cit.*—The idiomatic expression, *revenons à nos moutons* (i.e., "to return to our subject"), Poe awkwardly rendered literally as "But to our sheep," using it to return from a digression to the main subject, perhaps with what he considered humorous effect.

[88.] Edith Philips, "The French of Edgar Allan Poe," *American Speech* (1927), II, 270.

[89.] Gustav Gruener, "Poe's Knowledge of German," *Modern Philology* (1904), II, 125-140; Joseph C. Mathews, "Did Poe Read Dante?" *University of Texas Studies in English* (1938), XVIII, 123-136.

[90.] T. O. Mabbott, "The Source of the Title of Poe's 'Morella,'" *Notes and Queries* (January 9, 1937), CLXXII, 26-27; on Poe's knowledge of Spanish history, see also his review of J. F. Cooper's *Mercedes of Castile.* —For the theory that Angelo Poliziano, mentioned in *Pinakidia,* is the "Italian humanist on whose life Poe wrote his *Politian,*" see Nelda Budde, *The Reading of Edgar Allan Poe* (unpublished M. A. thesis, Lawrence, Kansas, 1946), p. 121.

[91.] Reid, p. 5.

[92.] Adolph B. Benson, "Scandinavian References in the Works of Poe," *Journal of English and Germanic Philology* (1941), XL, 73-90.

[93.] Killis Campbell, "Poe's Knowledge of the Bible," *Studies in Philology* (1930), XXVII, 546-551.

[94.] James O. Bailey, "Poe's 'Palaestine,'" *American Literature* (1941), XIII, 44-58.—Another main source for Poe's general information is the encyclopedia by Bielfield.

[95.] Quinn, p. 289.—John K. Moore, "Poe, Scott, and the 'Murders in the Rue Morgue,'" *American Literature* (1936), VIII, 52-58.

[96.] Carroll D. Laverty, "Poe in 1847," *American Literature* (1948), XX, 166-168.

[97.] Harrison, VII, xxxv.

[98.] J. S. Shick, "Poe and Jefferson," *Virginia Magazine of History and Biography* (1946), LIV, 316-320.

99.   Harrison, XIII, 5.

100.   W. F. Friedman, "Edgar Allan Poe, Cryptographer," *American Literature* (1937), VIII, 266-280.

101.   R. F. Almy, "J. N. Reynolds: A Brief Biography with Particular Reference to Poe and Symmes," *Colophon* (1937), II, 217-221; A. Starke, "Poe's Friend Reynolds," *American Literature* (1939), XI, 152-159.—Poe refers to Reynolds in *Autography*.

102.   Harrison, XIV, 177.

103.   *Ibid.,* XI, 206.

104.   Floyd Stovall, "An Interpretation of Poe's 'Al Aaraaf,'" *University of Texas Studies in English* (1929), IX, 106-133; Richard C. and Marie M. Pettigrew, "A Reply to Floyd Stovall's Interpretation of 'Al Aaraaf,'" *American Literature* (1937), IX, 439-445.

105.   Philip P. Wiener, "Poe's Logic and Metaphysic," *Personalist* (1933), XIV, 268-274; Laurence J. Lafleur, "Edgar Allan Poe as Philosopher," *Personalist* (1941), XXII, 401-405.

106.   Paul Valéry, *Variety* (tr. Malcolm Cowley, New York, 1927), pp. 128-131, 141, 146.

107.   George Nordstedt, "Poe and Einstein," *Open Court* (1930), XLIV, 173-180.

108.   Harrison, XVI, 292.

109.   Quinn and O'Neill, II, 1083.

110.   Harrison, XVI, 302.

111.   *Ibid.,* XVI, 310-311.

112.   The quotation is from a note in the text designated C by Mabbott, who refers to I Corinthians, XV, 28, "that God may be all in all."

113.   James O. Bailey, "Poe's Stonehenge," *Studies in Philology* (1941), XXXVIII, 645-651.

114.   F. O. Matthiessen, *The Achievement of T. S. Eliot* (New York, 1935), p. 40.

115.   Malcolm Cowley, "Aidgarpo," *New Republic* (November 5, 1945), CXIII, 608.

116.   H. L. Mencken, *Prejudices, Second Series* (New York, 1920), p. 59.

117. For the theory that "a tone of sober scientific accuracy" is a literary device in Poe's essays, see Charles C. Walcutt, "The Logic of Poe," *College English* (1941), II, 438-444.

118. Edward Shanks, *Edgar Allan Poe* (New York, 1937), p. 100.

119. William York Tindall, *Forces in Modern British Literature*, 1885-1946 (New York, 1947), p. 6—Before W. H. Pater, Poe had notions (perhaps from Bacon) about *bizarrerie*, according to Norman Foerster, "Quantity and Quality in the Aesthetic of Poe," *Studies in Philology* (1923), XX, 310-335.

120. Tindall, *op. cit.*, p. 20.

121. *Ibid.*—The British movement became identifiable with the elegance of Aubrey Beardsley, the exquisite refinement of Ernest Dowson, and the depravity of John Gray. Thomas Griffith[s] Wain[e]wright, whom Oscar Wilde described in *Pen, Pencil and Poison,* was a murderer. After the disgrace of Wilde, decadence as a literary movement became obscure in England.

122. Edwin Morgan, *Flower of Evil, A Life of Charles Baudelaire* (New York, 1943), p. 39.

123. Tindall, *op. cit.*, p. 225.

124. François Porché, *Chárles Baudelaire* (tr. J. Mavin, New York, n. d.), p. 225.

125. *Ibid.*, p. 156.

126. Rex Stout, "Grim Fairy Tales," *Saturday Review of Literature* (April 2, 1949), XXXII, 7-8, 34.

127. Christopher Morley, "Roderick Usher's Allergy," *Saturday Review of Literature* (April 16, 1949), XXXII, 30.

128. Oscar Cargill, "The Decadents," *Intellectual America: Ideas on the March* (New York, 1941), pp. 176 220.

129. John Ward Ostrom (editor), *The Letters of Edgar Allan Poe* (Cambridge, Mass., 1948), II, 459; hereafter cited as Ostrom.

130. Poe's concern about the proper situation in society for the artist was expressed in his review of Henry F. Chorley's *Conti the Discarded* (Harrison, VIII, 230), where

he praised poets as "the gifted ministers to those exalted emotions which link us with the mysteries" of Heaven.

131. My remarks on Poe in France, unless otherwise noted, are based on Célestin Pierre Cambiaire, *The Influence of Edgar Allen Poe in France* (New York, 1927), pp. 13-332.

132. E. D. Forgues, "Études sur le Roman Anglais et Américan—Les Contes d'Edgar A. Poe," *La Revue des Deux Mondes* (October 15, 1846), XVI, 366.

133. There is no evidence that Poe, who kept an eye on foreign citations of his name (as shown in his letter to Chivers, July 22, 1846), ever saw or heard of Forgues's essay (Quinn, p. 513 n. 34).

134. For an earlier translation of *Politian,* see William Little Hughes, *Contes inédits,* Paris, 1862; Mabbott's edition, *op. cit.,* p. iv.—Sainte-Beuve, Taine, and Louis Etienne are said to have disliked Poe's works; J. W. Krutch, *op. cit.,* p. 209.

135. P. Mansell Jones, "Poe, Baudelaire and Mallarmé: A Problem of Literary Judgment," *Modern Language Review* (1944), XXXIX, 236-246; Marcel Francon, "Poe et Baudelaire," *Publications of the Modern Language Association* (1945), LX, 841-859; Léon Lemonnier, "Baudelaire, traducteur du *Corbeau,*" *La Muse française* (1929), VIII, 701-705; Hazael Samuell Williams, *Baudelaire, Translator of Poe* (unpublished M. A. thesis, Southern Methodist University, Dallas, Texas, 1934), pp. 20-21 n. 1; and Léon Lemonnier, "Baudelaire et Mallarmé, traducteurs d'Edgar Poe," *Les Langues Modernes* (1949), XLIII, 47-57. I have not consulted Lois and F. E. Hyslop, *Baudelaire on Poe, Critical Papers,* State College, Pa., 1951.

136. J. C. French (ed.), *Poe in Foreign Lands and Tongues* (Baltimore, 1941), pp. 5-10.

137. Ramon Guthrie and George E. Diller (editors), *French Literature and Thought Since the Revolution* (New York, 1942), pp. 510 n. 28, 455.

138. Paul Valéry, *Reflections on the World Today* (tr. Francis Scarfe, New York, 1948), p. 153. John G. H. Meister, of the University of Pennsylvania, has now in preparation *Poe's "Eureka": A Study of Its Ideas, Sources,*

and Its Relationship to His Work; and in 1948 T. S. Eliot published *From Poe to Valéry,* a critical treatment of the influence of Poe's ideas.

[139.] C. H. Page, "Poe in France," *The Nation* (January 14, 1909), LXXXVIII, 32.

[140.] John Eugene Englekirk, *Edgar Allan Poe in Hispanic Literature* (New York, 1934), pp. 15, 56-85, 418-465; and the following papers by the same author, "A Critical Study of Two Tales by Amado Nervo," *New Mexico Quarterly* (1932), II, 53-65; " 'The Raven' in Spanish America," *Spanish Review* (1934), I, 52-56; and " 'My Nightmare.' The Last Tale by Poe," *Publications of the Modern Language Association* (1937), LII, 511-527.

[141.] John E. Englekirk, *The Song of Holland,* an In-edited Tale Ascribed to Poe," *New Mexico Quarterly* (1931), I, 247-269.

[142.] J. C. French (ed.), *op. cit.,* pp. 25-31.

[143.] John DeLancey Ferguson, *American Literature in Spain* (New York, 1916), pp. 55-86.

[144.] Samuel Putnam, *Marvelous Journey, A Survey of Four Centuries of Brazilian Writing* (New York, 1948), p. 119—For translations of Poe by Domingo Estrado, Guillermo Hall, and Maria Cruz, see Martin E. Erichson, "Three Guatemalan Translators of Poe," *Hispania* (1942), XXV, 73-78.

[145.] Muna Lee, "Brother of Poe," *Southwest Review* (1926), II, 305-312.

[146.] J. C. French (ed.) *op. cit.*—One may observe that Poe, at least in Central America, is sought today by readers other than critics and poets. In March, 1948, John Schnake, one of my students, showed me an editorial written by his brother Edward, a student of Canal Zone Junior College Balboa. In the school paper *Hot Air from the Tropics,* the author Edward Schnake commented as follows on the reading habits of himself and his fellow students: "I classed the students in the library into two distinct types. There are those who browse among the magazines on the table (the low browse) and those who browse among the books in the

balcony (the high browse). I didn't browse long, because
I don't read good (I read Poe)."

147. Carlos Dávila, "Poe y el centenario de la novela
policíaca," *America* (1947), XXXIII, 21-23.

148. C. Alphonso Smith, *Edgar Allan Poe* (Indianapolis,
1921), p. 5.

149. Abraham Yarmolinsky, *"The Russian View of American Literature,"* *The Bookman* (1916), XLIV, 44-48.

150. J. C. French (ed.), *op. cit., pp.* 11-21.

151. Malcolm Cowley, "Aidgarpo," *op. cit.*

152. Vladimir Astrov, "Dostoievsky on Edgar Allan Poe,"
American Literature (1942), XIV, 70-74.

153. Robert Magidoff, *In Anger and Pity, A Report on
Russia* (New York, 1949), pp. 228-229.—N. Bryllion Fagin, in
The Histrionic Mr. Poe (Baltimore, 1949), pp. 215 n. 69,
and 231, refers to the doctoral dissertation of the Russian
scholar M. H. Bobrova, *On the Prose of Edgar Poe* (in
Russian, Publication of the Irkutsk State Pedagogical Insti-
tute, 1937) and to the drama written in Russian by Valentine
Bulgakov, *Edgar Poe* (Prague, 1938).

154. As for Poe's knowledge of the German language,
Carl F. Schreiber ("Mr. Poe at his Conjurations Again,"
Colophon (1930), II, 1-11) states: "I am of the frank opinion
that Poe never read more than three pages of consecutive
German prose, if indeed he read that number."

155. J. C. French (ed.), *op. cit.,* pp. 22-24.

156. *Ibid.*

157. T. O. Mabbott, "German Translations of Poe's
'Raven,'" *Notes and Queries* (January 29, 1938), CLXXIV,
88.

158. *Ibid.*

159. C. Alphonso Smith, *op. cit.,* p. 7.

160. *Ibid.*

161. *Ibid.*

162. H. H. Ewers, *Edgar Allan Poe* (Berlin, 1905), p. 67.

163. Alfred Lichtenstein, *Der Kriminalroman* (Munchen,
1908), p. 9.

164. Charles W. Kent and John S. Patton (editors), *The
Book of the Poe Centenary* (Charlottesville, 1909), p. 74.

165. Friederich Depken, "Sherlock Holmes, Raffles und ihre Vorbilder," *Anglistiche Forschungen* (Heidelberg, 1914) XLI, 44.

166. C. Alphonso Smith, *op. cit.*, p. 8.

167. Leland Schubert, "James Wilson Carling: Expressionist Illustrator of 'The Raven,'" *Southern Literary Messenger* (1942), IV, 173-181.

168. Quinn, pp. 451-452. — In 1919 thirty copies of Elizabeth Barrett Browning's *Edgar Allan Poe, A Criticism with Remarks on the Morals and Religion of Shelley and Leigh Hunt* were printed in London for private circulation only by Richard Clay and Sons.

169. Frederic G. Kenyon (editor), *The Letters of Elizabeth Barrett Browning* (London, 1897), I, 249.

170. Donald R. Hutcherson, "Poe's Reputation in England and America, 1850-1909," *American Literature* (1942), XIV, 211-233.

171. For a comment on the passage, see Helen Simpson, *Edgar Allan Poe's Doctrine of Effect* (unpublished M. A. thesis, Southern Methodist University, Dallas, Texas, 1946), p. 106.

172. *Letters Chiefly concerning Edgar Allan Poe from Algernon Charles Swinburne to John H. Ingram* (London, Printed for Private Circulation, 1910), unpaginated; Caroline Ticknor, "Ingram—Discourager of Poe Biographies," *The Bookman* (1916), XLIV, 8-14.

173. Tennyson's statement was made in 1883; see the Memoir by his son, *Alfred Lord Tennyson* (London, 1897), II, 292-293.

174. Hutcherson, "Poe's Reputation in England and America, 1850-1909," *op. cit.*

175. C. Alphonso Smith, *op. cit.*, p. 23.

176. James McNeill Whistler, *The Gentle Art of Making Enemies* (New York, 1923), p. 161.

177. W. M. Rossetti, *Pre-Raphaelite Diaries and Letters* (London, 1900), p. 229.

178. *Ibid.*, p. 236.

179. *Ibid.*, p. 289.

[180.] Paull H. Baum (editor), *Dante Gabriel Rosetti: Poems, Ballads and Sonnets* (New York, 1937), p. 3 n. 1.

[181.] George Saintsbury, *Prefaces and Essays* (London, 1933), pp. 314-323.

[182.] Aldous Huxley, *Vulgarity in Literature* (London, 1930), p. 26.

[183.] Diana Trilling (editor), *The Portable D.H. Lawrence* (New York, 1947), pp. 671-672, especially p. 692.

[184.] F. O. Matthiessen, *op. cit.*, pp. 6, 41.—On Poe and James Joyce, see George Snell, "First of the New Critics," *Quarterly Review of Literature* (1946), II, 340.

[185.] On British interest in Poe during his lifetime, see J. H. Whitty, "Edgar Allan Poe in England and Scotland," *The Bookman* (1916), XLIV, 14-21.

[186.] Campbell, *op. cit.*, p. 37.

[187.] S. S. Rice (ed.), *Edgar Allan Poe: A Memorial Volume* (Baltimore, 1877), p. 13. But in 1830 Sarah J. Hale in *The Ladies' Magazine* thought Poe's recent volume boyish and feeble.

[188.] Carroll D. Laverty, "A Note on Poe in 1838," *Modern Language Notes* (1949), LXIV, 174-176; Samuel Longfellow, *Life of Longfellow* (Boston, 1886), I, 377; II, 150.

[189.] Lowell's "E. A. Poe" was published in *Graham's Magazine* (February, 1845); Quinn, p. 433.

[190.] Louis C. Jones, "A Margaret Fuller Letter to Elizabeth Barrett Browning," *American Literature* (1937), IX, 70-71.

[191.] "Olybrius" [Mabbott], "An Early Discussion of Poe," *Notes and Queries* (September 7, 1947), CXCI, 102; Pierre M. Irving, *Life and Letters of Washington Irving* (New York, 1869), IV, 275, especially 305.

[192.] Harrison, XIII, 1-2.

[193.] Rice, *op. cit.*

[194.] George Snell, "Poe Redivivus," *Arizona Quarterly* (1945), I, 55.

[195.] Rollo G. Silver, "A Note about Whitman's Essay on Poe," *American Literature* (1935), VI, 436.

196. Alice L. Cooke, "The Popular Conception of Edgar Allan Poe from 1850 to 1890," *University of Texas Studies in English* (1942), XXII, 145-170.

197. Tremaine McDowell, "Edgar Allan Poe and William Cullen Bryant," *Philological Quarterly* (1937), XVI, 83-84.

198. "Olybrius" [Mabbott], "Poe and the Artist John P. Frankenstein," *Notes and Queries* (January 17, 1942), CLXXXII, 31-32.

199. Rice, *op. cit.*

200. Horace Greeley, *Recollections of a Busy Life* (New York, 1868), p. 196.—On Poe's early fame in the West, see "Olybrius" [Mabbott], "An Early Discussion of Poe," *Notes and Queries* (September 7, 1947), CXCI, 102.

201. Anon., "Literature in the South," *The Outlook* (December 2, 1899), LXIII, 769.

202. P. E. More, "A Note on Poe's Method," *op. cit.*, p. 309.

203. Yvor Winters, "Edgar Allan Poe: A Crisis in the History of American Osbcurantism," *American Literature* (1937), VIII, 379-401.

204. The fictional portraits are based on such inaccurate testimony as that of Poe's enemy John Hill Hewitt, who once said: "The last time I saw Poe was in Washington; his appearance was anything but angelic. His features were bloated and haggard and he was the picture of 'un homme blasé.'" R. B. Harwell (ed.), *Recollections of Poe,* by John Hill Hewitt (Atlanta, 1949); Vincent Starrett, "One Who Knew Poe," *The Bookman* (1927), LXVI, 198; and "A Poe Mystery Uncovered: The Lost Minerva Review of *Al Aaraaf,*" *Saturday Review of Literature* (May 1, 1943), XXVI, 4-5, 25.

205. Among other studies of Poe, I may mention J. P. Fruit, *The Mind and Art of Poe's Poetry* (New York, 1899); John Macy, *Edgar Allan Poe* (Boston, 1907); Henry S. Canby, *Classic Americans* (New York, 1931); J. O. Bailey, *Pilgrims Through Space and Time* (New York, 1947); and Allen Tate, "Our Cousin, Mr. Poe," *Partisan Review* (1949), XVI, 1207-1219.

[206.] F. O. Matthiessen in *Literary History of the United States* (ed. R. E. Spiller *et al,* New York, 1948), I, 342.— Gerard Manley Hopkins early recognized the dipodic character of "The Raven." Brewster Ghiselin, "Reading Sprung Rhythms," *Poetry* (1947), LXX, 86-93.

[207.] Henry T. Tuckerman, *The Life of John Pendleton Kennedy* (New York, 1871), p. 376. Tuckerman is much nearer the real Poe than is Roy P. Basler in his Freudian study, *Sex, Symbolism, and Psychology in Literature,* New Brunswick, N. J., 1948. On psychological studies, see Philip Young, "The Early Psychologists and Poe," *American Literature* (1951), XXII, 442-454.

[208.] J. T. Buckingham, *Personal Memoirs and Recollections of Editorial Life* (Boston, 1852), I, 57; A. H. Quinn, "The Marriage of Poe's Parents," *American Literature* (1939), XI, 212.—Poe was buried October 8, not 9, 1849. John C. French, "The Day of Poe's Burial," Baltimore *Sun* (June 3, 1949), p. 14.

[209.] Like Poe, Baudelaire fabricated his adventures, one of his favorite sayings being "While I was in Calcutta," a place where he had certainly never been. François Porché, *op. cit.,* pp. 41, 51.—On Poe's love of make-believe, see Eola Willis, "The Dramatic Careers of Poe's Parents," *The Bookman* (1926), LXIV, 288-291.

[210.] Ostrom, I, 66-69.

[211.] Harrison, I, 344-346.

[212.] Ostrom, I, 12.

[213.] Mary Gove Nichols, *Reminiscences of Edgar Allan Poe* (New York, 1931), p. 12; originally published in the *Six Penny Magazine* for February, 1863; republished with accompanying letter by Mabbott.

[214.] Hervey Allen and T. O. Mabbott, *Poe's Brother. The Poems of William Henry Leonard Poe* (New York, 1926), pp. 21-22.

[215.] *Ibid.*—John Allan's letter was first discovered by Killis Campbell, "Some Unpublished Documents Relating to Poe's Early Years," *Sewanee Review* (1912), XX, 201-212.— The name is correctly either Allan or Allen.

[216.] For an account of Blaettermann, see Morgan Callaway, Jr., "The Historic Study of the Mother-Tongue in the United States: A Survey of the Past," *University of Texas Studies in English* (1925), V, 7-8.—On Poe's academic training, see Edwin A. Alderman, "Edgar Allan Poe and the University of Virginia," *Virginia Quarterly Review* (1925), I, 78-84; Joseph S. Shick, "Poe and Jefferson," *Virginia Magazine of History and Biography* (1946), LIV, 316-320; and Louis Sidran, "University of Virginia," *Esquire* (1947), XXVIII, 107.

[217.] Quinn, pp. 616-618.—According to Quinn (p. 618 n. 4), "Sartain makes no mention of Poe begging for laudanum, as Woodberry states, II, 309."

[218.] Ostrom, II, 400-403.

[219.] *Independent* (October 15, 1896), XLVIII, 1, 382.— Quinn (p. 694n. 91) cited also Thomas H. Lane, who knew Poe for several years, to the effect that the poet did not take drugs.—On Poe and English, see two papers by Carl F. Schreiber, "A Close-up of Poe," *Saturday Review of Literature* (October 9, 1926), III, 165-167; and "The Donkey and the Elephant," *Yale University Library Gazette* (1944), XIX, 17-19.

[220.] Carroll D. Laverty, "Poe in 1847," *op. cit.;* John W. Robertson, M. D., in referring to Poe's alleged use of drugs, likewise detected "no sign of it"; see *Edgar A. Poe, A Psychopathic Study* (New York, 1923), p. 67.

[221.] William B. Hunter, Jr., "Poe's 'The Sleeper' and *Macbeth*," *American Literature* (1948), XX, 55-57; T. O. Mabbott, "Poe's 'The Sleeper' Again," *American Literature* (1949), XXI, 339-340.

[222.] Quinn, p. 505.

[223.] Vincent Starrett (editor), *Edgar Allan Poe by Capt. Mayne Reid* (Ysleta, Texas, 1933), p. 5; Mayne Reid's *Memoir* was prepared for publication by his widow Elizabeth Reid in London in 1890; this reference is hereafter cited as Reid.

[224.] Hervey Allen, *Israfel, The Life and Times of Edgar Allan Poe* (London, 1927), II, 829; revised edition, two vols. in one (1934); anniversary edition, 1949.

225. L. A. Wilmer, *Merlin* (ed. T. O. Mabbott, New York, 1941); Floyd Stovall, "The Women of Poe's Poems and Tales," *University of Texas Studies in English* (1925), V, 197-209; and Émile Lauvrière, *The Strange Life and Strange Loves of Edgar Allan Poe* (tr. E. G. Rich, Philadelphia, 1935).

226. Frederick W. Coburn, "Poe as Seen by the Brother of 'Annie,' " *op. cit.*

227. Sydney R. McLean, "A Valentine," *Colophon* (1935), I, 183-187.

228. Reid, p. 5

229. Mrs. Frances Sargent Osgood, "Ida Grey," *Graham's Magazine* (August, 1845), XXXI, 83-84. T. O. Mabbott refers to Poe's "amour with Mrs. Osgood" in "The Astrological Symbolism of Poe's 'Ulalume,' " *Notes & Queries* (July 11, 1931), CLXI, 27.

230. Mrs. Osgood's "Ida Grey," *op. cit.*

231. *Ibid.*

232. Reid, p. 6.

233. Mrs. Marie Louise Shew said Poe's eyes were blue; Mrs. Susan A. T. Weiss reported them gray; and T. H. Chivers claimed they were hazel; A. P. Schulte and J. S. Wilson, *Facts about Poe* (Charlottesville, 1926), pp. 35-36.

234. Harrison, I, 348-349.

235. *Ibid.*, I, 356-357.

236. Frances B. Culver, "Lineage of Edgar Allan Poe and the Complex Pattern of the Family Genealogy," *Maryland Historical Magazine* (1942), XXXVII, 420-422; Mrs. Whitman's volume, *Edgar Allan Poe and His Critics* (New Brunswick, N. J., 1949) was edited by O. S. Coad.

237. Harrison, I, 355-356.

238. Letter of April 28, 1949, from Joseph Doyle, who is writing a biography of Woodberry. Both biographer and editor, Woodberry collaborated with E. C. Stedman in editing *The Works of Edgar Allan Poe* (Chicago, 1894-1895; New York, 1914).

239. Jacob E. Spannuth and T. O. Mabbott, *Doings of Gotham* (Pottsville, Pa., 1929), p. xv.

240. Philip Van Doren Stern (editor), "Introduction," *Edgar Allan Poe* (New York, 1945), p. xxxi. Stern is without authority in rearranging Poe's tales "Silence—a Fable" and "Shadow—a Parable" as free verse.

241. A. H. Quinn and Edward H. O'Neill (editors), "Introduction," *The Complete Poems and Stories of Edgar Allan Poe* (New York, 1946), I, 14; hereafter cited as Quinn and O'Neill.

242. William Hines and Edward Cottrell, "The University of Virginia," *American Mercury* (1948), LXVII, 194-202.

243. Frederick W. Coburn, "Poe as Seen by the Brother of 'Annie,' " *op. cit.*

244. My authority is E. G. Reuter, M. D., of San Antonio, Texas. Respecting Virginia's malady, Dr. Reuter says that if the cause of her hemorrhage had been a malignant tumor she would have died well within the year 1842 and not five years later.

245. The poet was seriously disturbed by his wife's condition. In a revealing unpublished letter (owned by Dr. Otto Fisher, Detroit 14, Michigan) Poe confesses that he was out of his head for a while after Virginia's death. Ostrom, II, 339; Quinn, p. 528.

246. Philip Van Doren Stern, "The Strange Death of Edgar Allan Poe," *Saturday Review of Literature* (October 15, 1949), pp. 8-9, 28-30.

247. Richard Beale Davis (editor), *Chivers' Life of Poe* (New York, 1952), p. 68.

248. N. Bryllion Fagin (editor), *Poe as a Literary Critic* (Baltimore, 1946), p. 3 n. 5.

249. *Ibid.,* p. 3.

BIBLIOGRAPHY

In this Poe bibliography, which covers over a century of publications, I have used a number of conventional abbreviations as well as a formal outline.

Abbreviations:

AL	-	American Literature
AN&Q	-	American Notes and Queries
BNYPL	-	Bulletin of New York Public Library
CE	-	College English
ELH	-	English Literary History
JEGP	-	Journal of English and Germanic Philology
MLN	-	Modern Language Notes
MLQ	-	Modern Language Quarterly
MP	-	Modern Philology
NEQ	-	New England Quarterly
N&Q	-	Notes and Queries
PBSA	-	Papers of the Bibliographical Society of America
PQ	-	Philological Quarterly
PMLA	-	Publications of the Modern Language Association of America
SLM	-	Southern Literary Messenger
SRL	-	Saturday Review of Literature
SP	-	Studies in Philology
UTQ	-	University of Toronto Quarterly

OUTLINE

1. EDITIONS:

A. Complete Works:

Dole, Nathan Haskell, *The Complete Works of Edgar Allan Poe*, London and N. Y., 1908 (10 vols.)

Griswold, Rufus Wilmot, *The Works of the Late Edgar Allan Poe: With a Memoir by Rufus Wilmot Griswold and Notices of His Life and Genius by N. P. Willis and J. R. Lowell*, N. Y., 1850-1856 (4 vols.).

Harrison, James A., *The Complete Works of Edgar Allan Poe*, Virginia Edition, N. Y., 1902 (17 vols.).

Ingram, John H., *The Works of Edgar Allan Poe*, Edinburgh, 1874-1875 (4 vols.).

Quinn, Arthur H. and O'Neill, Edward H., *The Complete Poems and Stories of Edgar Allan Poe, with selections from His Critical Writings*, N. Y., 1946 (2 vols.).

Richardson, Charles F. *The Complete Works of Edgar Allan Poe*, N. Y., 1902 (10 vols.).

Slater, Montagu, *The Centenary Poe; Tales, Poems, Criticism, Marginalia, and Eureka*, N. Y., 1950.

Stoddard, Richard H., *The Works of Edgar Allan Poe*, N. Y., 1884 (6 vols.).

Woodberry, George E. and Stedman, Edmund C., *The Works of Edgar Allan Poe*, Chicago, 1894-1895; N. Y., 1914 (10 vols.).

B. Selections:
1. Poems:

Alterton, Margaret and Craig, Hardin, *Edgar Allan Poe*: *Representative Selections, With Introduction, Bibliography, and Notes,* N. Y., 1935.

Campbell, Killis, *The Poems of Edgar Allan Poe,* Boston, 1917.

Clark, Harry H., *Major American Poets,* N. Y., 1936 (pp. 834-839).

Hutcherson, Dudley, "The Philadelphia 'Saturday Museum' Text of Poe's Poems," *AL* (1933), V, 36-48.

Johnson, R. Brimley, *The Complete Poetical Works of Edgar Allan Poe,* London, 1909.

Mabbott, T. O., *Selected Poems of Edgar Allan Poe,* N. Y., 1928.

———, *Al Aaraaf, Tamerlane, and Minor Poems,* N. Y., 1933 (1829 edition, Facsimile Text Society).

———, *Tamerlane and Other Poems,* N. Y., 1941 (Reproduced in facsimile from an edition of 1827; introduction covers known facts of Poe's life in 1826-27).

———, *The Raven and Other Poems,* N. Y., 1942 (Facsimile Text Society, from the Lorimer Graham Copy of 1845).

Stern, Philip Van Doren, *Edgar Allan Poe,* Viking Portable Library, N. Y., 1945.

Whitty, James H., *The Complete Poems of Edgar Allan Poe,* Boston, 1911 (rev. ed., Boston and N. Y., 1917).

2. Tales:

Anon., *The Complete Tales and Poems of Edgar Allan Poe,* The Modern Library, n. p., 1938.

Campbell, Killis, *Poe's Short Stories,* N. Y., 1927.

Mabbott, T. O., *Politian: An Unfinished Tragedy,* Richmond, Va., 1923 (drama).

——— and Allen, Hervey, *Gold Bug,* N. Y., 1928.

Varner, John G., Jr., *Edgar Allan Poe and the Philadelphia Saturday Courier,* Charlottesville, Va., 1933.

Wilson, James S., *Tales of Edgar Allan Poe,* N. Y., 1927.

3. Critical Works:

Moore, John Brook, *Selections from Poe's Literary Criticism,* N. Y., 1926.

Poe, Edgar Allan, *The Conchologist's First Book,* Phila., 1839-1840 (rev. 1845).

Prescott, Frederick C., *Selections from the Critical Writings of Edgar Allan Poe,* N. Y., 1909.

Seitz, Don C., *A Chapter on Autography,* N. Y., 1926 (an edition limited to 750 copies).

4. Letters:

Field, Eugene, *Some Letters of Edgar Allan Poe to E. H. N. Patterson,* Chicago, 1898.

Harrison, James A., *Last Letters of Edgar Allan Poe to Sarah Helen Whitman,* N. Y., 1909.

Ostrom, John W., *Check List of Letters to and from Poe,* Charlottesville, Va., 1941.

———, *The Letters of Edgar Allan Poe,* Cambridge, Mass., 1948 (2 vols.).

Quinn, Arthur H. and Hart, Richard H., *Edgar Allan Poe Letters and Documents in the Enoch Pratt Free Library,* N. Y., 1941.

Stanard, Mary N., *Edgar Allan Poe Letters Till Now Unpublished,* Phila., 1925 (letters in the Valentine Museum, Richmond, Va.).

II. Biographies:

A. Books:

Allen, Hervey, *Israfel: The Life and Times of Edgar Allan Poe*, N. Y., 1926, 1934, 1949.

Allen, Hervey and Mabbott, Thomas Ollive, *Poe's Brother: The Poems of William Henry Leonard Poe*, N. Y., 1926.

Cumston, Charles Greene, M. D., "The Medical History of Edgar Allan Poe," *St. Paul Medical Journal*, 1909.

Damon, Foster S., *Thomas Holley Chivers, Friend of Poe: With Selections from His Poems*, N. Y., 1930.

Davis, Richard Beale (editor), *Chivers' Life of Poe*, N. Y., 1952.

Fagin, N. Bryllion, *The Histronic Mr. Poe*, Baltimore, 1949.

—Gill, William F., "Some Facts about Edgar A. Poe," *Laurel Leaves*, N. Y., 1879.

—Hibbard, Addison, *The Book of Poe: Tales, Criticisms, Poems*, N. Y., 1929 (Introduction by Hervey Allen).

Keiley, Jarvis, *Edgar Allan Poe, A Probe*, N. Y., 1927 (Limited edition).

Leigh, Oliver, *Edgar Allan Poe, The Man: The Master: The Martyr*, Chicago, 1906.

Macy, John, "Biographies of Poe," *The Critical Game*, N. Y., 1922.

Moran, John J., M. D., *A Defense of Edgar Allan Poe, Life, Character and Dying Declarations of the Poet, An Official Account of his Death, by his attending Physician*, Washington, 1885 (Includes a fine engraved portrait by Sartain).

Quinn, Arthur H., *Edgar Allan Poe: A Critical Biography*, N. Y., 1941.

Schreiber, Carl F., "The Donkey and the Elephant," *Yale University Lib. Gaz.* (July, 1944) XIX, 17-19 (On some slanderous remarks by Thomas Dunn English about Poe.)

Spannuth, Jacob E. and Mabbott, Thomas Ollive, *Doings of Gotham*, Pottsville, Penna., 1929.

Stedman, Edward G., "Edgar Allan Poe," *Poets of America*, N. Y., 1885 (pp. 225-272).

Whitman, Sarah H., *Edgar Poe and His Critics,* N. Y., 1860 (also Providence, 1885; Oral S. Coad, New Brunswick, N. J., 1949).

Wilson, James Southall and Schulte, A. P., *Facts about Poe*: *Portraits and Daguerreotypes,* Charlottesville, Va., 1926.

B. Articles:

Alderman, E. A., "Edgar Allan Poe and the University of Virginia," *Va. Quart. Rev.* (1925), I, 78-84.

Bolton, Sara T., "On the Death of Edgar A. Poe," *Mother's Assistant and Young Lady's Friend* (Boston, Jan.-Dec., 1850), XIX-XX, 21-23.

Brigham, Clarence S., "Edgar Allan Poe's Contributions to 'Alexander's Weekly Messenger,' " *Proc. American Antiquarian Society* (1943), LII, 45-125.

Campbell, Killis, "Poe Documents in the Library of Congress," *MLN* (1910), XXXV, 127-128.

——, "Some Unpublished Documents Relating to Poe's Early Years," *Sewanee Rev.* (1912), XX, 201-212.

——, "Gleanings in the Bibliography of Poe," *MLN* (1917), XXXII, 267-272.

——, "Recent Books About Poe," *SP* (1927), XXIV, 474-479.

Coburn, Frederick W., "Poe as Seen by the Brother of 'Annie,' " *NEQ* (1943), XVI, 468-476 (Letters by Amos Bardwell, 1848 and 1851).

Culver, Francis B., "Lineage of Edgar Allan Poe and the Complex Pattern of the Family Genealogy," *Md. Hist. Mag.* (1942), XXXVII, 420-422.

Daughrity, Kenneth L., "Poe's 'Quiz on Willis,' " *AL* (1933), V, 55-62.

Davis, Richard B., "Poe and William Wirt," *AL* (1944), XVI, 212-220.

Dietz, F. Meredith, "Poe's First and Final Love," *SLM* (1943), V, 38-47 (Concerns Elmira Royster Shelton).

Evans, May G., "Poe in Amity Street," *Md. Hist. Mag.* (1941), XXXVI, 363-380.

Ferguson, Delancey, "Charles Hine and His Portrait of Poe," *AL* (1932), III, 465-470.

Forrest, William Mentzel, *Biblical Allusions in Poe,* N. Y., 1928 ("Christ" is mentioned 21 times while "devil" is referred to 155 times).

French, John C., "The Day of Poe's Burial," *Baltimore Sun* (June 3, 1949), pp. 14 (Oct. 8, not Oct. 9).

Gibson, T. W., "Poe at West Point," *Harper's* (1867), XXXV, 754-756.

Gill, W. F., "Edgar A. Poe and His Biographer, Rufus W. Griswold," *Lotos Leaves,* Boston, 1875.

Gravely, Wm. H., Jr., "Thomas Dunn English's *Walter Woolfe*—A Reply to 'A Minor Poe Mystery,' " *Princeton University Chronicle* (1944), V, 108-114.

——, "An Incipient Libel Suit Involving Poe," *MLN* (1945), LX, 308-311.

Hubbell, Jay B., "Poe's Mother; With a Note on John Allan," *Wm. & Mary College Quarterly* (1941), XXI, 250-254.

Laverty, Carroll D., "A Note on Poe in 1838," *MLN* (1949), LXIV, 174-176.

Mabbott, T. O., " 'Poe' on Intemperance," *N&Q* (July 18, 1942), CLXXXIII, 34-35 (An essay attributed to Poe in M. M. Mason's *The Southern First Class Book,* 1839).

Macy, John, "Biographies of Poe," *The Critical Game,* N. Y., 1922 (pp. 193-200).

Pittman, Diana, "Key to the Mystery of Edgar Allan Poe," *SLM* (1941), III, 367-377; 418-424.

——, "Key to the Mystery of Edgar Allan Poe," *SLM* (1942), IV (following sub heads: 'The Landscape Garden,' 19-24; 'Ebony Shadow Series. Metzengerstein,' 81-85, 143-149; 'The Two Ravens,' 149-157; 'Poe's "The Raven," ' 157-168).

Pruette, Lorine, "A Psycho-Analytical Study of Edgar Allan
    Poe," *The American Journal of Psychology* (1920),
    XXXI, 370-402.
Schick, Joseph S., "Poe and Jefferson," *Virginia Magazine of
    History and Biography* (1946), LIV, 316-320.
Starke, Aubrey, "Poe's Friend Reynolds," *AL* (1939), XI,
    152-159.
Stern, Philip Van Doren, "The Strange Death of Edgar Allan
    Poe," *SRL* (Oct. 15, 1949), pp. 8-9, 28-30.
Wegelin, Oscar, "The Printer of Poe's 'Tamerlane,' " *N. Y.
    Hist. Soc. Quar. Bul.* (1940), XXIV, 23-25 (Biographi-
    cal sketch of Calvin F. S. Thomas).
Wilson, James Southall, "The Young Man Poe," *Va. Quart.
    Rev.* (1926), II, 238-253.
Wimsatt, Wm. K., Jr., "Poe and the Mystery of Mary
    Rogers," *PMLA* (1941), LV, 230-248.

III. Poems, Tales, and Letters:

A. Poems:

Adkins, Nelson F., "Poe's 'Ulalume,' " *N&Q* (Jan. 14, 1933),
    CLXIV, 30-31 ("To the Autumn Leaf" (1837) compar-
    ed with "Ulalume").
Bailey, J. O., "The Geography of Poe's 'Dreamland' and
    'Ulalume,' " *SP* (1948), XLV, 512-523 (Both concern
    Poe's conception of a hollow earth).
Basler, Roy P., "Poe's 'Ulalume,' " *Expl.* (1944), II, 49.
———, "Byronism in Poe's 'To One in Paradise,' " *AL* (1937),
    IX, 232-236.
Baum, Paull F., "Poe's 'To Helen,' " *MLN* (1949), LXIV,
    289-297.
Bell, Landon C., *Poe and Chivers*, Columbus, O., 1931.
Belden, Henry M., "Observation and Imagination in Cole-
    ridge and Poe: A Contrast," *Papers in Honor of Charles*

Frederick Johnson, Hartford, Conn., 1928, (pp. 131-175).

_____, "Poe's 'The City in the Sea' and Dante's City of Dis," *AL* (1935), VII, 332, 334.

Booth, Bradford A., "The Identity of Annabel Lee," *CE* (1945), VII, 17-19.

Brown, Wallace C., "The English Professor's Dilemma," *CE* (1944), V, 379-385 ("To Helen" is superior to "Annabel Lee").

Campbell, Killis, "A Bit of Chicversian Mystification," *Univ. of Texas Studies in Eng.* (1930) X, 152-154.

Cargill, Oscar, "A New Source for 'The Raven,' " *AL* (1936), VIII, 291-294.

Coad, Oral S., "The Meaning of Poe's 'Eldorado,' " *MLN* (1944), LIX, 59-61.

Colton, Cullen B., "George Hooker Colton and the Publication of 'The Raven,' " *AL* (1938), X, 319-330.

Davidson, Frank, "A Note on Poe's 'Berenice,' " *AL* (1939), XI, 212-223.

Dudley, Fred A., "Tintinnabulation: And a Source of Poe's 'The Bells,' " *AL* (1932), IV, 296-300.

Durham, Frank M., "A Possible Relationship Between Poe's 'To Helen' and Milton's *Paradise Lost,* Book IV," *AL* (1945), XVI, 340-343.

Forsythe, Robert S., "Poe's 'Nevermore': A Note," *AL* (1936), VII, 439-452.

Gates, William Bryan, "Poe's *Politian* Again," *MLN* (1934), XLIX, 561.

Hall, Carroll D., *Bierce and the Poe Hoax,* San Francisco, 1934.

Hubbell, Jay B., " 'O, Tempora! O, Mores!' A Juvenile Poem by Edgar Allan Poe." *Univ. Colo. Studies,* Boulder, 1945 (pp. 314-321).

Hunter, Wm. B., Jr., "Poe's 'The Sleeper' and *Macbeth,*" *AL* (1948), XX, 55-57.

Jones, Joseph E., "Poe's 'Nicean Barks,' " *AL* (1931), II, 433-438.

Leary, Lewis, "Poe's 'Ulalume,' " *Expl.* (1948), VI, 25.

Mabbott, T. O., "Poe's Word 'Porphyrogene,' " *N&Q* (Dec. 2, 1939), CLXXVII, 403.

——, "A Lost Jingle by Poe," *N&Q* (Nov. 23, 1940), CLXXIX, 371.

——, "Poe's 'Ulalume,' " *Expl.* (1942), I, 25.

——, "Poe's 'To Helen,' " *Expl.* (1942), I, 60.

——, "The First Publication of Poe's 'Raven,' " *BNYPL* (1943), XLVII, 581-584.

——, "Poe's 'Raven': First Inclusion in a Book," *N&Q* (Oct. 9, 1943), CLXXV, 225.

——, "Poe's 'Israfel,' " *Expl.* (1944), II, 57.

——, "The Sources of Poe's 'Eldorado,' " *MLN* (1945), LX, 312-314.

——, "The Text of Poe's Play 'Politian,' " *N&Q* (July 14, 1945), CLXXXIX, 14.

——, "Palindromes (and Edgar Poe)," *N&Q* (Nov. 30, 1947), CXCI, 238-239 (Puzzle which interested Poe).

——, "Poe's 'Ulalume,' " *Expl.* (1948), VI, 57.

——, "Unrecorded Texts of Two Poe Poems," *AN&Q* (1948), VIII, 67-68.

——, "Poe's 'The Sleeper' Again," *AL* (1939), XXI, 339-340.

Newcomer, Alphonso G., "The Poe-Chivers Tradition Re-examined," *Sewanee Rev.* (1904), XII, 20-35.

Pettigrew, Richard C., "Poe's Rime," AL (1932), IV, 151-159.

——, and Marie M., "An Interpretation of Poe's 'Al Aaraaf' Answered," *AL* (1937), VIII, 439-445.

Pittman, Diana, "Key to the Mystery of 'Ulalume,' " *SLM* (1941), III, 371-377.

Pound, Louise, "On Poe's 'The City in the Sea,' " *AL* (1934), VI, 22-27.

——, "On Poe's 'The City in the Sea Again," *AL* (1936), VIII, 70-71.

Shockley, Martin S., "Timour the Tartar and Poe's 'Tamerlane,' " *PMLA* (1941), LIV, 1103, 1106.

Starrett, Vincent, "A Poe Mystery Uncovered: The Lost Minerva Review of *Al Aaraaf*," *SRL* (May 1, 1943), pp. 4-5, 25 (Review by John Hill Hewitt appearing in 1829 or 1830).

Stovall, Floyd, "An Interpretation of Poe's 'Al Aaraaf,'"
  Univ. Texas Stud. in Eng. (1929), IX, 106-133.
Triplett, Edna B., "A Note on Poe's 'The Raven,'" *AL*
  (1938), X, 339-341.
Turner, Arlin and Mabbott, T. O., "Two Poe Hoaxes by
  the Same Hand?" *AN&Q* (1943), II, 147-148 (Details of
  the New Orleans "Raven" hoax in 1870 bear unexpected
  likeness in method to the Giles story of "The Bells.")
Werner, William L., "Poe's Theories and Practice in Poetic
  Technique," *AL* (1930), II, 157-165.
———, "Poe's 'Israfel,'" *Expl.* (1943), II, 44.
Woodberry, George E., "The Poe-Chivers Papers," *Century
  Magazine* (1903), LXV, 435-447, 545-558.

B. Tales:

Abel, Darrell, "A Key to the House of Usher," *UTQ* (1949),
  XVIII, 176-185.
Allen, Mozelle Scaff, "Poe's Debt to Voltaire," *Univ. Texas
  Studies in Eng.* (1925), XV, 63-75.
Bailey, James O., "Sources of Poe's 'Arthur Gordon Pym,'
  'Hans Pfaal' and Other Pieces," *PMLA* (1942), LVII,
  513-535.
Basler, Roy P., "The Interpretation of 'Ligeia,'" *CE* (1944),
  V, 363-372.
Bayless, Joy, *Rufus Wilmot Griswold: Poe's Literary Exe-
  cutor*, Nashville, Tenn., 1943.
Benton, Joe, *In the Poe Circle*, N. Y., 1899.
Blair, Walter, "Poe's Conception of Incident and Tone in the
  Tale," *MP* (1944), XLI, 228-240.
Boll, Ernest, "The Manuscript of 'The Murders of the Rue
  Morgue,' and Poe's Revisions," *MP* (1943), XL, 302-
  315.
Boynton, Percy H., "Poe and Journalism," *Eng. Journal*
  (May, 1932), XXI, 345-352.
Bradley, Sculley, "Poe on the New York Stage in 1855," *AL*
  (1937), IX, 353-354.

Brigham, Clarence S., "Edgar Allan Poe's Contributions to *Alexander's Weekly Messenger,*" *Proc. Amer. Antiq. Soc.* (1943), LII, 45-125 (Data on Poe and cryptograms).

Campbell, Killis, "Three Notes on Poe," *AL* (1933), IV, 385-388.

Cherry, Fanny C., "The Source of Poe's 'Three Sundays in a Week,' " *AL* (1930), II, 232-235.

Clark, David L., "The Source of Poe's 'The Pit and the Pendulum,' " *MLN* (1929), XLIV, 349-356.

Friedman, William F., "Edgar Allan Poe, Cryptographer," *AL* (1936), VIII, 266-280.

Gruener, Gustav, "Notes on the Influence of E. T. A. Hoffmann upon Edgar Allan Poe," *PMLA* (1904), XIX, 1-25.

Hudson, Ruth L., "Poe and Disraeli," *AL* (1937), VIII, 402-416.

Hungerford, Edward, "Poe and Phrenology," *AL* (1930), II, 209-231.

Huntress, Keith, "Another Source for Poe's 'Narrative of Arthur Gordon Pym,' " *AL* (1944), XVI, 19-25.

Krappe, Edith S., "A Possible Source for Poe's 'The Tell-Tale Heart' and 'The Black Cat,' " *AL* (1940), XII, 84-88.

Laverty, Carroll, "The Death's Head on the Gold-Bug," *AL* (1940), XII, 88-91.

Lind, Sidney E., "Poe and Mesmerism," *PMLA* (1947), LXII, 1077-1094.

Mabbott, T. O., "Poe's Tale, 'The Lighthouse,' " *N&Q* (Apr. 25, 1942), CLXXXII, 226-227.

——, "Poe and Dr. Lardner," *AN&Q* (1943), III, 115-117.

——, "Poe's Balloon Hoax," *New York Sun* (Jan. 23, 1943), p. 6 (Poe's comment on Charles Green's plan to cross the Atlantic by balloon in *Burton's Magazine*, March, 1840).

Miller, F. De Wolfe, "The Basis for Poe's 'The Island of the Fay,' " *AL* (1942), XIV, 135-140.

Mohr, Franz Karl, "The Influence of Eichendorff's 'Ahnung und Gegenwart' on Poe's 'Masque of the Red Death,' " *MLQ* (1949), X, 3-15.

Moore, John R., "Poe, Scott, and 'The Murders in the Rue Morgue,'" *AL* (1936), 52-58.

Neale, Walter G., Jr., "The Source of Poe's 'Morella,'" *AL* (1937), IX, 237-239.

Rasor, C. L., "Possible Sources of 'The Cask of Amontillado,'" *Furman Studies* (1949), XXXI, 46-50 (Balzac and Bulwer-Lytton).

Schick, Joseph S., "The Origin of 'The Cask of Amontillado,'" *AL* (1934), VI, 18-21.

Scudder, Harold H., "Poe's 'Balloon Hoax,'" *AL* (1949), XXI, 179-190.

Taylor, Archer, "Poe's Dr. Lardner, and 'Three Sundays in a Week,'" *AN&Q* (1944), III, 153-155.

Turner, Arlin, "Sources of Poe's 'A Descent into the Maelström,'" *JEGP* (1947), XLVI, 298-301.

——, "Another Source of Poe's 'Julius Rodman,'" *AL* (1936), VIII, 69-70.

Wimsatt, Wm. K., Jr., "Poe and the Chess Automaton," *AL* (1939), XI, 138-151.

——, "What Poe Knew about Cryptography," *PMLA* (1943), LVIII, 754-779.

Wilson, James S., "The Devil Was in It," *Amer. Mercury* (1931), XXIV, 215-220.

Wilt, Napier, "Poe's Attitude Toward His Tales: A New Document," *MP* (1927), XXV, 101-105.

Worthen, Samuel C., "A Strange Aftermath of the Mystery of 'Marie Rogêt' (Mary Rogers)," *Proc. N. J. Hist. Soc.* (1942), LX, 116-123.

——, "Poe and the Beautiful Cigar Girl," *AL* (1948), XX, 305-412.

Wylie, Clarence P., Jr., "Mathematical Allusions in Poe," *Science Monthly* (1946), LXIII, 227-235.

Wyllie, John C., "A List of the Texts of Poe's Tales," in *Humanistic Studies in Honor of John Calvin Metcalf*, Charlottesville, Va., 1941 (pp. 322-338).

C. Letters:

Chase, Lewis, "A New Poe Letter," *AL* (1934), VI, 66-69.

Duffy, Charles, "Poe's Mother-in-law: Two Letters to Bayard Taylor," *AN&Q* (1943), II, 148 (Two begging letters written by Maria Clemm to Taylor in 1850 and 1859).

Mabbott, T. O., "The Letters from George W. Eveleth to Edgar Allan Poe," *BNYPL* (1922), XXVI, 171-195.

———, "Letters from Mary E. Hewitt to Poe," *Christmas Books*, Hunter College, New York, 1937 (pp. 116-121).

McCusker, Honor, "The Correspondence of R. W. Griswold," *More Books* (1941), XVI, 105-116, 152-156, 190-196, 286-289.

Ostrom, John W., "A Poe Correspondence Re-edited," *Americana* (1940), XXXIV, 409-446 (Letters to Joseph E. Snodgrass).

———, "Two 'Lost' Poe Letters," *AN&Q* (1941), I, 68-69.

———, "Two Unpublished Poe Letters," *Americana* (1942), XXXVI, 67-71 (Written to Hiram Haines, editor of the *Virginia Star,* in 1836 and 1840).

Thorp, Willard, "Two Poe Letters at Princeton," *Princeton Univ. Lib. Cat.* (1949), X, 91-94.

Vincent, H. P., "A Sarah Helen Whitman Letter about Edgar Allan Poe," *AL* (1941), XIII, 162-167.

Wilson, James S., "The Letters of Edgar Allan Poe to George W. Eveleth," *Alumni Bul. Univ. Va.* (Jan., 1924), XVII, 34-39.

Woodberry, George E., "Selections from the Correspondence of Edgar Allan Poe," *Century Mag.* (1894), XLVIII, 572-583, 725-737, 854-866.

IV. Critical Works:

A. Books:

Allen, Gay W., "Edgar Allan Poe," *American Prosody,* N. Y., 1935 (pp. 56-90).

Alterton, Margaret, *Origins of Poe's Critical Theory,* Iowa City, 1925.

Cooke, John E., *Poe as a Literary Critic,* ed. by N. Bryllion Fagin, Baltimore, 1946.

Evans, May G., *Music and Edgar Allan Poe,* Baltimore, 1939.

Jackson, David K., *Poe and the Southern Literary Messenger,* Richmond, Va., 1934.

More, Paul E., "The Origins of Hawthorne and Poe," *Shelburne Essays,* 1st. ser. N. Y., 1904 (pp. 51-70).

Shanks, Edward, *Edward Allan Poe,* N. Y., 1937.

Wallace, Alfred Russell, *Edgar Allan Poe,* N. Y., n. d. (Privately Printed. A series of Seventeen Letters Concerning Poe's Scientific Erudition in Eureka and his Authorship of *Leonainie).*

B. Articles:

Adams, Percy G., "Poe, Critic of Voltaire," *MLN* (1942), LVII, 273-275.

Adkins, Nelson F., " 'Chapter on American Cribbage': Poe and Plagiarism," *PBSA* (1948), XLII, 169-210.

Archibald, R. C., "Music and Edgar Allan Poe," *N&Q* (Sept. 7, 1940) CLXXIX, 170-171.

Bailey, James O., "Poe's Palestine,' " *AL* (1941), XIII, 44-58 (Poe's attraction to the bizarre and pseudo-learned).

———, "Poe's 'Stonehenge,' " *SP* (1941), XXXVIII, 645-651.

Benson, Adolph B., "Scandinavian References in the Works of Poe," *JEGP* (1941), XL, 73-90.

Boynton, Percy H., "Poe and Journalism," *English Journal* (1932), XXI, 345-352.

Breton, Maurice Le, "Edgar Poe et Macaulay," *Revue Anglo-Américaine* (1935), pp. 38-42.

Campbell, Killis, "Poe's Knowledge of the Bible," *SP* (1930), XXVII, 546-552.

Fagin, N. Bryllion, "Poe-Drama Critic," *Theatre Annual* (1946), pp. 23-28.

Foerster, Norman, "Quantity and Quality in Poe's Aesthetic," *SP* (1923), XX, 310-335.

Griggs, Earl L., "Five Sources of Edgar Allan Poe's 'Pinakidia,'" *AL* (1929), I, 196-199.

Hurley, Leonard B., "A New Note in the War of the *Literati*," *AL* (1936), VII, 376-394.

Jackson, David K., "Poe's Notes: 'Pinakidia,' and 'Some Ancient Greek Authors,'" *AL* (1933), V, 258-267.

———, "Poe's Knowledge of Law During the 'Messenger' Period," *AL* (1938), X, 331-339.

Lafleur, Laurence J., "Edgar Allan Poe as Philosopher," *Personalist* (1941), XXII, 401-405 (An exposition of *Eureka.*)

Laser, Marvin, "The Growth and Structure of Poe's Concept of Beauty," *ELH* (1948), XV, 69-84 (The influence of Coleridge, phrenology, and Shelley).

Lograsso, Angeline H., "Poe's Piero Maroncelli," *PMLA* (1943), LVIII, 780-789 (Data on the poet and musician whom Poe discussed in the *Literati* in June, 1846).

Mabbott, T. O., "A Review of Lowell's Magazine," *N&Q* (June 29, 1940), CLXXVIII, 457-458.

———, "Poe's Original Conundrums," *N&Q* (June 5, 1943), CLXXXIV, 328-329 (Reprint of two sets contributed to *Phila. Saturday Museum* in March and April, 1843).

———, "Evidence That Poe Knew Greek," *N&Q* (July 17, 1943), CLXXXV, 39-40.

Marchand, Ernest, "Poe as Social Critic," *AL* (1934), VI, 28-43.

More, Paul E., "A Note on Poe's Method," *SP* (1923), XX, 302-309.

Nordstedt, G., "Poe and Einstein," *Open Court* (1930), XLIV, 173-180 (Criticism of *Eureka*).

Norman, Emma K., "Poe's Knowledge of Latin," *AL* (1934), VI, 72-77.

O'Neill, Edward H., "The Poe-Griswold-Harrison Texts of the 'Marginalia,' " *AL* (1943), XV, 238-250.

Parkes, Henry Bamford, "Poe, Hawthorne, Melville: An Essay in Sociological Criticism," *Partisan Review* (1949), XVI, 157-165.

Pritchard, John P., "Edgar Allan Poe," *Return to the Fountains*, Durham, North Carolina, 1942 (pp. 26-43: Poe's debt to the classics).

Rede, Kenneth, "Poe's Notes: From an Investigator's Notebook," *AL* (1933), V, 49-54.

Rubin, Joseph Jay, "John Neal's Poetics as an Influence on Whitman and Poe," *NEQ* (1941), XIV, 359-362.

Stovall, Floyd, "Poe's Debt to Coleridge," *Univ. Texas Studies in English* (1930), X, 70-127.

Taylor, Walter F., "Israfel in Motley: A Study of Poe's Humor," *Sewanee Review* (1934), XLII, 330-340.

Walcutt, Charles C., "The Logic of Poe," *CE* (1941), II, 438-444.

Wilson, James S., "Poe's Philosophy of Composition," *No. Amer. Rev.* (Dec., 1926-Feb. 1927), CCXXIII, 675-684.

Wilson, Edmund, "Poe as a Literary Critic," *Nation* (1942), CLV, 452-453.

V. Reputation

A. France

Betz, Louis P., *Edgar Poe in der französischen Litteratur: Studien zur vergleichenden Litteraturgeschichte der neuren Zeit*, Frankfurt am Main, 1902.

Cambiaire, Célestin Pierre, "The Influence of Edgar Allen [*sic*] Poe in France," *Romanic Review* (Oct.-Dec., 1926), XVII, 319-337 (The first comprehensive treatment of the subject).

——, *The Influence of Edgar Allan Poe in France*, New York, 1927 (A development of the article mentioned beforehand).

Cargill, Oscar, *Intellectual America, Ideas on the March*, N. Y., 1941.

Carlill, H. F., "Philippe-Auguste-Mathias de Villiers de l'Isle-Adam," *Literature* (Aug. 5, 1899), V, 130-132.

Castelnau, Jacques, *Edgar Poe*, Paris, 1945 (A biography).

Clough, W. O., "The Use of Color Words by Edgar Allan Poe," *PMLA* (1930), XLV, 598-613.

Engel, Claire-Eliane. "L'Etat des travaux sur Poe en France," *MP* (1932), XXIX, 482-488.

Fontainas, André, *La Vie d'Edgar A. Poe*, Paris, 1919.

——, "Ce quont pensé d'Edgar Poe ses contemporains," *Mercure de France*, CCXXV, 312-323.

Forgues, E. D., "Études sur le Roman Anglais et Américain— Les Contes d'Edgar A. Poe," *La Revue des Deux Mondes* (Oct. 15, 1846), XVI, 341-366.

Françon, Marcel, "Poe et Baudelaire," *PMLA* (1945), LX, 841-859.

Jackowska, Suzanne d'Olivéra, *La Réhabilitation d'Edgar Poe et ses plus beaux poèmes en vers français avec texte anglais en regard*, Paris, 1933 (Contains twelve of Poe's poems done into French in rhyming metrical verse).

Jones, P. M., "Poe, Baudelaire, and Mallarmé: A Problem of Literary Judgment," *MLR* (1944), XXXIX, 236-246.

Lauvriére, Emile, *Edgar Poe, sa vie et son oeuvre, étude de psychologie pathologique*, Paris, 1904.

——, *The Strange Life and Strange Love of Edgar Allan Poe*, English version by Edwin Gile Rich, London, 1935 (Romanticized story).

Lemonnier, Léon, *Edgar Poe et la Critique Francaise de 1845 à 1875*, Paris, 1928 (Divided into four parts: 1. Le Héros Romantique; 2. Le Conteur Romantique;

3. Le Conteur Scientifique; 4. La Reaction du Bons Sens. Conclusion: Sardou, Gaboriau, Verlaine).

———, "Edgar Poe et la Théâtre de Mystère et de Terreur," *Grande Revue* (1929), CXXX, 379-396.

———, *Les Traducteurs d'Edgar Poe en France,* Paris, 1928.

———, *Edgar Poe et les Poètes Francais,* Paris, 1932.

Mason, A., *Contes Estranges,* illus. by de J. Wely, Paris, 1910.

Mauclair, Camille, *La Génie d'Edgar Poe,* Paris, 1925.

Page, C. H., "Poe in France," *Nation* (Jan. 14, 1909), LXXXVIII, 32-34.

Philips, Edith, "The French of Edgar Allan Poe," *Amer. Speech* (1927), II, 270-274.

Rasome, Arthur, *Edgar Allan Poe, A Critical Study,* London, 1910.

Schwartz, Wm. Leonard, "The Influence of E. A. Poe on Judith Gautier," *MLN* (March., 1927), XLII, 171-173.

Seylaz, Louis, *Edgar Poe et les Premiers symbolistes francais,* Lausanne, 1923.

Valéry, Paul, "Situation de Baudelaire," *Varieté* (1930), II, 141-174.

B. Spanish:

Catalan, Victoriano L., *Trilogia Doliente*: *Musset, Chopin, Becquer,* Buenos Aires, 1935 (Part five deals with Poe and Ruben Dario).

Dávila, Carlos, "Poe y el centenario de la novela policiaca," *America* (1947), XXXIII, 21-23.

Englekirk, John E., "The Song of Holland, An Inedited Tale ascribed to Poe," *New Mexico Quarterly* (1931), I, 247-269 (The Spanish Magazine *La America* for Oct. 8, 1883, printed *"The Song of Holland,"* an inedited tale of Edgardo Poe. This is analyzed as a Poe forgery contributed by Aurelien Scholl, a French writer).

———, "A Critical Study of Two Tales by Amado Nervo," *New Mexico Quarterly* (1932), II, 53-65.

———, *Edgar Poe in Hispanic Literature,* N. Y., 1934 (A

definitive treatment of Poe in Spain and South America.)

———," 'My Nightmare,' The Last Tale by Poe," *PMLA* (1937), LII, 511-527. ("Mi pesadilla," printed in 1902 as "the last tale by Edgar Poe," is unquestionably a hoax. This tale and an article on Poe were probably written by Francisco Zarata Ruiz).

Ferguson, John de Lancey, *American Literature in Spain*, N. Y., 1916.

French, John C., *Poe in Foreign Lands and Tongues*, Baltimore, 1941.

Johnston, Marjorie C., "Ruben Dario's Acquaintance with Poe," *Hispania* (1934), XVII, 271-278.

Lee, Muna, "Brother of Poe," *Southwest Review* (1926), II, 305-312 (Poe's influence on Jose Asuncion Silva).

Obligado, Carlos, *Los Poemas de Edgar Poe*, Buenos Aires, 1944.

Putnam, Samuel, *Marvelous Journey, A Survey of Four Centuries of Brazilian Writing*, N. Y., 1948 (pp. 115-119).

Torres-Rioseco, A., "Las teorias poéticas de Poe y el caso de Poe y el caso de José Asuncion Silva," *Hispanic Review* (1950), XVIII, 319-327.

C. Russia:

Astrov, Vladimir, "Dostoievsky on Edgar Allan Poe," *AL* (1942), XIV, 70-74.

Cowley, Malcolm, "Aidgarpo," *New Republic* (1945), CXIII, 607-610.

Magidoff, Robert, "American Literature in Russia," *SRL* (November 2, 1946), pp. 9-11, 45-46.

———, *In Anger and Pity, A Report on Russia*, N. Y., 1949 (pp. 228-229).

Yarmolinsky, A., "The Russian View of American Literature," *Bookman* (1916), XLIV, 44-48.

———, *A Treasury of Russian Verse*, N. Y., 1949.

D. Germany:

Babler, O. F., "Czech Translations of Poe's 'Raven,' *N&Q* (May 31, 1947), CXCII, 235.

Bonaparte, Marie, *Edgar Poe: ein psychoanalytique studie; mit einem vorwort von Sigmund Freud,* Vienna, 1934 (4 vols.).

Cain, Henry Edward, *James Clarence Mangan and the Poe-Mangan Question,* Washington, D. C., Catholic Univ. of Amer., 1929 (Mangan as a translator of German poetry; similarities between Mangan and Poe have been exaggerated).

Depken, Friedrick, "Sherlock Holmes, Raffles und ihre vorbilder," *Anglistiche Forschungen* (Heidelberg, 1914), XLI, 1-105 (Poe's detective stories).

Edmunds, A. J., "German Translations of Poe's 'Raven,'" *N&Q* (Feb. 5, 1938), CLXXIV, 106 (Translated into German in 1864).

Ewers, Hanns Heinz, *Edgar Allan Poe,* Berlin, 1905; N. Y., 1917 (Compares Poe with Hoffman and Heine).

Hippe, F., *Edgar Allan Poes Lyrik in Deutschland,* Munster, 1913.

Just, Karl Walter, *Die romantische bewegung in der Amerikanischen literatur: Brown, Poe, Hawthorne,* Weimar, 1910.

Mabbott, T. O., "German Translations of Poe's 'The Raven,'" *N&Q* (Jan. 29, 1938), CLXXIV, 88 (Cites translations to supplement those noted by Ingram in 1885).

Schubert, Leland, "James William Carling: Expressionist Illustrator of 'The Raven,'" *SLM* (April, 1942), IV, 173-181 (A German edition of "The Raven" appeared in Philadelphia in 1869).

Strobl, Karl Hans, *Worte Poes, Mit einer bibliographie von Moris Grolig,* Minden i. Westf., 1907.

Wächter, P., *Edgar Allan Poe und die deutsche Romantik,* Leipzig, 1911.

Wolff, Anne Lise, *Tod und unsterblichkeit*: *das leitmotiv von E. A. Poes werk,* Düsseldorf, 1937 (A critical interpretation of Poe's literary themes).

E. England:

Chase, L. N., *Poe and his Poetry,* London, 1913.
Eliot, T. S., *From Poe to Valéry,* N. Y., 1948.
Hutcherson, Dudley R., "Poe's Reputation in England and America, 1850-1909," *AL* (1942), XIV, 211-233.
Huxley, Aldous, *Vulgarity in Literature,* London, 1930.
Mabbott, T. O., "English Publications of Poe's 'Valdemar Case,' " *N&Q* (Nov. 1, 1942), CLXXXIII, 311-312.
Lang, Andrew, "To Edgar Allan Poe," *Letters to Dead Authors,* London, 1886.
Lawrence, D. H., "Edgar Allan Poe," *Studies in Classic American Literature,* from *The Portable D. H. Lawrence,* ed. Diana Trilling, N. Y., 1947 (first pub. 1923, 1930).
Robertson, John M., "Poe," *New Essays Towards a Critical Method,* London, 1889 (pp. 55-130).
Saintsbury, George, *Prefaces and Essays,* London, 1933 (Pronounces Poe a poet of the first order, pp. 314-323).
———, "Edgar Allan Poe," *Dial* (1927), LXXXIII, 453-463.
Slicer, Thomas R., "Poe—The Pioneer and Romantic Literature in America," *From Poet to Premier,* London, 1909 (Ch. I on Poe.)
Stevenson, Robert Louis, "The Works of Edgar Allan Poe," *The Works of Robert Louis Stevenson,* N. Y., 1925 (Vol. 5).
[Swinburne, Charles], *Letters Chiefly Concerning Edgar Allan Poe from Algernon Charles Swinburne to John H. Ingram,* London, 1910 (Printed for private circulation).
Ticknor, Caroline, "Ingram—Discourager of Poe Biographies," *Bookman* (Sept., 1916), XLIV, 8-14 (Ingram conducted a heated exchange with the American author of *The Romance of Edgar A. Poe,* Wm. F. Gill).

F. America:

Abel, Darrell, "Edgar Poe: A Centennial Estimate," *Univ. of Kan. City Rev.* (1949), XVI, 77-96 (His stories will endure longest).

Bayless, Joy, "Another Rufus W. Griswold as a Critic of Poe," *AL* (1934), VI, 69-72.

Braddy, Haldeen, "Poe the Peacock," *New Mexico Quarterly Review* (Autumn, 1949), XIX, 393-397 (Reviewed recent books by Fagin and Ostrom and emphasized Poe's flamboyance).

Brooks, Van Wyck, *The World of Washington Irving*, N. Y., 1944 ("Poe in the South," pp. 337-361, and "Poe in the North," pp. 443-456).

Brownell, William C., "Poe," *American Prose Masters*, N. Y., 1909 (pp. 207-267).

Campbell, Killis, *The Mind of Poe and Other Studies*, Cambridge, Mass., 1933 (Contemporary opinion of Poe, pp. 34-62).

Canby, Henry S., *Classic Americans*, N. Y., 1931 (pp. 263-307.

Cooke, Alice L., "The Popular Conception of Edgar Allan Poe from 1850 to 1890," *Univ. of Texas Studies in English* (1942), XXII, 145-170.

Darnell, F. M., "The Americanism of Edgar Allan Poe," *Eng. Journal* (Mar., 1927), XVI, 185-192 (Finds evidence of Americanism in Poe's ideals and individuality).

De Mille, George E., "Poe," *Literary Criticism in America*, N. Y., 1931 (pp. 86-117).

The Editors, "Poe's 'Ulalume,'" *Expl.* (1942), I, 8 (The Editors object to Aldous Huxley's "The Vulgarity of Poe"; they find his parody too full of feminine rhymes).

Foerster, Norman, "Poe," *American Criticism*, Boston, 1928 (pp. 1-51).

Gates, Lewis E., "Edgar Allan Poe," *Studies and Appreciations*, N. Y., 1900 (pp. 110-128).

Gordon, John D., "Edgar Allan Poe. An Exhibition on the Centenary of his Death, Oct. 7, 1849. A Catalogue of the first Editions, Manuscripts, Autograph Letters from the Berg Collection," *BNYPL* (1949), III, 471-491.

Greenlaw, Edwin, "Poe in the Light of Literary History," *The Johns Hopkins Alumni Magazine* (1930), XVIII, 273-290.

Gregory, Horace, "Within the Private View," *Partisan Review* (1943), X, 263-274.

Harwell, Richard Barksdale, *Recollections of Poe, by John Hill Hewitt,* Atlanta, 1948.

Laverty, Carroll D., "Poe in 1847," *AL* (1948), XX, 163-168 (Anonymous recollections of Poe in the *Home Journal,* 1860).

Mabbott, T. O., "Poe and the Artist John P. Frankenstein," *N&Q* (Jan. 17, 1942), CLXXXII, 31-32.

_____, "An Early Discussion of Poe," *N&Q* (Sept. 7, 1947), CXCI,·102.

McDowell, Tremaine, "Edgar Allan Poe and William Cullen Bryant," *PQ* (1937), XVI, 83-84 (A letter from Bryant in 1846 about Mrs. Clemm and Poe).

Miller, Arthur M., "The Influence of Edgar A. Poe on Ambrose Bierce," *AL* (1932), IV, 130-150.

Nichols, Mary Gove, *Reminiscences of Edgar Allan Poe,* N. Y., 1931 (Reprinted from the *Six Penny Magazine* (1863), with a bibliographical note by T. O. Mabbott, who says that Poe was introduced into her novel *Mary Lyndon).*

Parrington, Vernon Louis, "Edgar Allan Poe," *The Romantic Revolution in America,* 1800-1860, N. Y., 1927.

Parry, Albert, "The Lost One," *Garrets and Pretenders*: *A History of Bohemianism,* N. Y., 1933.

Schubert, Leland, "James William Carling: Expressionist Illustrator of 'The Raven,'" *SLM* (1942), IV, 173-181.

Silver, Rollo G., "A Note about Whitman's Essay on Poe," *AL* (1935), VI, 435-436 (Reproduces "Walt Whitman at the Poe Funeral," a short notice in Whitman's essay on "Edgar Poe's Significance").

Snell, George, "First of the New Critics," *Quar. Rev. Lit.* (1946), II, 333-340.

Trent, William P., "The Centenary of Poe," *Longfellow and Other Essays*, N. Y., 1910 (pp. 211-244).

Tuckerman, Henry T., *The Life of John Pendleton Kennedy*, N. Y., 1871 (Contains reminiscences of Poe).

Williams, William Carlos, "Edgar Allan Poe," *In the American Grain*, Norfolk, Connecticut, 1925.

Winters, Yvor, "Edgar Allan Poe: A Crisis in the History of American Obscurantism," *AL* (1937), VIII, 379-401 (Disparages the merits of Poe's writings).

VI. Bibliographies:

A. Books

Booth, Bradford A. and Jones, Claude E., *A Concordance of the Poetical Works of Edgar Allan Poe*, Baltimore, 1941.

Cambridge, History of Amer. Lit., II, 452-468 (Bibliography to Chap. XIV).

Heartman, Charles F. and Rede, Kenneth, *A Census of First Editions and Source Materials by Edgar Allan Poe in American Collections*, Metuchen, N. J., 1932 (2 vols.).

Heartman, Charles F. and Canny, James R., *A Bibliography of First Printings of the Writings of Edgar Allan Poe*, Hattiesburg, Miss., 1943 (First published in 1940).

Mabbott, T. O., *Index to Early American Periodical Literature* 1728-1870, New York Univ. Lib., 1941.

Robertson, John W., *Bibliography of the Writings of Edgar A. Poe*, San Francisco, 1934 (2 vols).

Spiller, Robert, *et al.*, *Literary History of the United States*, N. Y., 1948 (I, 342).

B. Articles:

O'Neill, Edward H., "The Poe-Griswold-Harrison Texts of the 'Marginalia,'" *AL* (1942), XV, 238-250 (Reprinted for the first time).

McElderry, R. R., Jr., "The Edgar Allan Poe Collection," *USC Lib. Bul.* (Jan., 1948), IV, 4-6.

Publications of Modern Language Association of America, American Bibliography, Current.

Wyllie, John C., "A List of the Texts of Poe's Tales," *Humanistic Studies in Honor of John Calvin Metcalf* Charlottesville, Va., 1941 (pp. 322-338).

INDEX